MW01067923

TRIUMPHS

OF TRANSFORMATION

TRIUMPHS

OF TRANSFORMATION

INSPIRING STORIES OF RESILIENCE AND LIFE CHANGE

CONTRIBUTING AUTHORS

JEN BAWDEN / JIM BEEBE / OSVALD BJELLAND
DR. ALEKSANDRA B. GAJER / DR. EDY GREENBLATT
ALI KATZ / JULIE LANCASTER / DR. EUGENE LIPOV
GEORGIANNE MCCONNELL / DENISE RUSSELL
STEPHANIE DE SARACHAGA-BILBAO AND MANY OTHERS!

THINK
TWICE
B O O K S

WASHINGTON, DC

THINK TWICE
B O O K S

Think Twice Books | www.thinktwicebooks.com

All trademarks are the property of their respective companies.

Cover Design by Garrett Miller
Interior Design: Jessica Angerstein

Cataloging-in-Publication Data is on file with the Library of Congress.

ISBN: 978-1-64687-193-3

Special Sales
Think Twice Books are available at a special discount for bulk purchases for sales promotions and premiums, or for use in corporate training programs. Special editions, including personalized covers, a custom foreword, corporate imprints, and bonus content, are also available.

1 2 3 4 5 6 7 8 9 10

To learn more about our curated community of
Triumphs of Transformation authors, their work,
and to connect with them directly, scan this QR code
to visit the Triumphs of Transformation website:

CONTENTS

FOREWORD

By Taryn Marie Stejskal, Ph.D.,
#1 Wall Street Journal Bestselling Author
Of *The 5 Practices of Highly Resilient People*

As a young girl, my maternal grandparents, who had summered in Minnesota since my mother was a girl, continued our family tradition by purchasing a lake home in Hackensack, MN. Each summer, after school was out, my parents would pack our car to the gills and make the annual two-day pilgrimage from our home in Ann Arbor, MI through the lower peninsula of Michigan, across the Mackinac Bridge, through the upper peninsula, and then drive through the state of Minnesota until we reached the town of Hackensack.

In Minnesota, the folklore stories of a giant woodsman by the name of Paul Bunyon are popular children's tales. For those of you who are unacquainted with Hackensack, the most notable aspect of this small lakeside town is that it is thought to be the original home of Lucette Diana Kensack, who in the folklore stories of Paul Bunyan, is also a fictional giant human and is said to be Paul's sweetheart. Hackensack's claim to fame as Lucette's birthplace is memorialized to this day with a 17-foot statue of Lucette welcoming all into the town.

Our lake home, perched on the edge of Birch Lake, just one of Minnesota's 10,000 lakes, had a main house with a screened porch, kitchen and dining area, living room, and two bedrooms. The property also came with a little guesthouse that had a kitchenette, with twin beds in a knotty pine lined back bedroom, and a pullout couch in the living room, where my parents slept during the summers. The pullout couch in the living room had a view of the lake through the big bay window, and during the times that my father returned to Ann Arbor for work, my brother and I would take turns sleeping on the pull-out with my mom.

One morning, when it had been my turn to sleep on the pullout, I opened my eyes at the first light of dawn and looked out across the lake, through the bay window. The sun was just beginning to peek over the horizon, and I could see bright pink fluffy clouds floating so low on the water that they looked like they might touch the surface of the lake. As I watched the first rays of morning sunshine illuminate the sky, I saw those low-hanging pink clouds gliding directly toward the guesthouse, until the frame of the bay window was filled only with the pink clouds billowing around the house. A moment later, those fluffy clouds, as quickly as they had come, were gone.

It was an other-worldly experience to see clouds of that vibrant color drift toward me and envelope our little house. That morning, still feeling elated by both the clouds' beauty and at the impossibility of what I had seen, I decided that pink clouds would be my sign from God. Pink clouds would be like God and my secret handshake, HIS way of communicating hope, possibility, and reassurance to me. From that time, until now, anytime I see pink clouds in the sky, even in the moments that seemed the most hopeless in my life, I allowed myself to believe that those clouds were a sign from God that everything was going to be alright.

I shared with you this seemingly unrelated story about my family's lake home and the clouds I saw one morning at sunrise because

I hope that the stories contained in this book will be your pink fluffy clouds. Most of us, if we're honest, have, are, or will go through something difficult, and in those moments of upheaval and uncertainty, we're very far from sure that things are going to be alright. I hope the stories you read will be the signposts you've been looking for that things are going to be okay.

Right now, more than ever, we need stories of triumph and transformation to illuminate our paths. I don't know anyone that isn't struggling with something, myself included. Oftentimes facing extensive challenge, change, and complexity, The Big 3 C's, as I call them, narrows the aperture of our focus until we are engaged so intently on the problem or stressor that we become myopic, and the issue is all we can see. It is easy to be blind to the array of possibilities that exist, to be unseeing when it comes to the potentiality for how we can heal, grow, evolve, and expand when the challenge at hand takes up all our available mental energy. Conversely, on the morning those impossibly fluffy pink clouds touched down right in front of my window, they blurred the world outside so that all I could see was the pink of the clouds themselves. This experience taught me that our vision is easily (forgive the pun) clouded by whatever is right in front of us. We can choose to focus on the difficulty all together or we can expand our lens and look for solutions, along with alternative perspectives and paths we hadn't previously considered.

Over the course of the last twenty years, to understand the concept of resilience, I have listened carefully to hundreds of people tell me their stories of how they faced The Big 3 C's. I have shared my own resilience stories from stages for hundreds of thousands of people. In sharing my resilience stories and listening to the stories of others, I've come to understand the magnitude of the power that each of our resilience stories carries. The stories we share with others about the times when we have faced our greatest difficulties are, in fact, the greatest opportunity to uplift, not only ourselves, but those around us including our friends, families, team members, colleagues, and neighbors.

One of The Five Practices of Highly Resilient People, that I uncovered through my work to understand the behaviors that foster resilience, is the practice of Grati-osity, a hybrid word representing the words for gratitude and generosity. I found that the people who faced challenges with the greatest resilience were the people who could engage in the practice of Grati-osity. First, they could look at a challenge, typically after some time has passed, and they can see the good in that challenge, even if they wouldn't have chosen it. Second, these people were able to share their resilience stories generously with others, after they'd had time for reflection, growth, and healing.

Generously sharing our resilience stories with others:

1. Solidifies our own resilience, so that we know better for the next time when we face a challenge the skills and tools that we used to effectively navigate that experience; and

2. encourages and offers hope to people outside of ourselves, in their darkest moments, so that when they hear our story, they receive the gift of a renewed belief in their capacity to face this difficulty and ultimately triumph.

When we share our resilience stories, we effectively engage in what I call human alchemy. Human alchemy is the magic that exists in the moments when we retell our resilience stories to others, effectively transmuting our darkest times of difficulty to become a light that we shine on someone else's path amid their own bleakness. Through our own healing, by retelling our resilience stories, we transform the darkness that had once existed in our lives into a light that gives others hope, and in doing so, whether we know it or not, we become part of someone else's survival guide.

Our stories matter. Your story matters. Yet so often the most meaningful resilience stories we can share with others, the stories that will foster the greatest cohesion and connection amongst our fellow humans, are the last stories we share with others because we fear we'll be judged for facing challenges. Facing challenges is not unique to any of us, rather, it is a collective element we all share within the fabric of our human experience. In this book you'll read stories about loss, rejection, disappointment, and disillusionment. The stories you read will be unique to each author. Yet, you'll be able to relate to the experience of each person's story on some level because their story taps into the universality of our shared human experience. The truest truth of what it means to be human is also the most easily forgotten: We are all deeply connected and more alike than we are different.

I am incredibly grateful to our authors for the tremendous courage, authenticity, and vulnerability required for them to share their resilience stories on the pages of this book. Unlike our authors, as you're reading this book, know that for you to heal, grow, and contribute at a higher level, you are not necessarily called to share your resilience story publicly. When contemplating sharing your resilience story early on, one of the most important decisions you can make is deciding who is worthy of hearing your story. You get to vet the people in your life that have earned the right to hear your story. The first few times you share your resilience story, it is tremendously important that the people you choose have the ability within themselves to both listen to you and truly hear you, to empathize with your experience, and support you in your growth. Some of your stories may not be for everyone, for the public, for the stage. Some of your stories may not be for anyone other than one other than a trusted companion or a small group of friends or family members. Know that the forum in which you ultimately choose to share your resilience story is your choice. As

I have shared my resilience stories and taught countless others to do the same, I tell people: You will be too much for some people. Not enough for others. These are not your people. Keep going until you are received by your tribe. Your tribe exists. They are out there looking for and waiting for you too!

No matter what, sharing our resilience stories with others amplifies hope, creates moments of deeper connection, and fosters the human alchemy of transforming the darkness of our experiences into a light that illuminates the path of others. The process of learning to share our resilience stories is a heroic act because it requires facing our fears and choosing bravery to get to a place where we can articulate our resilience stories. Giving voice to our pain, obstacles, and adversity requires commitment and conviction. When you engage in the process of sharing your resilience story, there are immense rewards: Those that share their resilience stories become beacons of hope within our society. No matter where you are on your journey, you've come to the right place. We're glad you're here. Thank you for being on this journey with us. We hope you enjoy these stories of triumph and transformation.

DENISE RUSSELL

United In Adversity: How Partnership Fuels Resilience

Carpe Diem

When I was twenty-five years old, my dad died. He attended a wedding and died of what appeared to be a heart attack the next day. He was fifty-six years old.

At the time, I thought this would be the end of everything I knew, and in some ways, it was. Death had raised the stakes; this was no dress rehearsal. Every significant life choice I've made since, and some not-so-serious decisions, usually starts with, "What's the worst that can happen?"

My story is one of fearlessness, a take-action attitude that has allowed me to grab life by the horns, seizing every moment with the boldness of a tequila shot.

Unicorns, Nespresso And Tom Brady

I'm writing this chapter following my first of two daily transcendental meditations, coffee consisting of two Nespresso shots with whipped cream, and half of a Lenny and Larry's soft-baked snickerdoodle cookie. My life and routines are nothing special.

So, "How do seemingly ordinary people do extraordinary things?" I ask myself this question often as I contemplate how I got to forty-eight years old. I've found that success comes to those not seeking it, a concept similar to love, money, or fame. Some people think it's luck, but like lightning, luck almost never strikes twice.

Building two global "unicorn" beauty companies at breakneck speeds was not done by me alone. I cannot tell you how to make millions of dollars precisely as I did, and I'm not so delusional as to think I've done this independently, because I haven't. Anyone who tells you that they have singularly achieved greatness is a fraud living in an egotistical illusion and most definitely a jerk. Even Tom Brady, the GOAT of all GOATs, has never stated he achieved greatness alone. Just like football, life is a team sport.

My quarterback is my husband and business partner, Ed Connaghan. We met in Las Vegas at a business conference when I was twenty-nine; I have never been the same. The rest is history. A Scottish accent and designer shoes wooed me, making me giggle as I write this. Oh, how times have changed.

Fake Farms And A Four Hour Work Week

When we first got together four years after we met, we had nothing and lived in El Paso, Texas, where I had just taken a full-time job to facilitate our relationship. Being an "alien" in Texas meant he could not travel outside of a twenty-mile radius and could not work until he had a visa. Ed, then my live-in boyfriend, played Farmville while I worked during the day. It annoyed me, but I knew it was only temporary. I'll always remember when he reached ten million dollars in the game and professed we would have bank accounts that read the same. He also told me he would take me around the world. Both promises seemed unrealistic at the time.

Roll The Dice

We rolled the dice again and opted to take a chance on entrepreneurial ventures. Ed needed a visa to do so. We got married in secret on his birthday at the little chapel of El Paso. It was insignificant, unromantic, and stealthy. There were no rings, no flowers, and no white dresses. We drank cheap champagne afterward and plotted our next move. His career as a digital farmer was over, and we were ready to take on the world. I quit corporate nonsense and read Timothy Ferris's *The Four-Hour Work Week*. We made our first $80,000 deal, which involved an espionage-like sale of shampoo, tickets to the Playboy Bunny mansion, and a fat, balding businessman who sold outdated cans of food to the penitentiary system in Florida—I can't make this stuff up!

Onwards and upwards, we packed our stuff and moved to Dallas, where we are today, taking innovative concepts and turning them into profitable realities. We are brand architects who create rapid global distribution for beauty brands. We have revolutionized haircare practices, achieved financial milestones, and positioned these companies to highly successful IPO and strategic sales, particularly with Olaplex and K18 Hair. In both cases, we are known for taking leadership roles, from brand creation to global market penetration, steering the companies toward substantial growth and market value.

Among the success of these companies have come momentous challenges and some amazing adventures. We have traversed the globe at least eight times, allowing me to see cultures and form perspectives that would be unthinkable through drinking around the world in Epcot or Netflix documentaries. The last twenty years have been a constant roller coaster of hustle, marked with endless bottles of Clicquot (We elevated our champagne game since El Paso.) and provided us with a financial means toward freedom.

Why, Winning And Work

Valuable insights I gained to succeed in business are from three prominent books: Simon Sinek's *Start with Why: How Great Leaders Inspire Everyone to Take Action*, Jack Welch's *Winning*, and *Principles: Life and Work* by Ray Dalio. Each book offers invaluable insights and strategies for running a successful business and creating a work-life balance through triumph. I still read these to find creative entrepreneurial inspiration, and I suggest you give them a whirl, as they can offer you more insights than I can.

Remember when I said you'd be a jerk to think you can do this alone? Well, there is a reason for this. It is the key to my resilience in this world, this life hustle, this journey in an energy-filled skin suit. I found my person, my soulmate, my mentor—and I found that thing that allows me to take chances and embrace change. I found the courage to take a chance on a fleeting opportunity: having my best friend, husband, and person with me, encouraging, challenging, and making me better. I found my resilience in the number two, the balance, duality, and partnership through teamwork, collaboration, and mutual support.

Find That Partner

Find that person or thing that inspires you to pursue success and the good life with a complete and all-encompassing attitude. Stay hungry, stay humble, and look to the left and lift someone up on their journey. Life is not a dress rehearsal; you have one shot at it. Every day is a clean slate that allows you to write and rewrite your story. Be a "RocknRolla," take the risk, roll the dice, and find the resilience in you.

JIM BEEBE

Sisu Is One Of Our Six Core Values

I have an undergraduate degree in business management and a master's in finance from Purdue University. And yet I'm the founder and owner of a strength and conditioning gym, Unbreakable Athletics Academy, in Plainfield, Indiana. How did I get here?

Kids, Loans, Divorce And Going All In

I left the private sector in early 2008 to earn my master's to advance further in the business world. Normally it's a two-year program. However, going without income with three young kids and a recent divorce meant I crammed it into one year's time. The real kicker was that those twelve months occurred during the housing-bubble crisis, a horrible time to work in finance and investments. Bank of America was being bailed out, which meant they left me high and dry my last semester on my student loan. There went $30,000 in loans onto a credit card at 29.9 percent because of the inflated rates. MBA graduate placement rates went from 94 percent to 28 percent that year. Well, big debts + kids + no income = networking day and night until I found a job upon graduation. And I did. I ended up at the largest bank of them all, JP Morgan(JPM) Chase. I bet heavily on one outcome, went "all in," and it paid off. That was the summer of 2009. I was thirty-four.

JP Morgan hired me as an associate in their private bank. This department serviced the high-net-worth clients, a smaller but very profitable niche of the bank. Clients needed to have a minimum of $5 million in assets or loans at JPM to work with our department. We made the wealthy clients wealthier and were paid to do so. Most of the financial world was in shambles, but JPM was advancing quickly. The career path was that after this nationwide hiring approach, the associates would carve out their own books of business, and we'd continue to build it if we were with the firm. The associate track was set for three years. Fast forward those three years, and it was almost time for the next chapter for a lot of us.

Life's Always Throwing Curveballs

Curveball. Many associates were slated to advance, which is an enormous cost to the bank. Therefore, JPM set a target for banking teams (bankers + associate + three specialists) to bring in $100 million (not a typo) in new assets and loans that year. It was a challenging task in Indiana and most anywhere. Well, you guessed it, most teams across the country did not. The few that did got to stay. Most others, including my entire team and I, ended up being forced out. Our $60 million in new "flows" that year was not enough. It was mid-2012. Now what?

I was thirty-seven. I spent fifteen years in the investment, banking, and finance world. I was good at making others wealthier and making the right bets on investments. I could connect with people and problem-solve their high-level finance issues. On the flip side, that stressful lifestyle and constant wining and dining left me physically very unhealthy. For most of my adult life, I weighed more than 270 pounds of mostly fat, couldn't run a mile, couldn't bench press much more than half my body weight, and couldn't back squat it either. I was consistently out of breath playing with my small kids, ages ten, eight, and six at the time. It was a recipe for a short and painful life.

Physical Change, Changed It All.

One great benefit from working at JPM was that I started to improve my health in late 2011 with the hit craze P90X. Then, in early 2012, I advanced to small group training and eventually CrossFit at a local gym. I was running 5Ks and improving my times. This wasn't hard to do when I started running at a pace of twelve minutes per mile. But over time, I completed some longer runs and eventually in 2012 managed a couple triathlons and a couple half marathons. That was when JPM invited me not to return.

I was at a crossroads. One thing that I learned at JPM was that most wealthy clients earned their fortunes by creating and running their own businesses and finally selling them. I coupled that idea with Steve Jobs's Stanford commencement speech on doing what you love. Well, I really liked math and problem-solving. But I always wanted to be an athlete, work with athletes, and be on a winning team in sports. I thought long and hard about it and decided to pivot my career and start a new chapter in the strength and conditioning world by opening a CrossFit gym.

I had some on-the-job training with the CrossFit gym where I trained. The owners took me under their wing. I went through the certification processes, passed the tests, and started to train a couple volunteers in my garage at home on the side. This was in late 2012. At the same time, I took one of my old MBA books on how to write a business plan off the shelf. And I got started. I analyzed the different demographics of where I needed to live in proximity to my children. I went through the typical SWOT (Strengths Weaknesses

Opportunities and Threats) analyses. There were spaces to rent, capital expenditures, and purchases to make. I had to put together budgets and estimates. And there was a need for financing. It was a brand-new endeavor in an unknown industry for me.

In the finance world, gyms are not sought-after prospects. It's a high-risk industry because most rather spend money on pizza and beer instead of making time to be healthier. Almost no bank would touch me. The plan was to secure half my financing from private lenders and the other half from a Small Business Administration loan. I was able to secure the first half relatively quickly. In a time of historically low interest rates, it helped that I ended paying 12 percent on the loan + 3 percent of all top-line revenue. It was a painful rate to pay but justified given the startup nature of the business. And then I also met Matt Smith, the small bank lender who guaranteed the SBA loan. Alright then. . . I was "all in" again, just this time with a gym.

Moving Forward Even With Roadblocks

I moved forward with a lease and started purchasing equipment. I started building out the space and could start eking out a small salary from the funding. Then right from the get-go. . . setback. Matt Smith was never going to secure funding for me. He made a lot of promises but never delivered. He left town and changed banks. I never heard from him again. The real issue was that I never should have moved forward without all the financing firmly secured. Absolutely my fault. So now I had half the funding needed to make this work. That's virtually a fatal blow to any small startup. However, there's no going back now. And March 7, 2013, CrossFit Unbreakable opened in Plainfield, Indiana.

I was a one-man show. I coached every session of the week. The first one started at 6:00 a.m. Most nights the last one ended at 7:30 p.m. Some were later. I had six sessions each day and a couple on Saturday and Sunday. When I wasn't coaching, I was trying to grow the business, handle the marketing, sales, and maintenance of the gym. It's a ten thousand square foot facility, and the building is more than fifty years old. The lack of funding meant I couldn't hire any staff. I was going to sink or swim solely on my own. And every week I had my three kids 50 percent of the time. They spent a lot of hours at my gym with me.

There is an enormous difference between making large investment decisions versus running a small business. The investment decisions take understanding the economics and finances into play and deciding. After two degrees and fifteen years' experience, that was relatively easy. And it should be by then.

Drink From The Fire Hose

Running a new business in a foreign industry takes a similar amount of knowledge and brainpower. And I didn't have a lot of that yet. Many will say they need roughly ten thousand hours of experience before truly becoming an expert in an area. It's true. And I was drinking through a fire hose cramming as much of the learning curve into me as I could.

I had no systems in place for billing, accounting, marketing, or even tracking clients' progressions. That's just for the business. At the same time, I was only certified in CrossFit to coach people. I was ten years behind on that knowledge as well. I was tasked with learning how to run the business and how to coach adults and kids to meet their health, wellness, and athletic goals. A common Navy SEAL mantra is "a good plan today is better than a perfect plan tomorrow." And

I subscribe to that. It was time to move forward and as quickly as possible. Then I had to adjust and correct equally as quickly. Just keep moving forward, inch by inch.

So You Want To Be An Entrepreneur?

The first year was very painful. The sheer workload volume alone had me beaten down. Add in the enormous mistake with the funding, and I was hanging on by a thread. I never had a billing system initially. Members would walk in with checks or cash on the first of the month to pay me. Anyone who came in mid-month paid a prorated amount. There were no contracts. I couldn't hire a lawyer. Consequently, there wasn't much financial accountability for members either. I naively believed that if "I built it, they would come." Well, some did. But that's not a sustainable business model. Fast forward to the end of 2013, and we are approaching the anticipated New Year's Resolution crowd. And then. . . another setback. Normally the January 1 members sign up at gyms in droves. Well, that first week of 2014 in Indiana, the entire state was under snow. A blizzard came through. It was one of the very few times the governor mandated the state shut down due to weather. That meant no first-of-the-month revenue. Many current members faded away because they regressed during the holidays and didn't start January 1. And the New Year's folks never came at all. Instead of great growth, I was in decline.

Money was really getting tight now. How tight? I had my car repossessed. I didn't have health insurance for three years. I was consistently late on all utilities and bills. Oftentimes, they'd get shut off and I'd have to reactivate them. However, I was always current on two things: my home mortgage and my interest payments to my gym lenders. I was still weighed down by the enormous student loan payments, credit cards, and still trying to raise three kids part-time. Instead of wasting the twenty-minute drive home, sometimes I'd sleep on the floor at the gym. I'd turn my heat way down in the winter and only have air conditioning at home in the summer when my kids were there. All the kids' birthday and Christmas gifts came from Goodwill. All my furniture except my bed was gifted to me. Sometimes I had to choose between buying gas or food.

No one gets strong from doing easy things. Ever. Mental and physical strength are forged by adversity.

One Book Changed It All

I kept at it. I kept drinking through the fire hose. I poured information and knowledge into me day and night on how to train people and how to run a business. A great colleague saved me in one area a couple years in. He introduced me to the book *Traction* by Gino Wickman. It guided me through all the areas for running a small business. It helped me define the company's core values, what our niche was, what separated me from others, how to set up operations, our culture, and more. The initial assessment test revealed a score of 22 percent. From there, the only direction was up. I started creating systems and processes for everything. Most days, I allocated time for reading, podcasts, seminars, etc. Tony Robbins states that "success leaves clues." He's right. So, I spent most of my time cramming in as much knowledge as I can and working day and night. And then I applied what I learned and evolved as quickly as I could.

For training athletes, I added certifications in powerlifting, strongman, and nutrition. I hired a sports performance coach for coaching student athletes and learned from him. I added seminars on West Side Barbell's conjugate system, Jim Wendler's 5-3-1 method, and more. Physically, I had to build my own hands-on experience at both ends of the spectrum. To that end, I've run six half-marathons, one in under two hours. I've also deadlifted over 600 pounds, carried 300 pounds in each hand, carried 800 pounds on my back, squatted 575 pounds, bench-pressed 335 pounds, and pressed 300 pounds over my head. I've dropped my weight to 225 pounds at 6'3" to run the half marathon and built it up to 320 pounds to compete at strongman and powerlifting, setting some modest state records. I know how to push it up or down depending on my goals and targets.

Unbreakable

What does that look like today? March 7, 2023 was my ten-year anniversary with the gym. Statistically, 4 percent of new businesses make it ten years. 96 percent fail. I have a staff of ten coaches. I have scores of adults no longer taking prescribed medications. Athletes have lost thousands of pounds of fat and gained thousands of pounds of muscle at Unbreakable Athletics. The bad aches and pains are replaced by the good aches and pains of muscle soreness. Over a hundred different times, athletes from my gym have set state or national records, been on podiums and competitions, survived military boot camps and first responder schools, and more. And a thousand more times the "average Joes" have moved outside their comfort zones, built a strong mental mindset, and reclaimed their health.

More than 10 percent of our high school seniors go onto play sports in college, and half are in Division I schools. Hundreds more of our student athletes simply move much better, are stronger, faster, and more resilient as well. They also develop the lost values of discipline, mental toughness, and accountability. As a child growing up without money, means, and resources, I had very little success in sports. I only played one year of high-school basketball and some recreational racquetball at Purdue. I was not a great athlete. Today, all three of my kids have earned varsity letters, some in multiple sports. My oldest plays division one football at Ball State. My second earned a full-ride academic scholarship to Alabama. My youngest is about to decide where he's going next. And to top it off, I married a true blessing of a woman, who I met at my gym.

I established a charity, The U Foundation. We raise and give away more than $50,000 annually to breast cancer, the military, and disadvantaged youth in athletics. Our breast cancer event in October 2023 raised $40,000 alone.

We evolved to Unbreakable Athletics Academy. We work with adults and student athletes on nutrition, CrossFit, sports performance, powerlifting, strongman, highland games, Olympic lifting, and mindset training. And it's just in a small suburb in Plainfield, Indiana.

Going forward we are expanding our reach by adding a new line of business called Athlete Builder. This new line is tasked to spread the knowledge and content we've learned over the last ten-plus years to high-school and college athletes as well as adults nationwide. We look at three components for the athlete's head and three for the body. For the head, we work to improve his/her Mindset, Knowledge about playing their sport, and their ability to work with Teammates (the coaches, Teammates on the field or court, and the support team). For the body, we improve how they Train, their Nutrition, and their Recovery. We identify the one "big mover" in each of the six areas daily. And we get them to execute and move forward. Our mantra is Forging Unbreakable Athletes.

Pain Teaches Us

The journey has been immensely painful. And the pain and lessons are requirements for the successes and much greater rewards received. Looking back, here are some tenets I know are true:

1. Sisu: It's an Unbreakable Athletics core value. It's a Finish word that roughly translates as grit, severe determination, and the belief of never quitting. Even if you're suicidal, you hang on and keep going. And it's critical for me. That means more than not giving up. For me it also means not giving up on the task at hand. See it all the way through to the end.

2. The other core values for Unbreakable Athletics as well as Athlete Builder are Integrity, Discipline, Teamwork, Kaizen (a Japanese business term for being 1 percent better in everything), and Enjoyment. We are Relentless in our application.

3. Learn every day. Get smarter immediately.

4. Get rid of your ego and develop better, more consistent feedback loops. This enables the Kaizen value to kick in and win.

5. Strive to add ten times more service and value than needed.

6. All in or not at all.

7. Win the Day means you must execute your daily priorities, your six athletic tasks, to win the long game.

8. The strength of the wolf is the pack. And the strength of the pack is the wolf. – Rudyard Kipling. You cannot be great alone. Find and work with strong-minded people.

9. No one is coming to save you. Own everything. Move forward.

10. You're only here once and for a short while. So "gotta go now!"

DR. EUGENE LIPOV, MD

A Story Of Resilience And A Peek At The Science Behind It

My Generational Trauma

Even before I was born, my DNA had been changed by trauma.

Epigenetics is the study of genetic changes due to generations of familial trauma—think of babies born into families that have lived in war-torn countries for generations. This kind of "generational build-up" of trauma can actually flip your genes on and off, modifying gene expression for at least two generations. This generational trauma does not permanently alter the DNA code, yet gene malleability does continue into adulthood of descendants, leaving them susceptible to a host of physical ailments, including post-traumatic stress symptoms (anxiety, hypervigilance, heightened reactions, depression, insomnia, and more).

My grandfather was a survivor of the atrocities committed in Ukraine in the early 1900s. My father was born in 1925 and went to fight in World War II. He was part of a squadron of ten thousand soldiers at the start of the war—only one hundred men from the squadron made it home.

Immersed in intense, long-term, life-threatening trauma affects an individual, obviously. But even when that individual is finally safe, far from danger, he or she often continues to behave irrationally, even violently. This person is exhibiting classic post-traumatic stress symptoms due to the injuries to his or her sympathetic nervous system that occurs with trauma. The physical injury or activation can now be seen on scans, which is why what you commonly hear referred to as post-traumatic stress disorder (PTSD) is now starting to be referred to as post-traumatic stress injury (PTSI). The family is then forced to deal with biologically driven erratic behavior from someone they love in what should be a safe household.

Over time, this behavior generates what is termed secondary PTSI in the family members. This means the partners and children in this household are not only dealing with epigenetic trauma affecting their DNA; their own daily experience is creating new trauma that is harming them not just emotionally but also biologically.

The reality behind this concept is only too real for me. The toxic mix of genetic predisposition and the trauma of living with a PTSI survivor affected me and my mother, who took her life when I was twenty-two. That single act changed my life forever. At the time of her death, I was doing a surgical internship at Cook County Hospital in Chicago. However, after her death, I could not go on as a surgical resident; the breath was knocked out of me. I simply existed over the next few years, operating on cruise control, surrounded by traumatized and ill people day and night. I was also receiving daily calls from my despondent father.

Yet . . . I knew I would make it through this dark time. I'd survived so much hardship already, growing up in Ukraine with a father suffering from PTSI. Then, nine months before my mother committed suicide, I was nearly killed in a boating accident. Just before starting at Cook County, I went on a celebratory trip to Mexico, only to be run over by a drunk fisherman and critically wounded by the propellor. Severe bleeding, barely controllable, led to an out-of-body experience. Talk about "what does not kill you makes you stronger." I left Mexico with two hundred stitches, severe pain, and a limp.

Then my mother took her life. Two years after my mother's death, I left surgery and became an anesthesiologist. At the time, I perceived anesthesiology to be a less prestigious career than surgery but made the change because I knew I wouldn't be able to sustain equanimity in the life of a surgeon.

The life events mentioned here, and the tenacity I took away from them, have led to me becoming arguably one of the top trauma doctors in the world as it relates to the sympathetic nervous system (SNS), the fight-or-flight response. That really started when I had the absolute honor of devising and explaining the mechanism of a fast and highly effective therapy for post-traumatic stress injury that works in minutes and may last for years. I took a century-old anesthetic approach originally called a stellate ganglion block (SGB) and made innovations that resulted in the more advanced version called the dual sympathetic reset (DSR). This approach is radically different from other treatments for PTSI due to its high efficacy and speed of onset, as well as lack of addiction potential. Quite simply, DSR seems to "reboot" a sympathetic nervous system (which includes the amygdala, the part of the system that controls the body's fight-or-flight response in the face of threat) that has become stuck in fight-or-flight by resetting the whole system.

Perseverance

During my years of intense research and studies around developing DSR, I learned a lot about neuroscience and molecular genetics, not to mention the true nature of PTS and how psychiatry was getting it wrong, labeling it a disorder instead of a biological injury. In my pursuit of changing the landscape of psychiatry, I came across a number of unbelievers. "SBG has been done since 1926. Who are you to find a new use?" How was it that no one else had discovered that the pain block could alleviate PTSI in all this time? I was challenged in medical journals and newspaper op-eds. I was even asked if I was a "crackpot" in a congressional hearing in 2010 before a veterans' subcommittee.

A number of people have asked me how and why was I able to persist on this path for seventeen years. Why persevere? Because now SGB and my DSR version are routinely used in military institutions to help soldiers with PTSI. At least five thousand military personnel per year receive the treatment. A large-scale study using functional MRI is being conducted to evaluate DSR at New York University (NYU). I know DSR/SGB has saved countless lives and relationships and reduced patient misery, as well as the misery of their loved ones.

Persevering was the right thing to do. In large part, I was driven by memories of my mother. Further, seeing the life-changing impact of DSR on my patients lives motivates me. My brother calls me "brother bulldog" due to my tenaciousness.

Look, I'm helping people. And I may have dealt with disdain and name-calling, but at least I'm alive . . . . Dr. Ignac Semmelweis challenged the medical establishment and was placed into a mental asylum and beaten to death within a month of being admitted. He'd had the audacity to insist that if doctors and nurses washed their hands before delivering babies, it would save lives. In 1866, twenty years after his death, doctors started washing their hands, and Ignac was widely considered the savior of babies. In my case, I am still working, designing studies, and serving as Chief Medical Officer at an international company known as The Stella Center, where miracles happen every day on three continents.

The Mechanics Of Resilience

Speaking of perseverance, that too has a biological component. Let's look under the hood, see how resilience works in our bodies.

Your body is designed to survive. Nature has built us a resilient machine. Perseverance in the face of threat is not just in your "head." Every part of your body, including your DNA, works together to help you come back from the biological impacts of trauma stronger and more resilient.

A great example of this is the hormetic effect. Hormesis is a term introduced in the nineteenth century to describe the effects of extracts of the Red Cedar tree (toxic to fungi) on wood-rotting fungi. Fungi exposed to low doses of this toxic substance increases growth and survival, as opposed to death at high doses. Hormesis has been described across plant and animal species, and hormetic effects such as this have been reported in neurological systems, where stress can fortify and optimize certain neural functions and may serve to protect neural systems in the brain. In this instance, literally what does not kill you makes you stronger. In humans, post-trauma adaptive responses have been recorded, including activation of growth factors, increased energy metabolism, stronger immune system, production of macrophages (helpful with immunity), autophagy (removal of old cells that makes us age), mood enhancement, and turning off bad genes in the DNA.

I did not ingest extracts from a Red Cedar tree, but like many humans, I have dealt with "toxins." In my case, the worst toxic substance I was dosed with long-term was trauma, growing up with a father exuding severe PTSI symptoms, almost losing my life when I was mangled by a boat propeller, and losing my mother to such a sad, unnecessary death. Surviving these horrifying traumas does have an upside—I am more resilient than many people I know. I had to be to survive. And now that resilience, that ability to persevere, helps others.

Keep in mind, the *absence* of adversity likely does not contribute to resilience to future insults. Indeed, exposure to controllable stressors is a major contributor to building resilience. So, try something new, get rejected, take a chance. Start building your resiliency. Take actions that will help build a tolerance for low doses of "toxin," or trauma. Within reason, of course.

You Can Do It

Many people avoid new situations (like giving a speech, going on a blind date, or going zip-lining) because they believe that they can not handle the stress. You can. *You can survive so much more than that*, if you have to. Your body wants you to survive. And if you continue to test yourself and build resiliency, the more endurance you will have in the face of new trauma.

Reading through this book, you will discover many inspiring stories of individuals who have had to persevere and what they did to survive. When I share how I continue to build on my own resilience, I like to use the mnemonic HERE: Humor, Exercise, Respect, Exploration. I hope it helps you on your own resilience journey.

Humor lets you connect. It has helped me in all aspects of my life, from treating patients to staying married to an amazing woman. In fact, published studies show humor has been associated with increased resilient responses in a number of populations, though gallows humor is associated with worse outcomes than other varieties. From a brain-scan perspective, humor has been shown to impact the amygdala (the part of the brain/SNS that controls PTSI) enough that you can actually see a positive brain change when you laugh.

Exercise produces endorphins (natural body opioids), making you feel calmer. There are also multiple beneficial physical impacts. Exercise reduces inflammation, physical hardiness, and feelings of mastery or self-esteem or self respect. Most significantly, from the neuroscience perspective, aerobic exercise is linked to increased volume in brain regions like the prefrontal cortex (where you do a lot of thinking) and hippocampus (where the memory is stored). These regions are typically decreased in individuals with a history of chronic stress or trauma.

Respect for self and others. I tell my friends I do not like to suffer, not if I have a choice. For example, prior to quitting my job at Rush University, I went out to a great French restaurant, had a glass of red wine, and then went to see my chairman. I made myself relax before engaging in an emotionally stressful situation.

Exploration. In this context, it means if you find yourself under duress, emotionally or physically, see what else is possible. If you are in a dead-end job, look around, even if the thought of a big change is scary. The mental upheaval that comes with change doesn't last long, but long-term physical and mental effects of unhappiness are real—daily microdoses of stress build up and can eventually induce PTSI just as if you suffered a major traumatic event. So do the scary thing, take the plunge. The same approach goes for many other things. You can drive your brain to where you want to go. Set a goal. Know that your body and mind have amazing tools to help you.

A common scientific definition of resilience is the ability to achieve a successful outcome in the face of adversity. Many believe that resilience is a way back to "normal" behavior after a trauma; it is, in fact, an active process that involves using a person's adaptive capacity to achieve a positive outcome. The trauma you survive changes you. Consider the plants thriving despite a toxic substance. You can come back from trauma even stronger than normal!

It should be remembered that stress is a key aspect of a healthy brain. Therefore, stress-induced changes in the brain after stress are neuroplastic adaptation (nerve change). Neuroplasticity (nerve growth) describes the process of our ever-changing brains even into our nineties.

Trauma can activate "bad" genes and deactivate the "good ones." However, what you think matters, and the reversal of trauma effects is possible. I am currently conducting a study that is based on the fact that PTSI can speed up the aging process and can be measured accurately by an epigenetic clock (GrimAge clock). This clock has a very high predictive ability regarding the speed of aging and death. Thankfully, the treatment of PTSI can reverse the speed of aging and delay death. *Resilience can change your DNA function.* Further, mindfulness-based stress reduction and meditation increase functional connectivity—they keep the brain evolving by adopting beneficial fluid intelligence and improve function in aging people.

Lack of resilience comes with a high cost according to rat experiments. When faced with a predator they could not escape, the brains of defeated rats versus non-stressed rats revealed atrophy of the hippocampus. The hippocampus is a region of the brain important for spatial learning and memory, and it plays a role in the regulation of the HPA (cortisol) axis. Hippocampus is the most sensitive to stress in both humans and animals, and a loss of hippocampal volume is associated with risk for brain disorders such as PTSI and memory loss. The ability to exercise has had profound effects on reversing some of the negative behaviors observed after stress in rodents.

Exercise has also been seen to restore the underlying neurobiological changes associated with stress susceptibility in humans, so let's get on a treadmill! Extended periods of exercise increase hippocampal function. Neural plasticity, or making new nerve connections, has shown that biology is not destiny—you can change it for the better. As you've read, yes, the brain can maadapt, considering epigenetics, but also *adapt*, depending on life experience and what you do after trauma.

For adults, a number of interventions have been created to boost resilience in groups likely to face trauma in the course of their working lives (e.g., soldiers and firefighters). These approaches often involve training in job-specific skills to enhance the sense of control under stress, as well as improve relaxation, mindfulness, and other more general stress-management approaches.

It is also clear that resilience has neurobiological correlates in those brain regions like the hippocampus and prefrontal cortex that support complex cognition and memory, sociality, and successful coping. Interventions and education that increase function in these regions will in turn contribute to resilience. Other brain regions, such as the amygdala, tend to be hyperreactive in vulnerable people; thus, interventions that reduce amygdala activity, such as DSR and other trauma interventions are likely to promote resilience, as will leaning into the elements of my mnemonic HERE (described above).

In Summary

Resilience is controlled by our genetics, our personal trauma, and the actions we initiate to bolster ourselves. Biology is not destiny. Genes can be switched on or off. The sympathetic nervous system, including the amygdala's fight-or-flight mechanism, can be rebooted, shutting down symptoms of PTSI. Exposure to trauma can actually make one stronger and able to do better with the next trauma. Having a mindset based on resilience can make the garden of the brain grow.

I would like to leave you with a parable told to me by my father, a story that has kept me going through the worst times:

Two frogs fall into a jug of milk. The first frog closes his eyes and says, "I guess it is time to die." He allows himself to sink and drowns. The other frog cries out, "I will fight until the last possible moment!" He moves his legs, kicking out, churning to keep his head above the milk. "I will not drown," he says, exhausted, but he keeps kicking. Eventually, he realizes the milk has thickened into butter and he is able to get enough purchase to jump out.

Do not give up. Keep kicking! Your brain and biological systems can help you, if you let them.

DR. EDY GREENBLATT, PH.D.

Learning To Dance In Your Own Body: Confessions Of A Resilience Guru

One of the most important life lessons I ever learned came during my time as a graduate student in Dance Ethnology at UCLA. It wasn't just about dance; it was about resilience—learning to thrive within our own unique circumstances. This lesson came to me in a freshman ballet class led by the legendary Margaret Hills, a master ballet mistress and Fellow of the Royal Academy of Dance.

Embracing Our Unique Bodies

At the end of the first class, Ms. Hills lined up each perfectly shaped, fit, and talented 18-year-old dance major. To the first student, she said, gesturing towards her ribs, "It appears you took singing lessons when you were younger." The young woman nodded. "Those lessons changed the shape of your chest. As such, in ballet, when you raise your arms like this" – she demonstrated – "you'll need to turn your chest slightly away from center to compensate."

She moved to the next seemingly perfect dancer. "It appears the ratio of your thigh to lower leg length is higher than average. This puts you at risk for knee injuries when dancing on pointe. You'll want to..." And so she continued, showing each seemingly perfectly proportioned student in the class how she could learn to dance safely and effectively in her own body.

Learning To Thrive Within Constraints

This experience taught me a profound lesson.   That each of us has unseen challenges and imperfections. That no one is perfectly suited to the roles they play or the goals they set, no matter how things appear from the outside. We must each learn to dance in our own body, simultaneously embracing our uniqueness while graciously adapting to our personal and professional constraints.

The Art Of Resilience

To dance effectively in our own bodies means that we must become and remain strong and flexible humans on every level. Personal resilience, the ability to succeed and triumph over life's challenges, large and small, requires a lot of luck and some skill. Most importantly, we must become experts at knowing the exact behaviors and conditions that restore us and deplete us. This is a key finding of my research, starting with my PhD studies and continuing through the last 20 years of professional coaching and consulting. Resilience isn't about pushing through difficulties; it's about having a deep understanding of ourselves – physically, socially, spiritually, psychologically, and emotionally – and using that knowledge to fuel everything we want to do.

About a third of us have a powerful combination of self-awareness and the capacity to manage ourselves and our situations effectively, consistently making sound decisions that prevent burn-out and help us thrive. The rest of us need help. Often, this involves figuring out a personalized resilience plan and getting the support we need to implement and maintain it.

When we recognize our worldview and assumptions, are clear about our values, know the conditions and behaviors that restore and deplete us, and have the knowledge and tools to support ourselves, we thrive. This understanding and application are not just theoretical concepts – they are the foundation for a life well-lived, and they are essential for true resilience.

Transitioning From Dance Culture To Corporate Culture

To dance well in our own bodies, we must KNOW all aspects of ourselves and what affects us. This includes recognizing what we think and our worldview, and how these shape our experiences. I received an accelerated lesson in this when I arrived at Harvard Business School, where I knew, going in, that I would be an outlier. I was the second oldest in my MBA section and wasn't even an MBA student – I was there to earn a Joint PhD in Organizational Behavior. My education and professional experience had been in the arts, education, and travel, not business. I did not come from privilege. My father's mental health problems led to my parents' divorce when I was young. Inadequate diagnosis and treatment in the VA hospitals left him to struggle with PTSD and subsequent homelessness until he died. My mother was a concentration camp survivor who came to the US as a college student and refugee. She made the best of a difficult life that included work-induced burnout and early disability. We faced financial and social difficulties. My brother and I started earning money in our young teens having developed a robust work ethic as children helping mom with home-based businesses. As she became increasingly ill, we took care of her in every way possible. Through my PhD studies, I now had a chance to end decades of family struggle. I was joining the business world, transitioning from dance culture to corporate culture.

Thinking 100 Miles Outside The Box

I arrived for my first day dressed in appropriate MBA student apparel, accessorized by a gorgeous, deliciously scented white ginger lei. I'd received it on my way back from Western Samoa, where I had spent two weeks with other dance scholars documenting the quadrennial Festival of Pacific Arts. My outsider-ness became apparent immediately.

The majority of the seventy students in my section came from companies and industries I knew nothing about. They had worked for McKinsey, Bain, Goldman. They did M&A were CTOs. As everyone else just nodded knowingly, I sat reminding myself that I had five years to learn. I did recognize a few military roles: Navy SEAL, F-16 pilot. I knew Kellogg made cornflakes and Canadian Glacier bottled water. Finally, Jordy said he'd worked in "PNG." Ah! Great! PNG I knew. I was excited. At the break, I made a beeline for the PNG guy. Bedecked in my fragrant white flowers, I bounced over and introduced myself.

I told him how I'd just come back from working with guys from Mt. Hagen during the festival. I shared how we'd documented their dance performance preparation – putting the boar's tooth through their large nasal piercings, and carefully inserting the tens of precious bird feathers into their ceremonial headdresses after painting the red, yellow, and black curves around their eyes. Jordy gaped at me open-mouthed. I was already feeling the weight of being an outsider. Now, it was amplified when my excitement about Papua

New Guinea was met with a blank stare. After an additional quizzical glance at my lei and what seemed like an eternity, he politely said that it all sounded quite interesting, but he didn't understand why I was sharing those experiences with him this minute. I responded, "Well, you said you worked in PNG. I figured you were familiar with Papua New Guinean culture even if you worked in Port Moresby. What did you do there?"

Jordy smiled like an indulgent parent and said, "I worked at Proctor and Gamble in Cincinnati, Ohio. We call it P&G. You know, Mr. Clean, Dawn dish soap?" I turned red. My heart sank. I apologized for the confusion, asked him a few more polite questions, and walked away.

The subsequent days, weeks, and months were difficult. It became clear that it was not just my lack of business knowledge and experience that set me apart. At HBS, my thinking wasn't just outside of the box, it sometimes fell off the page and extended into the next city. I excelled in the Leadership and Organizational Behavior class where the best solution to the case problem just jumped out at me. I was puzzled by why it took others so long to work it through. I accepted the backhanded compliment when the Financial Accounting and Control professor chastised fellow students for failing his exam by saying that even Edy, who had no business doing so, had passed the midterm.

The Impact Of Our Worldview And Assumptions

It became clear that in two distinct ways, I experienced the world very differently from my colleagues. First, my worldview was entirely different from their assumptions about people, money, communication, human behavior, and global possibilities. In the context of business school studies, I soon realized that I had to release a number of unproductive assumptions. Marketing class, for example, was an emotional rollercoaster. As an artist, I saw robust marketing and sales as untrustworthy and embarrassing behaviors. If you are good enough, someone will discover you. There is no need to shout and pester people. That self-limiting and judgmental assumption was an error. I suffered through marketing class trying to learn important tools while challenging my deep-seated personal myth.

Years later, working at McKinsey & Co. revealed more communication blind spots. After months of angst, I still didn't understand the "code" my colleagues and superiors spoke in. In the dance world, "you might think about ..." was a mentor's gentle encouragement to explore my capacity and find a better solution. At McKinsey, "you might think about ..." meant "do it or your annual review will report that you don't collaborate well." Again, I didn't know enough about myself and my assumptions to respond and perform as effectively as I would have liked. These blind spots created stress and anxiety, both for me and for those around me, because none of us could reconcile how people so committed to collaborating could have such trouble interacting. As I gained more clarity about my world view and my expectations, I became more resilient. The process, painful as it was, made me better able to help others on similar journeys.

Integrated Thinking

The second dimension on which I was different from my colleagues was how I process information and generate hypotheses. I have since realized that as a trained dance anthropologist, I think with my entire being—not just with my mind, but with my body, heart, and soul as well. This kind of integrated thinking is uncommon in corporate America. It's not that I can't separate thought from emotion or the present from the future. I can. It's that I am able to view things both separately and holistically. Similarly, I don't just imagine what it might be like to be in a situation looking from the outside in. I can experience myself in the situation as well. In dance, I am known for my capacity to adopt any cultural or personal dance style. It is easy for me. I just 'embody' the dancer I want to emulate. This superpower allows me to often understand and anticipate what others, present or hypothetical, might experience – physically, psychologically, socially, cognitively, and emotionally. And, this approach became the basis for my PhD research on burnout prevention in 24/7 service workers. Ultimately, my native ability led to research advances and the development of personal resilience tools, in some cases, decades before positive psychology and employee resilience were "a thing". These were important steps in my learning to dance in my intellectual body. The dance anthropologist's world view, which made me an outlier in my field, enabled me to help employees find burnout solutions otherwise unavailable to them.

The Importance Of Revisiting Definitions

Our self-definitions and values take shape early in our lives. Our childhood experiences, our education, and our first jobs create a set of expectations and narratives. Some of those serve us well and help us to excel and innovate. Some work well in emergencies but fail us in 'normal life.' To be happy and resilient, we must constantly revisit not only our narratives, but also the very definitions of the words we use in those narratives. Your worldview is the integration of your beliefs about yourself and others with your beliefs about how the world operates for you and others. The words you use to describe those beliefs must be precise. When you say PNG, do you mean a culturally extraordinary Melanesian island nation, the home of the Huli people, or a $400 billion global consumer goods company and home of Charmin's bears? Do those you work with share your definition? Turning inward, are your definitions of happiness or success precise enough to help you transform your life into what you want? Are you really after happiness, or is it contentment you seek? What do you need in order to re-energize and restore yourself? Do you really need to get back to running? Or is it that you crave some time for yourself, a cardio-vascular challenge, 40 minutes outdoors without your phone, or all of these? To create an effective resilience plan, you need to disentangle what you call your restorative event (running) from its characteristics (40 minutes of uninterrupted alone time, outside, getting an endorphin kick). A clear understanding of the behaviors and conditions you need to thrive will launch you towards a sustainable resilience plan.

Dancers As Masters Of Resilience

Dancers know that each performance is different, that there is no perfection, and that we have to keep looking at what we have done and making small adjustments if we want to do them better in the future. We never dance a dance the same way twice. We are always working with a slightly different body, audience, stage, partners, surfaces, and costumes. We perform with ever-changing health challenges, family issues, priorities, and financial concerns.

Dancers use their hard-won strength and knowledge to execute the choreography, while being open to necessary real time improvisation. We push on our limits while being careful not to harm ourselves or others in the process. Dancers are masters of resilience.

You Are The Lead Dancer In Your Life

You, too, are a dancer in life. What do you need to learn in order to best dance in your body? Which narratives that you inherited from mentors or family would you be better off without? Which definitions of self that served you in the past might need revision to carry you into your future? Is there an internal artist, politician, superhero, nurturer, youngster, or philosopher whom you need to consider more regularly in your daily work or play? When we understand the root causes of what limits, supports, depletes, and restores us, we can amplify the good in our lives and reduce our liabilities' effect on us. You're all set to do so.

Commit To Embracing The Resilient Dancer Within

I have been named the #1 Global Resilience Coach by Thinker's 50 Global Coaches. Respected professionals call me Dr Edy, a resilience guru. Yet, I am and will always be a dancer. Finally, I am no longer afraid to be an outsider and will no longer hide my dance anthropologist's identity. For decades, I have successfully run an effective workshop called World Class Leadership Through World Dance. Through it, a few thousand people, from MBA students to global industry leaders, have learned key leadership and team effectiveness lessons. But, out of fear, I have largely kept the program a secret that I only offer to clients and colleagues who already know me. So, now you know.

I hereby commit to using the strengths and lessons from my dancer core unabashedly in the service of all that I do. I already actively bring them into my coaching. They are built into Resilience Oasis ™, my mobile app and process that provides affordable, personalized resilience assessment, coaching and action planning to employees so they can better dance in their own bodies. I'm now all in as a dancer, leading the employee resilience revolution!

It's not enough to merely survive or go through the motions, hoping things will improve. Resilience requires deliberate action. We must learn to dance in our own body, consciously exploring our worldviews, releasing outdated assumptions, and embracing those that strengthen us. Understanding what restores and depletes us—physically, emotionally, psychologically, and spiritually—is essential. If this doesn't come naturally, seek help from coaches, technology, and colleagues! Then, make the decisions that prevent burnout and help you thrive!

Resilience is a dance—an ongoing, evolving performance that demands deep self-awareness and commitment to values, learning, action, health, and happiness. In the dance of life, challenges can usually be rechoreographed for the better.

Join me on this journey. Resilience, self-awareness, and continuous growth are universal principles. We each have our own "bodies" to dance in—unique circumstances, strengths, and challenges. By embracing and working with them, we can dance more gracefully through life.

Try answering this question. What would it look like to truly dance in your own body, align your actions with your deepest values, and meet your own needs in a way that restores and sustains you? If that vision is appealing, you are not alone. I am here to guide you, not just as a coach or consultant, but as someone who has leapt along this path and knows the power of embracing who you truly are. Being an outsider, embracing my unique perspective, and listening to my body and soul have become my strengths. These qualities enable me to help others find their own resilience.

Embrace who you are, and know that you are resilient. Dance joyously in your own body, rewrite the narratives that no longer serve you, and step boldly into the life you are meant to live. Clear away the deadwood in your mind, nurture the seedlings of hope in your heart, and soon you'll hold the bouquet earned by a life well danced. Resilience isn't just about bouncing back—it's about thriving, growing, and finding joy in life's dance, no matter the music. And that's a dance we can all master, one step at a time.

ALI KATZ

Inheritance Redefined: Healing My Inherited Victim Consciousness And Becoming A Powerful Creator Of Reality

Recognizing My Reality

Twelve years ago, I was emotionally, spiritually, and financially bankrupt. My inner psyche had been ruptured by conflict between my mind and heart, stuck in a war that I couldn't seem to reconcile. A war of the masculine and feminine, my heart and mind, two distinct parts of myself: Ali and Alexis. I hated myself, and most of the people around me.

As I sit here writing this, I am overlooking the ocean, close enough to see the waves crashing on the shore. I live with five of my best friends, one of them is the young female COO who is running my portfolio of legal and financial education companies while she raises her own child and three of them are the most beautiful, heart-centered, trustworthy men I know. I'm about to begin working on a creative project I've been dreaming of for years, and this year our companies will generate over $10 million in revenue.

Back then, even though I had won all the awards and accolades on the physical plane, it became clear I had won the wrong game. Or at least, that's what I thought for so many years as I grappled with the perpetual question: "Is there something wrong with me?"

I had played by all the rules, checked all the boxes: graduated first in my class from Georgetown Law, secured a six-figure paycheck at one of the best law firms in the U.S., gotten married, had a child, and bought a house with a white picket fence and a tire swing in the front yard, in Redondo Beach, California. On paper, I had achieved the American dream. I was twenty-nine years old and beginning to wonder if I had made a gigantic mistake.

Underneath all those checked boxes, I felt a crushing loneliness, a painful void that I couldn't seem to fill no matter how much I accomplished. Something essential was missing, even as I'd dutifully checked off each milestone society had told me would bring fulfillment. It wasn't until I began uncovering the layers of victim consciousness I had inherited from my father and maternal grandmother that I realized I had been pursuing the wrong prize entirely. The true path to wholeness lay not in worldly accolades, but in the radical reclamation of my identity as a powerful creator of my own reality.

Find Your Church

During that time of deep loneliness, a gnawing thought began to echo in my mind: "Find a church, find a church, find a church." But that idea didn't make any sense to me. I had been raised Jewish, and the two people I loved most in the world, my father and maternal grandmother, both seemed to believe that God was for "stupid" people, not for intelligent, successful individuals like me. Why was I suddenly feeling this pull toward something I had been taught to dismiss?

Instead, I decided I'd focus on finding a preschool for my daughter. She was at home with her father all day, while I commuted an hour away in Los Angeles traffic, still nursing, still pumping breast milk, and often getting calls throughout the day with her crying in the background. There had to be something better the two of them could do.

I asked my husband to take our daughter to the local parent participation co-op, Manhattan Beach Nursery School. I scanned the phone list he brought home, and one woman's name flew off the page at me. That was weird.

"Who's JoAnne?" I asked.

My husband shrugged. "Just some bitch."

"What? Why is she a bitch?"

"Oh, I saw her at AA the other night, and she ignored me."

I didn't think of it again until two weeks later, as I was sitting at my desk pumping milk, and the phone rang. It was JoAnne.

She was calling around to all the moms to arrange for playdates. I didn't know about synchronicities back then, but I did know that something felt shocking to my system.

This was the same woman whose name had flown off the page at me, and now she was calling me out of the blue.

I told her I was the working parent, so not available for park playdates, but that my husband was at home with our daughter and had seen her at AA, so they should get together. She was overjoyed. They would meet at a nearby park and get to know each other. I was overjoyed at the thought of my daughter and her dad having friends instead of sitting at home all day.

JoAnne would become my first real adult friend and my first spiritual teacher. But at first, I had no idea about the spiritual part. While I had been hearing that repetitive thought, "Find a church," I had an aversion to the idea of God. And every time JoAnne and I got together, she'd talk about God. Incessantly. My stomach would twist each time she uttered the word.

Remember, I had been raised to believe that God was for "stupid" people, not for me. And yet, if I was so smart, and I didn't need God, why was I so unhappy, lonely, and broken, even though I had done everything "right"? There must be something I didn't understand, and maybe this "God" thing was the answer. . . .

When JoAnne suggested I check out Agape International Spiritual Center, a church she attended regularly, I decided to give it a try. The minute I walked into Agape, I knew I had found exactly what my mind had been trying to get me to look for when it kept repeating, "Find a church."

I was home.

The energy was unlike anything I had ever experienced. A palpable current of love and possibility pulsed through the giant warehouse, beckoning me deeper.

As the service began, the congregation began to sing songs that I somehow felt as if I already knew, and something deep stirred within me. Something about this place resonated with a deep, long-forgotten part of myself.

I wasn't alone anymore.

Rev. Michael Bernard Beckwith spoke about God in a way that made total sense to me. He described God not as some distant, judgmental figure, but as the love intelligence that governs the universe. And most incredibly, he helped me to see that I am God—the hands, feet, heart, soul, and body of God—and that God could only operate through me and each of us.

This concept was revolutionary to me.

It meant that I didn't have to do it all alone, that I could relax some of the weight on my shoulders and give it over to a power greater than myself. What a relief! I wasn't separate from the divine, but an integral part of it. I began to see glimmers of how this understanding could transform my life in ways I had never imagined.

In the weeks and months that followed, I immersed myself in the teachings at Agape. I learned about the power of intention, the law of attraction, and the science of the mind. I began to understand that my thoughts and focus had the ability to shape my reality and were in fact already doing so. I began to wonder: If my mind was this powerful, what could I manifest if I directed it with clear, purposeful intention? But I also began to wonder how I'd allowed myself to get into a situation where I felt so lost, confused, and alone when I wasn't at Agape.

Is There Something Wrong With Me?

"Is there something wrong with me?" Once again, the thought echoed through my mind.

This time, the question wasn't just a thought stuck on loop in my mind, but instead a turning point in my journey. I began to accept that there *was* something wrong. What I heard Rev. Michael speak of was so deeply resonant and true, yet it didn't seem to align with the way life or my relationships felt.

The incongruity was most evident when I left Agape each Sunday, as the people who had been singing, hugging, and crying minutes before now jockeyed for their position in the food line or cut each other off in the parking lot with scowls on their faces.

If I was truly the creator of my own reality, something *was* wrong. But I didn't yet know what it was, and if I was going to discover what it was and heal it, I'd have to turn toward it to find out. But where was I supposed to look?

At first, I thought the answer was to look outside at the people around me. Maybe it wasn't me at all, but them. That's what I had learned from my father and my maternal grandmother, Nan. If something was wrong, it must be "them"—the people around me who were to blame. Certainly, it must be my husband. Or my kids. Or the partner I worked for. And, later, the staff I hired.

So, I'd begin the process of upleveling all of them. If I could just get my husband to come to Agape with me. Or, if I could get us to a better house. A better sitter for my kids. Better work. My own business! And a better team. I did everything I could to fix all of it, and all of them. I learned to use the power of my mind to create a new reality.

Manifestation?

I manifested the perfect house, steps from the beach, on one of the coveted walk street roads in Hermosa Beach. I wrote it in my journal: three bedrooms, washer/dryer, wood floors, max rent of $2,500/month, on the walk street. We rented our Redondo Beach home, and moved onto 20th street two months later.

After my second child, Noah, was born, I manifested the perfect circumstances to decide I would leave the BigLaw firm and the security of my six-figure paycheck to create my own law practice, a business I never dreamed of having but was clearly my next step. The journey of how that came to be is detailed in my book *The New Law Business Model Revealed: Build a Lucrative Law Practice That You (and Your Clients) Love.*

I manifested the perfect office setup, in which I would build my law practice into a business I loved. I manifested the perfect first team member, Susan, a former teacher at my kids' school, who knew nothing at all about business, but had a huge heart and desire to serve.

And I also manifested all the perfect troubles:

- My husband, an alcoholic and rage-aholic who always just seemed to want to get away;
- A near inability to be alone with my kids without all the energy draining from my body, with no understanding of why it was so hard for me to be with them;
- The weight I was holding onto after both kids and the lethargy I felt every Sunday;
- The team that was constantly failing me, including a team member who stole from me and then sued me when I fired her, an associate lawyer who missed getting a document signed during deathbed planning and left me subject to a lawsuit from the heir who was harmed as a result, and even another team member who tried to steal the entire practice from me, preying on my naive, newly burgeoning spiritual beliefs of trusting everyone without verification.

I couldn't understand. Why was it all so difficult? I had such good intentions, and yet at every turn it seemed that life was challenging me in ways that left me lost and confused.

I thought I was a good person with a good heart, and in one respect, life seemed to be rewarding me.

As I went through a divorce with my husband, I had my first million-dollar year in business by finding my way to stop the conflict between us and give him what he needed.

At the same time as I was selling my law practice to the wrong lawyer, who would later give it back to me without paying me in full for the purchase and stick me with a $250,000 debt I'd take on to close the business in the right way, I built a second million-dollar business, an online training company.

As I was getting sued by a former employee, I wrote a best-selling book on legal planning for families and began appearing on television regularly as a family, financial, and legal expert.

Through it all, though, I knew something still wasn't right, and I needed help to figure out what it was.

Plant Medicine

It was around that time I felt the call to the plant medicine ayahuasca. This was back in September 2009, well before plant medicine became the common staple of healing it is known to be now.

Through significant resistance, I found myself in a downtown Los Angeles warehouse with twenty others, ready to "purge" anything not aligned with the life I wanted to create.

Back then, though, I didn't know anything about purging or alignment. I just knew that what I had been doing, even though it created so much external success, was not working for me at all on the inside.

My ayahuasca experience showed me a dream I'd spend the rest of my life pursuing.

I envisioned people living on land, in harmony, growing food, raising children, working together. As I felt it, a world that works for everyone. I had never experienced anything like it in my own reality, and yet as I felt it through ayahuasca, I knew it was what I desired to create. I had no idea what that would take, but I said yes.

Voices In My Head

Over the following few months, I systematically got to experience every single way I was creating the exact opposite of that world. I got to see the ways my leadership and my choices were self-centered, not we-centered.

It all came to a head as I sat on the soundstage of the Nancy Grace Show. I had spent hours getting down to the studio and into hair and makeup to gossip about Tiger Woods's divorce. Normally, this ritual was one in which my mind would be silent, my ego satisfied that I was living my purpose, on my path, doing exactly what I should be.

But this time, it was very different. As the camera was about to turn to me, I heard a loud, booming voice in my head:

"Alexis, what are you doing?" the voice yelled at me. "You are about to go on national television to gossip about another human being. You are contributing to the world negatively, one thousand percent. You can never do this again."

Wait, what?!

Through my confusion, I delivered my message on the show and left the studio with the clarity that I would have to leave Los Angeles.

Days later, I found myself in Denver to speak to the law school class of my best friend, who lived in Boulder.

She lived on a cul-de-sac, walking distance to a public school for my kids. Our kids were best friends, and there was a house for rent on the lake two houses down from hers—twice the size and half the rent.

We Were Moving To Boulder

I didn't know exactly why life was taking me to Boulder, but by then, I had begun to get good at listening beyond what I could see on the surface and following what I heard.

My early days in Boulder were full of extreme confusion, internal tension, and a significant amount of "woe is me" finger-pointing and blame, with glimpses of a new future reality that showed me what I desired beneath it all: Connection with land. Community. Learning to feel. My heart as the guide, and my mind a tool in service to my heart.

But I was quite far away from all of that, and the glimpses I received created a profound contrast that often left me in despair at how far away I was from the life I dreamed of having.

"What is wrong with me?" I wondered even more often now. "Why can't I appreciate what I have? Why isn't it enough?"

Now, with hindsight, I can see clearly.

Life needed to break me down completely so I could see what I otherwise would have blocked out with powerful defense mechanisms created by a mind that believed it had all the answers.

What I've come to discover is that the mind developed in childhood, and the success that results from that mind, can be a powerful protector that keeps us safe—and stuck—behind an armored wall of surface, feel-good victories, shielding us from the full range of a life truly worth living.

Intimacy, connection, and true love are on the other side of that wall.

Who Am I, Why Am I Here And What Is Mine To Do?

My mind was particularly strong. It's why I went to law school and was able to graduate first in my class. I barely let myself feel anything for those three years. I made very few friends and didn't care that most of the class shunned me because I was such a "gunner" with my hand raised at the front of the room in every class session.

I just put my complete self into proving I could be as smart as everyone else.

My heart is sensitive and tender, and she spent many years in deep disappointment about what life is. . . and what we have become. My mind needed to protect her and keep her safe. But in the process, it became over-developed. Too powerful. And disconnected from the truth of my actual desires. My heart. My body. My soul.

Until I could get these four parts of me all into alignment—mind, heart, body, and soul—all unified, I would constantly be in a state of incongruence and no matter how much success I experienced or money I had, it would never be enough.

I had used my mind to create the most success I possibly could, and it wasn't it.

Moving to Boulder led me to walk away from everything I had created, fire just about everyone I was paying, and move to a farm so I could live for a year asking three questions: "Who am I, why am I here, and what is mine to do?"

I needed to ask these questions without money motivating my choices. I needed to find out what was true if my mind wasn't in the driver's seat.

I needed to learn to feel my heart and let her lead.

- Would I even still want to be a lawyer?
- Why did I go to law school?
- Would I want to train lawyers?
- Was my work valuable?
- Was I just like my father, a con-artist who stole from people because he didn't think he could create real value?
- What would I choose to do if money weren't motivating me?

The answers shocked me.

Nothing had been a mistake at all. I went to law school and became an estate planning lawyer so I could discover the truth about inheritance and estate planning. I needed to see just how broken it was so I could fix it. I needed to face the possibility that I was just like my father to understand that I came here as the evolution of him to heal what I inherited and create a new future reality. And that, in fact, we all have.

This realization marked a crucial juncture in my path.

Inheritance Redefined

I began to see how the patterns of victimhood and blame I had inherited from my family were operating in my own consciousness, even as I was learning and discovering profound spiritual truths.

I discovered that this is a common purpose we all share: to heal what we've inherited in service of creating a new future reality.

If we want life to change, we must change it through ourselves. We are the eyes, hands, mouth, heart, and body of God. We are the evolution, and that evolution begins with looking at what we've inherited honestly, so we can stop the behaviors from continuing to perpetuate through us and ripple throughout the world.

I knew that if I wanted to truly embody the principles I had first discovered at Agape, I would need to do the deep inner work of confronting and healing these inherited narratives. It wasn't enough to simply point the finger outward; I had to take radical responsibility for my own life and experiences. I knew that if I truly wanted to transform my life and step into my full potential as a conscious creator, I would need to do the inner work to heal and release these limiting narratives.

It wasn't enough to simply understand the principles of manifestation and divine connection intellectually. I had to embody them, to root out the stories of lack, unworthiness, and powerlessness that had shaped my life for so long.

And so, with a mix of trepidation and resolve, I began the journey of excavating my own consciousness, layer by layer.

I knew it would be a challenging and often uncomfortable process, but I also knew that it was the only way to create the life of authentic joy, connection, intimacy and purpose I yearned for.

As I took my first steps down this path of fierce self-honesty and transformation, I had no idea just how much I would uncover about myself and my lineage.

My ancestors had been powered over, forced out, and needed to cheat, steal and lie for their own safety and protection. They passed on an inheritance of scarcity based decision-making and fear that I've identified as "Money Dysmorphia" and I vowed to recognize this distortion inside myself, so I could heal what I inherited and create a new future reality.

I've taken this vow into my life and work, creating a new model for legal and financial planning that shifts our paradigm from zero-sum games and win-lose dynamics into a paradigm of "all-win" systems that support our collective, thriving future because of how we choose to engage with each other, and use our collective resources for good.

The individual and collective relationship we've inherited around our resources of time, energy, attention and money (our TEAM resources) is ready to be healed. Our legal and financial advisors can learn this path of healing and transformation, do their own work, and help their clients to do the same. With the help of advisors trained in the model I'm creating, we can come to see our inheritance as the conduit for personal and family healing at the deepest and highest levels, and together create the legacy our ancestors prayed we would discover.

Inheritance redefined.

ADRIENNE DENESE, M.D., PH.D.

From Communism To Consumer Sales

I was born in Hungary during the height of communism. Life was grim for a kid during that time. No TV, no fashion, no shopping, no parties, no dances, no movies, no games... nothing. There was literally nothing else for a kid in communist Hungary to do—except study.

We had two hours of television broadcasting a night, one channel only, and it was mostly heavily censored news.

However, on Saturdays between three and four o'clock, life as we knew it stopped for one hour. Western pop music was broadcasted! We were glued to the radio listening to the Beatles, in awe, for that one magical hour each Saturday afternoon.

Food shopping was equally unexciting. You cannot even fathom what a grocery shop looked like during the height of communism. I lived next door to one as a child, so I remember as if it was yesterday. It was a simple, rectangular store with no middle aisles given that there was nothing to display. No fruits, no vegetables, nothing but potatoes, cabbage, and onions. One wall was covered with uniform bags of government-brand flour and sugar. The opposite wall had bags of salt and a few bottles of oil and vinegar. There was one brand of soap, one brand of shampoo, one brand of toothpaste and Vaseline. No face cream, no lipstick, no makeup, no deodorant, no laundry detergent.

The milk and butter came at eight in the morning. I knew that because a line immediately formed outside the store and stretched around the corner until all the goods were sold. Bread came at noon. The line was even longer then.

When I was five, it was my job to run and stand in line as soon as possible because bread sold out as fast as it came. I proudly stood in line for milk and butter, I brought home the bread at noon every day, and I felt that I was making a great difference in the household. It helps to live in a small world, where you feel you can master it all, at least for a few happy years.

Family

My grandmother was the most influential person in my life. She was solid, predictable, never left the house, worked incessantly, and was always there for me. She got up at five every day, chopped wood, fed all the wood-burning stoves in the house, fed the chickens and pigs, collected the eggs, cleaned the house, made pasta from flour and water, cooked, baked, made elaborate meals several times a day, did laundry by hand (no washing machine), and tended to a vegetable garden and about fifty apple trees. At night, she peeled piles of apples for jam and pie or knitted sweaters for me. I remember watching her hands, wondering how they never ever seemed to stop.

Whatever was soft, nurturing, and pleasant in my life came from my grandmother. She also taught me the value of hard work. She used to say that there is never enough time in the day—and absolutely no time to be idle! She made sure I was always busy studying.

My father was a very intelligent man. He read everything he could get his hands on, and whatever he read he remembered. He was remarkably worldly, well informed, and razor-sharp in his political predictions. He grew up before communism took hold in Budapest, a privileged child of a prominent tax lawyer. He was sixteen when the Second World War broke out. He lived through the bombing of Budapest and the bombing of Dresden in Germany. He walked home from Germany through Austria to Hungary. He literally came home on foot at the end of the war by himself. He was only nineteen years old. He never talked about what he saw, and he never recovered from the experience. He became a bitter, opinionated man who suffered from depression for most of his life. His emotional burden must have been unbearable.

My mother had the face of an angel, and she acted like one. She was a national sports champion in sprint and high jump. She trained incessantly—that is all she wanted to do. She was charming, charitable, naïve, kind, selfless, and truly angelic.

Whenever I think of my mother, one incident always comes to mind. We had a tall wrought-iron gate in front of our house in the small town where I was born. It was a well-made iron piece, ornate with many flowers and about two stories high, it dated back to well before communism. I was about five years old when I finally figured out how to climb up to the very top. When I tried to show my grandmother how well I could climb, she nearly fainted and ordered me never to do it again. I expected something similar from my mother. However, she remained calm, applauded when I got to the top, and told me, "As long as you hold onto something with one hand, as long as you hold on really tight, you can climb up as high as you want."

So, I climbed up all the gates and all the fences, barn roofs, and tool sheds that I could find—always holding on really tight with at least one hand—and I felt that I could master anything.

When I was nine years old, my aunt began to make her famous bee pollen face cream for the ladies in the neighborhood. I was right there "helping" her. During the height of communism, any kind of private enterprise was strictly forbidden, so we had to work behind closed doors and drawn curtains. Soon, my aunt's creams became so well known that dozens of women came to buy it, at night, in secrecy, knocking on the kitchen window.

Eventually, the police came one night, confiscated all the creams, and shut us down. My aunt just narrowly escaped going to prison. I will never forget that night. It was frightening when the police came, but when I look back, the joy of helping my aunt to make the creams and seeing the enthusiasm of the ladies as they clamored to buy them is what comes to mind.

Study, Study, Study

Except for the bright, brief, and exciting episode of cream-making, most of my childhood memories are of studying.

I completed a Ph.D. in neuroscience at the young age of twenty-three and made plans to come to America to study medicine. My father spent his entire life's savings on a one-way airplane ticket to New York. He had forty dollars left, which represented a lot of money to him, so he gave it to me for "spending money," As I later found out, the ride from the airport was more than forty dollars.

I came to the U.S.A. by myself at age twenty-three with forty dollars in my pocket, not knowing a single soul here. No relatives, no friends, no acquaintances, nothing. It was the single most difficult thing I had ever done, but I felt there was no choice. I could not see myself listening to news or reading books and newspapers rewritten by the ruling party for the rest of my life.

It still gives me chills to remember saying goodbye to my family at the small-town train station. I remember my grandmother struggling with tears; I had never seen her cry before. We all thought we were seeing each other for the last time.

When I arrived in New York, I stayed with a pen pal at first. Then, after about eight months of unimaginable struggle for survival, I landed a postdoctoral fellowship at the University of Pennsylvania. It did not pay anything at first, but they gave me room and board, and the University had a medical library that was beyond comparison. It was open until midnight each and every day, even Sundays. I spent endless hours there trying to make up for lost time.

The head of the department at Penn was baffled by me at first. He had never seen anyone who asked for nothing and worked around the clock. I guess he had never been to Hungary. He liked me a lot, and eventually we published many scientific papers together, detailing how the right and the left sides of the brain differ from each other and how the brain organizes sustained attention (vigilance) responses.

Based on the publications, one day, I was invited to give a lecture at the Neurology Department of Beth Israel Hospital at Harvard Medical School on the brain studies that we conducted at Penn.

On a Tuesday, very early in the morning, I went to Boston. When I arrived, I was in bad shape. I vomited from nervousness in the taxicab on the way to Harvard. When I arrived, I went to the bathroom, cleaned up, looked in the mirror, and something clicked in my head. I felt that I had nothing to lose, so I turned it all around.

The lecture went really well. Fifty people, all in white coats at Harvard's top teaching hospital, clapped enthusiastically. The head of the department, a man of few words, stood up, called the lecture brilliant, and offered me a fellowship at Harvard right then and there. I accepted it, mostly because I was hopelessly in love with him by the end of the evening.

The love story went nowhere, but Harvard was wonderful. It taught me how little I really knew and spurred me to go to medical school.

A few years later, I got into Cornell Medical College on a full scholarship, and for one day, the day I received the letter of acceptance, I felt truly light and happy. It did not last long.

I was the oldest in my class (age thirty-two) and felt totally out of place among my bright, young Ivy League classmates. For the first time, I began to experience the uneasy realization of getting older, so I began to develop an overwhelming interest in antiaging medicine.

Let's Get To Work

After completing medical school and residency at Cornell Medical College and New York Hospital, I opened an anti-aging medical practice in Manhattan, a few blocks away from my alma mater.

All the wise ones told me: Nobody opens a practice right after residency; you are sure to go out of business. While I thought that this was entirely possible, I opened my antiaging practice anyway. I laid the tile in the hallway myself to save money, painted and hung wallpaper during the day, while at night I worked in the emergency room as a doctor to cover renovation costs.

Anti-aging medicine must have been an idea whose time had come because a few months later the *New York Times came to my office on their own accord and wrote a two-page article about my clinic in the Sunday Times (1998). Two days later, I was on Good Morning America, on 20/20 shortly after, and experienced an avalanche of television and magazine interviews (maybe fifty) over the next few months.*

As I was seeing my patients seeking to ward off aging, interestingly enough, they all settled on the same question at the end of the conversation: What can you do for my skin?

I tried to introduce already existing doctors' skin-care brands into my practice, but somehow, they fell short of my expectations, so I hired a highly experienced chemist, and we began to experiment in my kitchen.

We worked out a handful of formulations based on the most advanced active ingredients I could identify. I often used multiple times the percentage of active ingredients compared even to high-end commercial brands because I figured if I wanted to see a visible change in the skin, I needed to use unusually high levels of active ingredients. The formulations were very expensive, but I did not care. I had to face my customers in my office daily, so it was imperative for me to be able to show them visible results.

Next, we took our formulations to a well-respected cosmetic manufacturing facility for manufacture.

I remember the first time when I went to pick up the manufactured goods. I took my SUV, figuring I would bring them to my basement.

I arrived at the factory, and someone pointed to an actual mountain of boxes to be picked up. I apologized, ran out, rented a truck, and rented the largest storage unit I could find. I finished loading the storage unit shortly after midnight, and on the way home, I was pondering if this qualified as the most stupid move I had ever done.

Well, as it happens, we emptied the storage unit in less than a year and kept renting more and more units.

Celebrities began to frequent my office to pick up my skin-care or asked us to hand-deliver the goods to their Upper East Side townhouse while they were abroad. Lots of magazine publicity followed, and women came from great distances to find out more about my cosmetics.

One day, the TV shopping channel QVC paid me a visit and asked if I could present on television. The mere thought of being in front of millions of viewers gave me shivers, so I immediately said "no." But the young buyer kept coming back and finally told me that she might lose her job if she could not get me on board, so I agreed.

At first, I was like a deer in the headlights on live television. But with practice, training, and some hypnotherapy, I became one of the most successful skin-care lines ever in QVC's history, receiving a Rising Star Award and countless Customer Choice Awards over the past twenty-two years.

A few times a year, QVC asks you to prepare a Today's Special Value kit, orders fifty thousand to seventy thousand of that same kit, and expects you to sell them all in one single day. It is not easy, as you can imagine, and there is a lot at stake, but I succeed most of the time.

When I see the convoy of forty-foot trailers leaving my warehouse toward QVC, all full of merchandise that I will have to sell in one day, I often think of the night when I hand-loaded the first batch of products into a storage unit that I hastily rented and questioned my own sanity all the way home that night.

As it turns out, it was not a foolish mistake after all. In retrospect, it turned out to be the most important decision I ever made. Life will take you to places and directions that are unexpected.

Could I see myself becoming one of the top selling products on QVC while growing up in Hungary? Absolutely not, but life has taught me that there are always challenges, there are always uncertainties knowing this makes navigating this beautiful existence easier.

AMBER CAUDLE

The Shadows And Joys Of Hunger

Not unlike most newborns, I came into this world wide-eyed, slightly terrified, and screaming, apparently almost intelligibly, "I'm hungry!" It seems that most first-time mothers seek the advice of lactation experts to get newborns to latch on properly so the milk flows easily. But we didn't need any assistance; I seemed to know just what to do. Back then, there was no recommended set schedule for nursing (feeding on demand), and I took the demand part to mean that any time I cried, I was fed; a plentiful supply of milk always appeared. Little did anyone suspect that those first feeding forays contributed to the defining purpose and meaning for my life's path.

Cherry Pie And Sugarplums

My most indelible childhood memories around food are cooking with my grandma when I was not yet three years old. To this day, I can still salivate and even conjure up the aromas of the cherry pies baking in her kitchen. I can still feel the effort it took to stretch onto my tiptoes on that kitchen stool, making myself just tall enough to reach the cutting board to help roll out the freshly kneaded dough. I am giving you the embodied details of these kitchen adventures because I have had years to reflect, and I can now see that those experiences were an opening, a portal into a world of unbelievable wonder and enchantment. In my mind's eye, it was all magic, and visions of sugarplums were always dancing in my head. Each dish prepared together was a lesson in love. The best part, of course, were the endless opportunities for tasting, my favorite being the extra pie crust, warm and oozing with sugar and butter, which was all mine for the asking.

I'm pretty sure—as strange as it may sound— that the love of food was in my genetic coding, that my career as a chef was already etched into my very being. Could it also be true that those beloved cooking adventures were the beginnings of my decades-long complicated relationship with food? It is a heavy question to ponder. But had I considered it earlier in my life, maybe I would have blamed myself less harshly, behaved less radically and loved myself more deeply.

Sugar, Friend Or Foe

By the tender age of eight, I found myself in a delicate yet deliberate tug-of-war with my trusted confidant—sugar. My parents, on a health kick, began restricting sugary delights, and I found myself engaging in what I would call survival tactics. I remember the secret thrill of sneaking candy from a friend's house, taking it home, and stashing it under my bed away from the prying eyes of my parents. Did I experience shame and regret for my actions? Maybe just a twinge. But all I could process was the comfort and safety these escapades always delivered. I was simply taking care of myself.

Throughout my terrible teens, my questionable eating habits continued, and not just with the sugary treats, but with portion control as well. I labored under the belief that my hunger, my cravings, were simply a physical need. It didn't occur to me to curtail my eating until one day in gym class, in the dressing room, I remembered my gut-wrenching reaction when I suddenly became aware that my body was more developed than seemingly everyone around me. I was filled with a deep sense of insecurity and shame, even to the point of thinking I was deeply flawed and unworthy. Somehow, thinness became equated with happiness, and if I could not have the body I wanted, I must have done something terribly wrong.

During my high school years, I attacked the problem with a vengeance. I started to obsessively count calories, which threw me head-first into any and all restrictive diets in an attempt to mold my body into the ideal I had envisioned. When the diet tactics didn't pan out, I tried the fasting/starvation route, which led to binge eating, starving, and binging again. I was trapped in that vicious cycle that carries with it self-loathing and deep despair. Life had lost its meaning; I scarcely knew who I was. All I could think of was the punishment I was enduring simply by depriving myself of the very thing I loved the most—food.

As disheartening as that all sounds, I could not pull away from the calling of my life's destiny! Throughout my high school years, I worked at various fast- food venues which always supplied me with an abundance of sugary treats. So upon graduation, I set off to Auburn University, where of course, I chose a major in hotel and restaurant management. I loved it, especially the ventures into the back of house, the kitchen, when I was supposed to be studying the management, front-of-house side of things.

Found My Home Out West

But gratefully, opportunities come when we least expect it. I headed out west, to Ft. Collins, Colorado, where I had been offered an apprenticeship in a four-star Italian restaurant. Within days, my newfound passion kept luring me to the back of the house, where, in my opinion, all the magic was happening. Fortunately, the chef never stopped my relentless trips into the kitchen; I think he even sensed the possibilities of my innate talent. So it came to pass that there, amid the heart-beat of culinary creation at its finest, I found a home. I became fully immersed in the art of Italian cooking, which still today holds a piece of my heart.

Three years passed quickly by. How was my disordered eating (as I have since labeled it) showing up, one might wonder? Clearly it was still with me. Food was everywhere: new creations to taste (You can't create unless you taste— and taste), and yes, some after-hours partying added to it. As I look back, I knew I was gaining weight, but somehow, it wasn't the obsessive focus of my life. As I said, I was in heaven, envisioning my life as a renowned and respected chef.

And then, my chef came to me with the amazing opportunity to open a Mediterranean restaurant in Hermosa Beach, California, and to make me the executive chef! I couldn't pack my bags fast enough. At Mediterraneo, I poured my heart and soul into this all-encom-passing and somewhat daunting venture. The relentless work hours, coupled once again with the partying culture, tested my limits. Here I was, same song second verse, living out my deep love for and, at the same time, intense struggle with food. Yet, most importantly, I was achieving success and recognition in the culinary world of the South Bay, so I continued giving it my all.

My Body Was Telling Me Something

And it took my all. The ceaseless pace and rather grueling lifestyle led me to a critical point of collapse. Plagued by excessive weight gain, fatigue, pain, inflammation, hopelessness—Did I mention it all?—brought me literally to my knees. Following hip surgery for a torn labrum, the result of compulsive over-exercising, I knew I stood at a crossroads; something, everything needed to change. But how? Give me a challenge, a hardship to endure—but not this; I couldn't do it. I felt I had tried all avenues; all I could manage was crying myself to sleep every night, wondering if I could ever stop eating.

Luckily for me, a friend visiting me in the hospital one afternoon mentioned a spa she had recently attended. Perfect. I found myself journeying to the desert, drawn to this detox-fasting retreat center known for its myriad healing practices. I was a little leery of fasting—been there, done that—but I trusted the universe and went with an open heart and mind. On my arrival, I entered my room and found a book by David Elliott, *Healing, on the bedside table. This book became a beacon, illuminating a path toward self-love—a concept that, I must admit, was foreign to me. More than just words on a page, this book introduced me to new avenues of self-exploration and healing practices (e.g., breathwork, journaling, visualization, affirmations, walking a labyrinth) on what I now refer to as pathways to my spiritual awakening. Parts of myself were revealed to me that I had never confronted. During my last walk in the labyrinth, at the end of my stay, I heard a gentle voice in the desert breeze whispering encouraging messages: "You have been abusing food your whole life. It is time to start looking at the healing benefits of food." And just as gently and sincerely I replied, "Show me the way. I am ready."*

A New Me, A New Adventure

Upon returning from the desert, I felt like a totally different person. One thing resonated with absolute clarity: It was time for me to reclaim my power from food and, in that process, foster a healthy and loving relationship with my body—and my calling. This realization was a turning point. My passion for healing myself and others through the nourishing properties of food became an all-consuming mission. But how could I realistically make that happen? I intuitively knew I couldn't stay at Mediterraneo much longer, but I just couldn't walk away from the restaurant I had helped birth and still passionately loved.

So I Waited For A Sign

One serendipitous afternoon, exhausted after a late-night shift, I indulged in a much-needed nap on my living room couch. When I awoke, feeling refreshed and apparently emboldened, I stepped outside and spotted my neighbor, who happened to be the owner of a quaint little café, close to the beach. In a spontaneous burst of curiosity mixed with a little courage, I approached her and heard myself blurt out, "Do you want to sell your café?" To my astonishment, she paused for a moment, and then said she had been pondering that very idea! I hardly remember saying anything back to her. I turned, ran inside and hurriedly got a call off to my mother while visions of customers wrapped around the cafe were already dancing in my head. Could we do this? Her words were a beacon of trust and reassurance, reminding me that I had manifested this opportunity and now the universe had stepped in. Just forty-five days later, in December 2012, The Source Café opened its doors——yes, to a line of customers wrapped around the corner—and yes, because of a vision I had dared to dream.

It's hard to believe that we are in our twelfth year at The Source Café, and I am continually filled with gratitude at the reported impact it has made on people's health—and happiness—every day. It has been a joy to behold. Often, customers will ask how this all came about, and slowly I began sharing my story which gradually led to more formal speaking engagements. My eyes were opened to the power of storytelling. After a talk, people would approach me, tears in their eyes, sharing how deeply my words resonated with them, offering them a glimmer of hope. It was through these exchanges that I recognized the capacity of our stories to serve as catalysts for healing and connection. Yet oddly, I felt like I wasn't getting my whole story out; somehow, I wasn't telling the whole truth. I wasn't holding back; I just felt a part—a big part—of my story was missing.

Going Deeper

Meanwhile, my disordered eating had not magically gone away, and even in the midst of creating and serving the healthiest food on the planet, I was often out of touch with my own body. In fact, I began to think it was impossible to trust my body. All my white-knuckling attempts to control my eating were only digging me into a deeper hole. I wondered if I could help anyone when I couldn't even help myself.

Ever since leaving the desert spa, as broken open as I could imagine, I instinctively knew I needed to go even deeper. And so, as often happens, in the course of events, I found The Institute for the Psychology of Eating. Immediately after beginning the program, my over two-decade struggle with food came into clearer focus: My disordered eating behaviors were symptoms of deeper, underlying issues. Eating itself was never the root problem. It took an honest dive into the depths of my soul to uncover why I had been escaping and numbing myself with food. I had to let go of limiting beliefs that were keeping me small and dimming my true light.

And then it dawned on me: This was the part of my story that I somehow knew had been missing—the unconscious questions I had been carrying with me all along. I realized that my relationship with food was a medium through which more profound, unresolved issues sought to express themselves. I must admit, in the beginning, this process was not a very pretty picture, but it is one that I have come to accept, understand, and fully embrace.

Many enlightening interventions came into play, but among all the treasures I uncovered, my most prized discovery happened when I reconnected with an unknown, long-forgotten, neglected part of myself—my inner-child archetype, whom I affectionately named Sally. Bless her heart, she had been abandoned and pushed to the sidelines, her existence denied, which only led her to desperately act out to capture my attention. When I began to approach her with curiosity and compassion, acknowledging her presence and needs, I understood that she was only trying to keep me safe. She pushed me to my edges, helping me discover the root causes of my pain, my traumas, which gave me the courage to find my true voice. Whenever compulsions arose, I engaged with curiosity, leaning in, and pausing instead of reacting impulsively. I learned to listen, trust, be comfortable with discomfort, and accept that pain is temporary; it is not who I am. We were—and still are—partners in this continuing journey of healing and self-discovery. Together, we gratefully connect with this beautiful vessel, my body, in new ways—acknowledging, accepting, and truly loving her for the first time.

Sexy Food

With this newfound sense of self-love and acceptance, I embarked on another soul project: publishing my now best-selling cookbook, *Sexy Nourishing Food to Heal your Mind, Body, and Soul. After years of teaching cooking classes at The Source Café, customers continually asked for a cookbook, inclusive of all the many meals we had partaken of together. I was thrilled to do it; it was my gift to the culinary world, espousing my favorite philosophy: What we put in our bodies matters, one delicious, life-changing bite at a time!*

So here's the next wild idea that popped into my head: I still felt there was something missing in my life's calling—my reason for being here, for sharing my expertise and my story. I felt I could do more, reach more people, and help open more doors. One of my dear friends was a business coach, and she sparked my curiosity about the art of coaching. Could I coach people, empowering them to reclaim their power over food while cultivating love for their bodies. . . and be a chef at the same time? I instinctively knew that my pain and suffering were meant to be shared as a source of strength and inspiration for others on their healing paths. It all suddenly seemed to fit together in my mind. And just to validate my decision, The Institute for the Psychology of Eating offered a certification program which perfectly fit the bill. After graduating, I started my coaching business, Nourish Your Power, the fulfillment of a long-awaited, deep-seated vision of my soul.

Transformations

In the collaborative process of coaching, I have been privileged to witness remarkable transformations. My clients gradually released the heavy burdens of self-judgment and shame that had long clouded their self-worth. But often, the concern of worthiness seemed to surface. Someone would say, "I have read about people who have overcome impossible odds to achieve their goals. What am I whining about? I just can't seem to stick to a diet. I have to try harder."

My consoling but unwavering advice was this: "Don't compare your pain, your anguish, to someone else's. If uncontrolled eating and disrespecting your body are ongoing issues, then know that you have been wounded in ways you may not yet know. And when your dark shadows threaten to consume you, know that it is your inner child crying out, asking you to search for the answers and to give you assurance that you are never alone."

I am eternally grateful for every twist and turn, every challenge and triumph that has led me to where I am today. My journey has underscored the importance of embracing our imperfections, celebrating our uniqueness, and honoring the inherent beauty within each of us. There are still days when self-acceptance feels elusive, but together we can navigate these moments with greater love, compassion, and grace, knowing that pain is transient if we remain present and listen.

Am I still as ravenously hungry as the day I was born? Absolutely, in countless ways I never dreamed possible! I am hungry to continue to broaden the passions of my life's journey, to tell my story and hear yours, and hungry to make a difference in the world—one nourishing, sexy bite at a time.

So to you, dear reader, I extend an invitation to take the first step toward your healing. Know that you are deserving of love, worthiness, and fulfillment. Life is filled with highs and lows, pain and joy, but it is in our responses to these challenges that our true selves are revealed and celebrated. Embrace your journey with open arms, recognizing that each step forward is a step toward wholeness and freedom.

May you discover the incredible power that lies within you.

May you always know you are worthy of love and happiness.

May your life overflow with nourishment and abundance.

DAVID LOWRY

From Crisis To Clarity: Lessons Learned And New Perspectives "Call 911!"

These two words concisely summarized my first day as the President and Chief Executive Officer of a hospital and health care system in western North Carolina.

I'm a physician. I've spent most of my career providing care for critically ill hospital patients. Managing medical emergencies is my forte: running code blue events, performing emergency procedures in the intensive care unit, even responding to in-flight emergencies while on vacation. To be honest, I'm a bit of an adrenaline junkie. I perform at my peak during a crisis. But this situation was completely different. I was the person in trouble.

I decided to become a doctor when I was in high school. My father spent a career in the navy, and both of my older brothers are combat-decorated military officers. They assumed that I would be a military officer, and they were right. I attended medical school on an Air Force scholarship, completed an internal medicine residency, and served at the United States Air Force Academy hospital. After leaving the Air Force, I settled in western North Carolina, working as a hospitalist physician and serving in a variety of medical staff leadership positions. I never dreamed that my career would veer away from clinical medicine toward a formal leadership position.

A New Role

Several years ago, a colleague encouraged me to become a Chief Medical Officer. I wanted to use my clinical experience to help develop health care strategy, so I knew that this would be a good fit for me. After switching to this new role, I returned to school, completing an MBA and a fellowship in Transformational Health Care Leadership. I wanted to learn everything possible as I started on this new career trajectory.

Two years ago, I was encouraged to apply to become the President and Chief Executive Officer of UNC Health Caldwell. This organization is a component of the University of North Carolina Health System in the western North Carolina foothills, consisting of a hospital and over thirty practices and facilities spanning a three-county area. The interview process was long, providing ample time to prepare a personal development plan. I knew that personal resilience would be critical for success—maintaining work-life balance to maintain peak performance; regular exercise; plenty of sleep; a healthy diet; and time for family, friends, and hobbies, so I developed a "resilience plan."

I was selected as the new President and Chief Executive Officer late in 2023 with a start date of January 2, 2024, following the retirement of the existing CEO.

This is when my resilience plan imploded.

Just A Normal Day

I came to work on January 2, 2024 eager to get started. I completed an aerobic workout before sunrise and left for work. The day was fast-paced, consisting of back-to-back meetings, phone calls and strategy sessions, capped off by a late afternoon appointment at a local fitness center to start a strength training program. A friend from work had encouraged me to start a strength training program, even placing a series of scheduled workouts on my calendar. This seemed like a great idea. After all, mid-afternoon exercise increases energy levels and would help me function at peak performance; I knew the data: endorphin release, dopamine increase, etc. It was part of my "personal resilience plan."

My friend met me at the gym, introduced me to the trainer, and helped me complete an easy workout. I showered in the locker room and dressed, knotting my tie, ready to drive back to the office, finish off a few things, and then head home. I was feeling a little proud of how I was managing my first day as the new CEO, blazing through meetings and calls at high speed while finishing a "two-a-day" workout.

Then my world fell apart.

Blindsided By Pain

As soon as I stood to leave the locker room, car keys and cell phone in hand, I suddenly experienced the most intense, blinding, bone-crunching pain of my life. Intense pain surged across my entire right leg. I couldn't breathe. I felt like I was going to pass out. I sat down on a wooden bench, rolling onto my back while trying to stretch out my leg. My first thought was that I had a severe muscle spasm, but this felt exponentially more severe than anything I had ever experienced before. An elderly man clothed only in a white gym towel wrapped around his waist towered over me and said, "Son, are you having a heart attack?"

Through clenched teeth I said, "No, I'm okay." But I was lying. My thoughts were racing.

"I have to get back to work!"

"I don't have time to be sick!"

"Maybe I can drive to the emergency room?"

As several other people ran in to check on the "guy having a heart attack in the locker room," two things dawned on me: 1. I wasn't having a heart attack, but something was seriously wrong, and 2. I was totally incapacitated.

I finally broke down and told the gathering crowd "Call 911!"

Within minutes, an EMS team arrived, and I was transported to the emergency department at my own hospital. A STAT MRI confirmed the diagnosis: an acute L4-L5 disc herniation with severe impingement of the nerve root. "Severe" is a nonspecific adjective, but in my case, severe meant "really, really bad." In effect, the L4-L5 nerve root was crushed.

The L4-L5 nerve branches off the spinal cord in the lower back. It travels through the vertebral bone and extends down the leg, controlling motor and sensory function. In addition to excruciating pain, I lost much of the motor function in my right leg. I was admitted to the hospital, and a spine surgeon was consulted. He recommended urgent surgery to decompress the crushed nerve, so I went to the operating room.

Reality Check: From Leader To Patient

I don't remember much about the next few days, although I recall trying to text instructions to my teammates as soon as I was out of the recovery room. In retrospect, this sounds absurd but is very predictable behavior for those who know me well. I couldn't grasp that I was incapacitated; I had a job to do, and nothing was going to get in the way.

I was discharged home after a couple of days and slowly began to understand the extent of my injury. My right leg didn't work. I could barely stand, and I needed a walker just maneuver from my bed to the bathroom. Going up and down stairs? No. My leg collapsed with every attempt. I was shocked when a physical therapist came to my house. "I don't really need this, do I?" I asked my wife, Dana.

After an extensive evaluation, the therapist gave me a series of exercises to do while lying flat on my back. One required me to lift both arms from horizontal to vertical. I told Dana with frustration and anxiety, "I jumped out of airplanes when I was in the military! I was a long-distance runner in high school and college! Now, all I can do is raise my arms above my head?!"

About a week after surgery, Dana had to run an important errand that would take a few hours. She was concerned about leaving me alone, but I assured her that I would be okay. Of course, contrary to her instructions to rest on the sofa, I sat up and spent three hours sending and answering emails. I became more and more uncomfortable, so I finally grudgingly decided to stop working, put an ice pack on my leg, lie down, and watch an action series that I had been binging on. I settled on my favorite sofa, but when I raised my arm to aim the TV remote, I dropped it. It bounced across the hardwood floor and slid several feet, disappearing from view and out of reach. I literally broke down and cried, knowing that I had hit rock bottom.

I slowly improved over the next few weeks, gaining some strength in my leg, but I didn't return to baseline. I pretended that I was well and pushed myself harder than I should have. I like to jog down a back stairwell near my fifth-floor office, but one day, my leg collapsed and I fell a few stairs. I didn't do serious damage, but my surgeon was alarmed. Subsequent tests revealed that I had residual nerve compression.

To make a long story short, I had a second surgical procedure last week. The procedure went well; the tissue compressing the nerve was removed, and I have already noticed some improvement in my leg pain. It may take weeks or even months for the nerve to heal, but the surgeon is optimistic. I am frustrated by the lengthy list of post-operative restrictions, but this time, I am following them to the tee.

So, what has happened to UNC Health Caldwell over the past few months, while I have been in and out of the hospital?

Vision In Action

I developed a vision statement before I officially started as CEO. I shared it with my leadership team and with our entire organization. I shared it with Dana, my friends, colleagues in the UNC health system, community leaders, my board of directors, and anyone else who would listen.

My team has been amazing! They have taken "the ball" and run with it. The results have been amazing!

I want us to provide state-of-the-art medical care by hiring the best and building depth. Our catchment area extends into some rural, underserved areas in the mountains of western North Carolina, and I want every North Carolinian to have access to the best medical care. Over the past few months, we have added two pulmonary medicine specialists. Two additional surgeons have been hired for our orthopedic practice. Our behavioral health services continue to grow with the addition of a pediatric behavioral health specialist.

We have reengaged with our community, improving relationships with our local government leaders. Several of our senior leaders are volunteering and serving with local community organizations. One coaches a youth football team. Another attends a local senior center as an Elvis impersonator. I have started reading books for a class of first-grade students.

We are building a great culture where excellent patient care takes center stage but where we still have fun! I helped our team deliver 140 dozen donuts to all of our teammates earlier this month as we celebrated National Donut Day. It wasn't really about donuts. It was about telling our people, "We see you. You matter and you are important."

I have encouraged my team to innovate and think outside of the box, and I am astounded by what has happened. It has been exciting to see that the vision I communicated early on has been embraced and borne fruit. I want to think that this has happened despite my health issues. But maybe some of this has happened because of what happened to me.

Pivot And Rewrite

So, what about my resilience plan? How is it doing?

Boxer Mike Tyson famously said, "Everyone has a plan until they get punched in the mouth." I can certainly relate.

I still want to achieve work-life balance. I want to have time for self-care, time for exercise and sleep, time to spend with my wife and family. But I have learned that rigid and overly structured plans can make me fragile rather than resilient. Expectations can end up as "premeditated disappointments."

So I am trying to be less rigid in my approach as I develop a new paradigm for resilience: Pivot and rewrite the story.

How am I rewriting my story?

1. I realized how important it is to be present.

Visibility is critical: walking the halls, talking to those on the front line, making observations. As a new CEO, I intended to schedule time to get out to the medical practices and the nursing units every day, but my plan fell apart. But did it really? I didn't anticipate that emergency surgery would give me a front-row seat and a special window into the workings of my organization. The truth is that I couldn't have come up with a better way of seeing our operations firsthand. It was like I was starring in an episode of *Undercover Boss taken to an extreme. I saw a lot and learned a lot.*

I was deeply touched when a housekeeper told me, "I want to make your room look nice. You have so much stress, and I want to be able to help take some of it away. I know that a clean room will help".

I became the world's biggest fan of whiteboards. These dry-erase boards hang on the wall of each patient's room and are updated throughout the day, listing the name of each nurse and doctor on the treatment team as well as the day of the week and the date. It only took one time of awakening in pain and realizing that I had lost track of the time, date, my location, and my nurse's name, to become the world's biggest whiteboard fan.

I gained a new appreciation for the bedside nursing shift report process. I felt safe and protected when the day-shift nurse stood at my bedside and gave a detailed report about me to the oncoming night-shift nurse.

2. I learned to trust my team.

Sometimes the best action a CEO can take is to get out of the way. My intent as a new CEO was to know everything and do everything. This goal collapsed immediately. All I could do while lying in the emergency department was whimper. This is a far cry from leading a board meeting or negotiating a contract. Each person on my executive team dropped by to check on me after surgery, and they all said the same thing: "Don't worry. We've got this.

Everything is going to be okay." I am learning that my role is not to control everything and know everything. I am surrounded by a great team of talented, motivated professionals. I am learning how to help them succeed.

3. I learned to be more empathetic.

What about my friend, the one who encouraged me to start strength training and scheduled me to meet with the trainer? I learned that after my surgery, she was sobbing in her office. She felt responsible. She dropped by my room, trying to hold back tears. I reassured her, "This is not your fault. What if I had been out alone, hiking in the mountains? I would be dead." I reminded her that her intention had been to help me and that she had insisted that I started the strength training in a safe, monitored setting. "It's not your fault at all." Her tears stopped; she began to smile and said, "Thank you." I realized that even though I was stuck in a hospital bed, I could still be an encourager and help others feel better.

4. I learned to be more thankful.

It is amazing how thankful I became when I was totally helpless. Even the smallest things brought me a bit of joy. I thanked the housekeeper, the nursing aids, the person who brought my meals, the nurses, the physical therapist and everyone else I could. Something remarkable happened; the more people I thanked, the more I wanted to thank people.

The relationship between our organization and our county government has been strained for several years. I knew that this stemmed from a variety of causes ranging from unaligned goals and objectives to perceived slights and criticism from years gone by. Even though this situation predated my tenure as CEO, it was clear that I needed to fix it—but I didn't know what to do.

A week or so after my surgery, I was thinking about what had happened in the gym. I remembered lying on the floor of the fitness center locker room, screaming in pain. I was frightened. I even thought that I might die. When the paramedics arrived, one said, 'It's going to be okay. We're here to help." They were professional, calm, and kind. They made me feel safe.

I wrote a letter to our county manager telling him how thankful I was for the high-quality emergency care I received. I also expressed gratitude for his leadership in providing such great resources for our county. A few weeks later, I was scheduled to attend a meeting with some of our county leaders. I was apprehensive and anxious, knowing the contentious relationship that existed between our organizations.

As I sat down, a county official said, "Thank you so much for your note!" The meeting did not go as I had anticipated. It was lighthearted, respectful, and collegial. The problematic relationship with our county government has been dramatically different over the past few months. I can't take all of the credit for the improvement in this relationship, but I am convinced that thankfulness, gratitude, and praise have helped.

5. I learned that my job is a marathon, not a sprint.

I have always been fascinated by the slow pace of correspondence in Colonial America. A letter sent from Boston to London would take several weeks to arrive, and the response would be equally long. I would have had a difficult time living in that era. I like action and forward progress. I don't like "going slow." It surprised no one that I was impatient following surgery. I didn't allow the necessary time for recovery. I should have taken a few weeks off of work, but instead, I started working from home on post-op day five. This may have slowed my recovery and played a role in the need for another operation.

I will pay better attention this time: working a little slower for the next few weeks, delegating, letting my team do the great work that they do. I want to stay the course over the long haul. I'm not invincible, and progress takes time. After all, every Super Bowl has a half-time, a time to regroup and rest before starting again. Sometimes the best part of the game is in the second half and even the final minutes of the fourth quarter. I want to be in the game until the final whistle.

Pivot and rewrite the story.

ALEKSANDRA GAJER

From Darkness To Light: A Journey Of Health, Healing, And Transformation

I had to learn what health is not before I could understand what it truly is. And sometimes life has a way of teaching us exactly what we need to learn. Today, I enjoy a healthy body, mind, and spirit. I am grateful for a full and beautiful life where I get to be a lighthouse for people who have lost sight of their own health and wellness. And I am grateful for the journey that brought me here, despite—or perhaps because of—the many ups, downs, and unexpected turns. I believe today that it is only because I have known great darkness that I can appreciate the light that shines so brightly in my life.

Navigating Change And New Beginnings

At age seven, I loved riding my bike on the narrow, poorly paved streets of my neighborhood in Poland. My knees were covered with scrapes and bruises and my days were filled with friends, family, and laughter. I lived in a house with my parents and a big, warm extended family. Despite the austerity that communism imposed upon us, I was surrounded by love, connection and care. When my parents told me we were moving to New York, I couldn't comprehend how my life would change. "What language do they speak in New York?" I remember asking my parents.

Upon arriving on Long Island, I found myself surrounded by an abundance of "things." The environment felt crowded with toys, overflowing grocery stores, and endless shops and commercials. Hearing English for the first time, I often felt lost amid the hustle and bustle. Meanwhile, my parents, who were just twenty years old when I was born, were bravely navigating this new chapter alongside me. My father's position in the Mathematics Department at SUNY Stony Brook not only provided us an escape from the oppressive Communist regime in Poland but also opened doors to opportunities I would not have otherwise had.

At seven years old, however, I couldn›t fully grasp the complexity of our situation. I sensed that life had become harder. We were in a new country where I didn't speak the language, my parents were adjusting to a different culture, and I missed the close-knit bonds of my extended family and friends back in Poland. Our living situation reflected our adaptation: We resided in a modest two-bedroom apartment on campus, sharing it with another couple. Initially, I shared a bedroom with my parents, while our roommates occupied the other room. While we pursued the promise of the American Dream, we longed for the simplicity and familiarity of Poland. Although initially planning to return, my father's career opportunities in the U.S. led us to make it our permanent home. As we settled into our own place, our quality of life gradually improved.

I was a shy kid and a head taller than my classmates. I felt a strong awkwardness with my peers even after my English improved. I excelled in school and skipped the second grade. My father's job in academic mathematics took us to many university towns around the country. From New York, we moved to California, then Texas, then Baltimore, challenging any roots I had begun to set down. As I approached my teen years, my shyness turned into restlessness. Perhaps it was something in my genes combined with the instability of frequent moves, but when my neighbor offered a beer at the age of twelve, I found that the gnawing pit of discomfort deep in my belly was somehow relaxed as the liquid warmed my body. Over time, as my peers made positive choices, I gravitated toward those that provided temporary relief. Despite my darker habits, I excelled academically, skillfully concealing my struggles behind straight-A report cards. Assured by my academic performance, my parents chalked up occasional missteps to the normal process of growing up.

Substance And Struggle: The Deepening Descent Into Darkness

What I didn't know was that each time I dissolved the deep discomfort that plagued my soul with substances, it grew deeper, stronger, and more entrenched. When I was fifteen, my parents divorced, adding more fuel to the fire that I tried to drown with drugs and alcohol. The divorce led to further moves, and the substances became the one reliable factor in my life. Although I knew I was not drinking normally, I believed I could stop when I wanted to. I was having fun, and when I grew up, I would put this behind me and have a career, family, and life. But my drinking put me in situations of danger, which created more lasting trauma that further knotted my insides. I became more reckless and more willing to do dangerous things to avoid feeling.

In 2000, I was accepted to Boston University for college, where I entered as a math major. Inspired by my father's career, I was drawn to and excelled at math and science. Shortly after starting college, however, I found that my party-focused lifestyle was incompatible with the rigorous schoolwork required to get a degree in mathematics. I changed my major to psychology, in hopes of discovering what drove my destructiveness and finally fixing it. What had once been recreational drinking and substance use had evolved into a daily habit, necessary for mundane tasks like cleaning or socializing. I distanced myself from my family and anyone who would see how bad it was. I knew it was killing me, but I also believed that the monster I was drowning would overtake me if I stopped. I tried various ways of controlling it, always failing eventually. My fight against drugs and alcohol was all-consuming and exhausting. In moments of exasperation, I cut my wrists and prayed for the courage to cut deep enough to let all the pain out. Luckily, I could never drive the knife that deep.

At the age of nineteen, I could feel that I was close to death. There was a thin, gray line that seemed to separate my life from the blackness beyond, and I knew I was dancing and stumbling around it. There were several near misses where I thought it would all end, but I somehow woke up and took another breath. I needed to hold a part-time job to support myself during college, and that had become impossible. In the summer of 2002, I took my final exam in Statistics II and took a taxi directly from the classroom to McLean Hospital, where I was admitted. Although I met many people who offered me help, I was not fully ready to accept it. I went back to my chaotic life and spent a few months in and out of hospitals and programs mostly keeping my troubles private. Eventually, my mother learned more of the truth about what was happening in my life. She firmly told me that I must come home, and in my confused haze, I boarded a midnight Greyhound bus from Boston to Washington, D.C., where my family picked me up and dropped me off at another hospital. Luckily, this was to be my last.

From Desperation To Renewal

As the haze cleared that last time twenty-one years ago, I met people who had also navigated their way out of the crushing world of addiction. Many of them were living exceptional, productive lives that inspired me. For the first time, I was able to set my ego aside and listen, wholeheartedly, to how these people recreated their lives. I am grateful to say that I have not touched alcohol or any mind-altering substance since that time. The beating I endured from addiction gave me the gift of desperation and an open mind. The people in the treatment programs taught me how to say "yes" to life again, which I embraced. During my first weekend out of rehab, my mother invited me to join her at a meditation retreat. I embraced the practice, and it became the seed from which my daily meditation routine, which I maintain to this day, was born. I moved in with my mother and sister and after taking a semester off, I transferred to George Washington University to finish college.

At the age of twenty-one, I had to rebuild my life and learn how to live. I had to discover what to do with my feelings, boredom, and occasional happiness. The blank slate was unnerving, but I also realized I had a second chance at life. I became immersed in an amazing recovery community. I read countless books and sat quietly while I watched the storms of emotions pass within me. I found that if I sat with my emotions, firmly rooted in the ground, they would pass. Clear skies awaited me after the storms. My meditation practice grew stronger, and the simple joys of life became sweeter. For much of my life, I had tried to bypass hard emotions. I learned that the only way to get past something is to go through it. Learning to stay was a most valuable lesson. Despite the pain and trauma I endured, I became incredibly happy and grateful. I attended more retreats and made more meaningful friendships and connections than I ever had before.

Redemption Through Medicine And A New Beginning

As I started to feel more certain and grounded in my recovery and new life, I felt an overwhelming desire to give back to society. Overcoming my profound struggles taught me so much about returning to health—both physically and emotionally—that I wanted to share what I had found with others. I rediscovered my passion for learning and finished college with top grades. In the last semester of my senior year, I grew uncertain about my career path in psychology. I missed the rigor of math and science that I enjoyed in my early education. I decided to take a chemistry class to see if I could still excel in the sciences. I loved the material. To my surprise, I earned the top grade in a seminar of 250 students. This experience led to an epiphany: Medicine was the perfect combination of what I liked most about psychology and the sciences. I set my sights on medical school, and I never looked back. Medicine, I felt, was the ultimate redemption for the lost years in my early life.

While most people spend much of their twenties having fun while building a career and perhaps a family, I was on a mission to rebuild my life into something extraordinary for myself and others. Over the next several years, I worked full-time and took prerequisites for medical school at night. I spent endless hours studying, volunteering, and reading. I continued to work on my inner life. My healing came slowly and in phases, like the peeling of an onion. I learned to be present with my sometimes overwhelming feelings and emotions, whatever they were.

In 2007, I enrolled in a master's program in Physiology and Biophysics at Georgetown University to improve my chances of acceptance into medical school. I took medical school classes and was laser-focused on performing at my absolute best. I was accepted to the University of Maryland School of Medicine. I got married after my first year of medical school. My life finally seemed to be coming together exactly as I had hoped.

Balancing Ambition And Self-Care

Nothing in life is completely black and white. Medical school allowed me to actualize my potential in a powerful and meaningful way. I set hard goals and achieved them, gaining more faith in myself and my abilities. I loved learning the intricacies of how the human body works and applying that knowledge to help others. However, I put a lot of energy into being what I believed people wanted me to be—the perfect medical student, the perfect wife. To optimize my performance, I learned to ignore and extinguish the signals from my own body and mind. I worked through hunger, fatigue, anger, and sadness. The more I ignored my own needs to be a great doctor, the more I was rewarded with accolades.

At the end of my third year of medical school, I gave birth to my first son. My pregnancy was complicated, and I was forced to go on bed rest. I delivered a beautiful, healthy baby boy and experienced a love beyond what I thought possible. Despite my immense love for my son, I faced debilitating postpartum depression, and the period of bed rest threw me off cycle with my medical school class, causing me to wait an extra year to apply for residency. I had initially planned to pursue a demanding general surgery residency, but after my son was born, I could no longer bear the idea of working eighty-hour weeks for seven years and missing his early childhood. During an emergency medicine rotation, I discovered that this field was a perfect match for my interests and temperament. I enjoyed the rush of saving lives in dire situations and appreciated the organized chaos of the emergency department. I graduated with top honors from the University of Maryland, was inducted into the Alpha Omega Alpha Honors Society, and matched at my top choice for residency at George Washington University.

In residency, I worked long, unforgiving hours in a highly stressful, life-or-death environment. Residents are trained to be doctors first and humans second. We learn to forgo sleep and food, hold our bladders, and ignore our personal needs for the sake of doctoring. We train to be effective under any conditions. We are taught to give our energy to the sick and hope there is enough left over for our loved ones when we get home. This process results in a metamorphosis in which we enter as students and emerge as doctors ready to take on the great responsibility of fending off death and disease. Although this process led to incredible personal and intellectual development as I stepped into my sacred role, I knew along the way that it was taking something from me that I likely was not going to get back. I felt that I was shedding my skin to step into this role, and an important part of me was going with it.

An Unexpected Turn In The Road

At the end of my first year of residency, I became ill. It started with headaches. Initially, I could manage them with ibuprofen during my shifts, but soon this was no longer enough. The pain in my head became so intense that I couldn't focus. Then, I became overwhelmed by an incessant fatigue and malaise, as if I had the flu all the time. About a month prior to this, I had spent time hiking in Vermont. Despite seeing countless doctors, no one was able to figure out what was wrong. I couldn't explain what was happening, and it became increasingly difficult to push through at work and at home. Eventually, I was forced to take a month off work. It was a time of crisis, and I was unsure if or how I would finish my training. I was determined to get better, but the path to health was unclear. Fortunately, I had a physician mentor in residency who encouraged me to explore diagnostics and treatments outside mainstream, conventional medicine.

I started working with doctors in integrative medicine and learned that there was a different lens through which health and disease could be viewed. The stress of my schooling, my growing disconnection from myself, and lack of regular nutritious food and predictable sleep made me susceptible to illness. Through advanced testing, I was diagnosed with Lyme disease. Traditional Lyme disease testing only picks up 29 to 40 percent of cases when done early, and mine was initially negative. I began treatment, but my improvement was painfully slow. It became my mission to understand how to heal my body and return to health. I intuitively knew that Lyme disease was only a part of the puzzle and that my lifestyle over the previous years had taken my body and mind out of alignment. Medical school and residency taught me a great deal about disease and its treatment, but I realized that I actually knew very little about health. It became my personal mission not just to study disease, but to understand health and the conditions necessary to cultivate it.

It has been a decade since I faced my health crisis. I am now thriving in the best health of my life and possess a deep understanding of health and illness that I wouldn't have otherwise gained. Despite enduring sickness without a clear solution, the experience was a catalyst for significant personal and professional growth. My recovery wasn't always linear and often felt frustratingly slow. During my last year of residency, I gave birth to another child. I completed my residency and began working as an attending physician in the emergency department. Unfortunately, my marriage did not survive my extreme work hours and illness. Through life's ups and downs, I continued to be a student of how health can be restored and maintained under the most difficult conditions.

I will always be grateful for the years I spent doing the sacred work of emergency medicine—being present for people during the worst moments of their lives. I had the chance to make miraculous saves and honed a skill set that meant the difference between life and death. Working in the emergency department taught me so much about health and disease and even more about the human condition. In most cases, however, I could do little to alter the course of the disease due to long-standing irreversible changes caused by poor lifestyle (diet, nutrition, movement, stress) and a lack of guidance and support.

A New Opportunity

When I met a physician who wanted to sell his medical practice, I knew that life was presenting me with a singular opportunity. I established the Gajer Practice with the mission of integrating everything I had learned from my personal journey through illness and health, as well as from treating the sickest patients in the healthcare system. Up to this point, I had been on a path of two parallel educations: my mainstream, Western, medical education, and my simultaneous study of a more integrative approach to health and wellness that I applied to myself and my loved ones. My practice offered me the opportunity to integrate these deeply lived worlds into my health manifesto.

In medical school, I was taught about thousands of diseases, each neatly categorized into separate organ systems, with specific specialists, drugs, and sometimes surgeries. While many health conditions could be cured or greatly improved, there were also many quick fixes and band-aid solutions that relied too heavily on medications. Only in hindsight did I realize how much influence lobbyists and industry had over my medical education. There was an implicit understanding that if there was a disease, there would be a pill to fix it. Unfortunately, much of the time, the pill did not actually fix anything, only masked or managed the symptoms. Sometimes the pill or procedure made things worse or caused other problems. This felt shortsighted to me and became unacceptable when my own health was at stake. It was also incongruous with my experience of recovery in my early life. I knew that our bodies had the innate wisdom to heal themselves and, when supported correctly, could start functioning properly again. For each ailment, a root cause could be found if one looked carefully enough.

I now know that health is much more than the absence of disease. Symptoms appear to alert us to areas where we are out of balance. They should not be masked or ignored. My symptoms in my youth and again in residency signaled loudly that I needed to pay attention and make changes. We are fortunate to live in an age where research and knowledge exist about how to bring our bodies into balance and produce health, but unfortunately, we don't learn much about this during medical training. Health and well-being are predicated on a few simple factors that need to be aligned. These factors sound simple, but modern life doesn't always make them so.

Eight Foundational Pillars

I discovered that addressing eight foundational pillars allowed me to live a healthy and balanced life, and helping others align these pillars would also produce good health and well-being. The eight pillars do not have to be done perfectly. Our bodies possess incredible innate wisdom about themselves; sometimes, we just need to slow down and listen to their messages.

1. Humans experience real health and well-being when we have a robust metabolism, balanced gut microbiome, controlled inflammation, and stable hormones. Every seven years, all the

cells in our bodies turn over and are built anew. Much of the blueprint for this regeneration comes from the foods that we eat. Fueling our bodies with whole, minimally processed foods creates conditions for a healthy metabolism, a balanced gut microbiome, controlled inflammation, and stable hormones. Conversely, engineered foods harm our health and contribute to illness, fatigue, and anxiety and depression.

2. Human bodies thrive when they move regularly. No drug or supplement outperforms exercise, and maintaining healthy muscle mass through exercise is a critical factor to reduce risk of illness, metabolic disorders, and cognitive decline.

3. Stress can be positive when balanced with purpose and joy, but chronic stress leads to dysregulation and illness. Addressing this requires activities that regulate the nervous system and reset stress responses.

4. Sleep is often undervalued but crucial for repairing tissues, regulating hormones, and strengthening the immune system. Chronic sleep deprivation increases the risk of various health conditions. Through coaching and lifestyle changes, people can optimize their sleep for better health.

5. Excessive inflammation from exposure to certain foods, cosmetics, or inhaled substances can lead to autoimmunity, cancer, and mental health problems. Being mindful of our exposures is essential for reducing inflammation.

6. Humans evolved with natural sunlight and temperature variations. Spending excessive time indoors under artificial lights and maintaining constant temperatures can lead to illness. Regular exposure to sunlight and temperature variations such as sauna or cold plunge promotes better health.

7. We are social creatures and cannot enjoy real health without community and connection. Though we live in a culture that favors individualism, we need each other to heal and stay healthy. Like everything else in the natural world, we are implicitly connected to each other. Loneliness and isolation not only hurt our hearts but also have a measurable impact on the cells of our bodies when we lack connection.

8. To achieve real health, we must connect with ourselves and our deeper purpose, as our bodies and minds are intricately linked. Life's inevitable highs and lows affect everyone, and our ability to face these experiences directly influences our happiness and health. Each person is unique, and we must courageously examine both our dark and light sides to fully inhabit our lives. Only then can we genuinely contribute to others and live purposefully, ultimately defining our health.

Embracing Growth

As I reflect on my life journey, I am grateful for my relentless desire to keep growing. Despite many instances where I wanted to stop and hide, an intangible force pushed me to continue. I appreciate the innate wisdom of my body, which urged me to explore all the places where I had abandoned myself. With the guidance of many great teachers, I became curious about my body's messages and learned to embrace my bio-individuality as my greatest strength. Through introspection and perseverance, I discovered that health encompasses far more than the absence of disease; it is a delicate balance of physical, emotional, and spiritual well-being. My journey, fraught with trials and setbacks, led me to a holistic approach to health that integrates the wisdom of both conventional and integrative medicine. By recognizing the interconnectedness of lifestyle factors—such as nutrition, movement, stress management, sleep, environmental exposures, community, and mindfulness—I uncovered the fundamental pillars of health and well-being. Now, in the current chapter of my career and life, I am committed to sharing this knowledge and guiding others on their path to healing and wholeness. Adversity may have shaped my past, but embracing these challenges has led me to my true calling—to be a beacon of hope and transformation for those seeking to reclaim their health and vitality.

GEORGIANNE MCCONNELL

Transformation From The Inside Out
My Story Of Love Reclaimed

My story begins like many others you've probably heard before. It tells of a woman finding her footing in a world filled with hopes and expectations, pressures to be, to act, to show up in a certain way. It speaks of a woman desperately wanting to be desired and deeply *loved* yet going about it from a misguided place, searching for it in all the wrong places, never receiving what she truly yearned for. . . until, of course, she did. It is through my own metamorphosis, my own empowered transformation, that I uncovered the strongest, most resilient version of me: a woman burning bright with passion, intention, and a full appreciation for the magic of life.

At first glance, my story could be considered one of divorce and relationships that unraveled at the seams. A recounting of a woman picking up the pieces time and time again. On the surface, those are the facts, yes. But it's also so much more than that. Immensely more. It's a story of divorce, but divorce as a catalyst that launched me toward the uncovering of myself. I began a journey of looking myself deep in the eyes and slowly but surely, loving what I saw.

This is in no way a story of love lost, not how I perceive it.

This is a portrayal of love gained, love transmuted, love reclaimed. Through all of my experiences, I was brought back home to myself, realizing I already had everything I needed within me, without seeking external validation from a partner.

You see, growing up, I spent years and many relationships trying to please the men in my life, to be what they wanted, to show up in a way that was comforting and expected—something I'm sure was passed down, on some level, from woman to woman in our lineage and then, of course, onto me. It was ingrained in me, and so I did all of this. I was the adoring wife, the wife who played the role perfectly, molding myself into whomever they wanted, until I drifted so far from who I was that I couldn't stand it. I didn't even know who I was among it all. If this was the advice women were living by, why was it not leading to contentment? Why was I feeling like I was slowly dying inside? It felt like happiness was constantly eluding me, slipping from my fingers when I tried to hold it close.

Before John

John, who finally appeared to be everything I was looking for, my missing piece in this puzzle of happiness. He strolled back into my life as the opportunity I longed for, the chance to get it right this time, to play the role better, to be truly connected as one—all in the search for that fulfilled life. I was ready. I wanted this. I wanted the idea of it. The picture of a meaningful life that had been promised to me somewhere along the way. So, disregarding the lingering voice within, the one that begged to be heard, that spoke of my true desires, I dove into this marriage with John as the woman he wanted me to be. I was nurturing, supportive, showing up for every moment together. . . until that became utterly unsustainable and nothing like I'd hoped it would be. I could no longer live this way. I was dying inside.

I remember the first time I told John I was unhappy. He didn't want to hear it. He shoved it off that time and the other fifty times I attempted to share my truth. Something wasn't adding up in this new life we'd created. I sensed it, and he likely did too. He didn't know what to do with this woman who was now so different from the one he married. He chose denial and control, and I withdrew, unable to come to terms with my internal scarcity, the feeling of never being enough for him. I didn't have enough gusto to pretend anymore. The role of the perfect, adoring wife felt impossible and all wrong now.

I stopped saying anything. I stopped sharing my thoughts, my needs, the inner parts of myself that were screaming to be witnessed. A space formed between us, one that became harder and harder to bridge. There wasn't a single moment when I realized the expanse between us was unbreachable, but there I was throughout our emailed divorce discussion, drained on a deep soul level, wondering what kind of divine planning this truly was. John was supposed to be the man of my dreams, "The One," so to speak, the partner I'd share the rest of my days with. So how did we end up *here* of all places? How had this happened?

Deep down, I knew those answers. The truth was slowly revealing itself to me and I was finally ready to look at it. I was ready to face what I hadn't been able to for so long: myself.

Our divorce discussion was conducted entirely through email with our mediator, who happened to be a good friend of ours. I was eager not to cause waves as we split our financial accounts. John was intent on sending hurtful remarks my way, ones he knew would hit their mark, and there I was, *still* trying to please him. On some subconscious

level, I still wanted him to like me, to think fondly of me. With everything we'd owned together, John claimed I should only receive the
two pieces of jewelry I brought into the relationship, despite all the
time, money, and energy I had contributed over the years. We had
four sons between us. I managed the household, took care of the
kids, worked full time during our entire relationship, and had even
built my own successful financial advising business. How could he
feel that I had not contributed to our assets and lifestyle during these
thirteen years? Email after email, he berated me. He complained that
I was not worthy of *any* of our assets. Unable to take any more, I
broke down and acquiesced to his demands. And yet, as I did, the
universe finally seemed to intervene, to stir something within me.
As I sent the email to John and our mediator, agreeing to much less
than I deserved, the email did not go through to John, returning with
an error message.

You Are Entitled To More

*It's time to receive what you truly are entitled to. It's time to receive what
you deserve and are worthy of, when it comes to abundance and with everything else*, it seemed to say, loud and clear, and I was *finally* listening.
That email error message—or divine intervention, one could say—
allowed me to stay strong and claim my fifty percent of our assets,
enabling me to move to Arizona with my son, purchase a house, and
begin what would become the pivotal point of my transformation, of
my awakening.

Yes, I *was* entitled to assets from my chapter with John, and
I stepped into my power to claim them. But I was also worthy of
other valuable things I'd never been open to receiving before. It was
time to break the tired cycle and ancestral patterning that had been
passed down for generations. Life, I found, did not revolve around

losing yourself in pleasing a man or draining your true essence for the sake of a "partnership." My divorce opened my eyes wide, and I began to see that there was much more awaiting me. I saw glimpses of true *fulfillment*, and it was nothing like I'd once perceived it to be. It came from the inside out. It emerged from within as I started to design a life I actually adored. I began to cherish the woman I was, outside of any husband. Because she was *free*; she laughed more; she felt expansiveness in her heart, excited to begin each day. I forgot that life could feel gentle and playful and bursting with vibrant aliveness. Day by day, I remembered. As I adapted to my new life in Arizona, I began to hear the voice within me, the inner truth that spoke clearer than it ever had before, now that I was listening. I felt the nudge to reconsider who I was. Who was I really? Who did I *want* to be? I had spent a lot of time picking up the pieces after each heartbreak, but I hadn't considered the fact I already held something very precious and unbroken within me: my self-worth. It shone like a beautiful gem, whole and resilient, wise and powerful. My self-worth was growing the more I believed in it.

I mourned the relationship that ended with John. Endings can be complicated. But this one was a gift. It introduced me to this woman who was much braver, more spontaneous, more free-spirited, more *deeply connected*, than I ever let her be. I found my way back to myself.

Arizona Awakening

Without a doubt, Arizona woke me up. It ignited a fire within me. In its ever-knowing, high mountain desert energy, my new home illuminated the core of who I was. This fire helped me successfully battle a bout of cancer that has thankfully resolved. In my healing, I dove deeper into my spirituality, attending numerous conferences and workshops. I even chose to become certified as a Reiki master during this time. I also worked with an energy healer, Carol, who helped further clear my limiting beliefs and subconscious blocks. We even worked through past life patterns, ones that I wasn't surprised to discover stemmed back to relationships with men.

I was letting go of a lot and in the process, I was gaining so much.

I reignited my love for road trips. Traveling this way, in my car, with a podcast, good music, or just the internal rhythm of my own thoughts, was incredibly grounding for me, something I'd forgotten somewhere along the way. During my thirteen-plus years with John, I stifled this desire because he didn't like "gratuitous" driving. But the thing was, I *did*. Mindless driving was not what I was doing. These were soul drives for me, my sacred space to just *be*. I loved exploring new places and all the space in between them.

One place specifically, Zion National Park in Utah, has been my favorite national park for over twenty years. At the start of our relationship, John and I planned a weekend getaway in this breathtaking pocket of nature, and he enjoyed himself, truly. Yet we never went back. After the divorce, I made a point to drive there for a weekend visit. I felt such immense freedom driving there, staying in my cabin, spending two days hiking and taking in the majesty of the steep red cliffs, breathing in the silence and healing solitude. I realized then how much I missed being in nature, exploring new and familiar places and celebrating my life and the limitless possibilities ahead of me. I felt restored and renewed by returning to these things I loved dearly.

Since moving to Arizona, I would get up in the early hours of the morning and drive to places like San Diego, Long Beach, Pismo Beach, Santa Barbara, Sedona, and Bryce Canyon. I even took a trip to Weaverville, California with my mom, revisiting the place we had lived in 1975, reconnecting me with a younger version of myself in quite divine timing. My trips on the road woke up my spirit. They were the times when I felt the deepest connection to myself, my vibrant inner child, and the energy of the universe guiding me forward.

A Time For Me

I dedicated this time for me, for no other reason than the fact that I enjoyed it. Every six to eight weeks, I'd drive to visit my oldest son in Reno, Nevada, leaving early in the morning to make the twelve-hour road trip. We'd have the loveliest dinner out, followed by a few days spent laughing, reminiscing, talking about life, and then I'd drive back home once more. I made other trips like this to visit family and friends all over the country. I even embarked on a magical, spiritual journey with a group to Egypt—all as a way of exploring and filling my immense desire to see as much of the world as I can.

The thing was, I had set myself free—arms-spread-wide free. The symbolism of my cherished Honda Accord, which carried me through tens of thousands of recorded miles, was not lost on me. I had put in the time, recorded my road miles to learn my powerful relationship and life lessons, and now I was flying free, soaring down whichever path felt truest, my heart leading the way. There will always be lessons and experiences, yes, but I now know just how supported I am.

Life opens up in unexpected, beautiful ways when you're living in your most authentic, vulnerable expression of you. Maybe there's a romantic partner who will walk into my life, loving me for exactly who I am, supporting me in my truest desires. But I'm perfectly okay either way. I've released any expectation around partnership because the relationship I have with myself is where I'm pouring my focus. It's my absolute number one priority. Because when I allow myself to be me, connecting into the well of love I feel for myself, remembering how very worthy I am—traveling, road-tripping, finding my next adventure, building my business, enjoying time with family and friends—life always feels magical and alive. So I'm going to keep dancing in that energy. I'm going to lean further into those places.

Throughout my story of love reclaimed, my truth rings loudly, flowing through every fiber of my being.

I am enough.

I was always enough. I am worthy of a life that feels vivacious and supportive, exciting, and joyful. I can be *me*, fully and truly, and have everything I need in that. When you've uncovered this, the rest, all the other abundance and prosperity that emerges, is just a beautiful, deserving bonus.

So, after all the bumps in the road, I will keep driving. I will keep exploring the largeness of life, knowing that no matter where I go next, I've arrived back home to myself. And honestly, it's the best love story I ever could have written.

HEATHER MACK

Surrender; Surf The Wave Of Life Without Trying To Control The Ocean Of Existence.

My life has been blessed but also extremely challenging. Though I initially grew up in Rhode Island, I don't remember much about my childhood. Due to my father's work, my family moved frequently, and by the time I was in third grade, we had lived in six different places. I do remember how sad I felt to be repeatedly forced to leave my friends and start over in a new school, though. Yet these days, I see those experiences as a gift, having allowed me to learn at a young age the nature of impermanence and the value of nonattachment, adaptation, and resilience. It turns out that my youth was preparing me to learn what would become the most valuable lesson of my life: surrender, the ability to surf the wave of life without trying to control the ocean of existence.

From Rhode Island, my family moved to Connecticut, where my parents built the house where I would spend the rest of my childhood. My mother worked multiple jobs to afford our lifestyle, one of them being military service for thirty years. I have a deep respect and admiration for her dedicated service, especially her time spent in Iraq. When my mother was away, my brother and I spent quality time with our father. We called them "Daddy Days," those times when he would take us shopping and let us get whatever we wanted. Unfortunately,

Daddy Day also sometimes involved dad drinking heavily and taking his aggression out on us. Like many parents, he treated us much as his parents had treated him. It was only later, through years of therapy and self-work, that I came to learn something deeply useful from this abuse: how to turn pain into strength and resilience.

Partying, Pills And Treatment

As a teen, I started partying, which led me to become addicted to diet pills, caffeine pills, and alcohol. Hanging around the "cool kids" at school, I eventually found myself in a situation where a man forced himself on me while I was intoxicated. Afterward, I spent over a decade blaming myself before finally accepting what had happened. My habit of engaging in negative self-talk was nothing new; it had begun at a young age, serving as a means of attention-seeking.

Instead of pursuing my passion to become a fashion designer, I opted for a business degree in college. It was then, while attending a small college, that I began to explore my newfound freedom without knowing how best to use it. My twenties were all about living for the moment, which for me involved coping, numbing, and dancing with the idea of ending it all. While struggling with bulimia, I numbed myself daily with alcohol and drugs, taking upward of forty milligrams of Adderall a day.

It wasn't until my mid twenties, during a rehab stint for my eating disorder, that I began to scratch the surface of the trauma I was enduring. Discovering solace in yoga and meditation, I slowly brought clarity to how I had been treating myself. I began embracing self-care, immersing myself in spiritual teachings, and started to respect myself more. I realized that whatever energy I brought to my life, life always brought more of that same energy back to me.

Although it all began in Boston, the real transformation awaited in the next chapter of my life.

As I learned to embrace my freedom in healthier ways, my life began to get more expansive, interesting and exciting. In January of 2016, I left the toxicity I had become accustomed to and moved from Boston to Los Angeles. It was there that I slowed down my drinking and started cycling. I began doing endurance rides where I would cycle upward of a hundred miles, waking up at 4:00 a.m. to bike before work. Endurance rides quickly turned into sprint triathlons, and soon enough, I managed to participate in seven races over two years. I was so invested in my training that it led me to cut back on my drinking while also improving my eating disorder. Slowly but surely, I was learning how to love myself.

As things improved internally, I also started to witness improvements externally. I met a boy and quickly fell in love. It was all lining up like a fairy tale, until it wasn't. After seven months, I began to see how unhealthy our relationship actually was and ended it, only to find another one much like it. It would take me five years to realize that my choices had been deeply rooted in a fear of abandonment, combined with a lifetime of conditioned codependency.

Burning Man

Catalyzed by a recent breakup, one of the most pivotal moments of my life was attending Burning Man in 2019. Despite the scarcity of tickets, just two weeks before the event, my unwavering belief and preparation led me to a serendipitous opportunity to be there. The experience itself was mind-blowing, revealing a community united in openness and creativity. It not only showed me a new way of life, characterized by independence and authenticity, but also introduced me to individuals like

Dr. Taryn Marie, whose kindness and guidance reshaped my understanding of compassion and self-expression.

After Burning Man, going back to daily life was challenging. I remember, right before returning to work, sitting in the office parking lot crying, thinking how I couldn't do this anymore. I couldn't be a cog in the wheel of a corporate powerhouse, contributing to the destruction of our planet. The whispers of my intuition were getting louder and I began to follow their guidance more closely. I discovered the Japanese Ikigai chart, a Japanese term that blends two words: *iki* meaning "to live," and *gai* meaning "reason," which translates to "a reason to live." I journaled with this idea, and as I began journaling about fulfilling my life's purpose, I sought out opportunities to be helping people and the environment, growing spiritually, healing, and expressing my care and compassion. Right after doing so, I manifested a perfectly aligned gig at a wellness consulting business, geared toward the betterment of individuals and the planet.

See You At The Top, My Journey With Nature

As 2020 unfolded, life's journey became more intense. I took the opportunity presented by the pandemic to pursue a new passion: mountain climbing. My first "fourteener" (the name given to mountains over fourteen thousand feet) was in August of 2020. Reaching the top of Mount Langley after fifteen hours of hiking, I felt an overwhelming sense of accomplishment. As my friends pointed to Mount Whitney, the highest mountain in the contiguous United States, in the distance, I said, "I'm doing that next!", entirely unaware that I had to reserve a permit in advance. Yet by that time, my manifesting skills had become so refined that I was able to hike the peak exactly two weeks later, permit in hand.

There was no stopping me now. As I wrote in my journal at the time, "My true essence comes alive when I'm in nature. I feel so complete being with her." And so my love affair with Mother Nature blossomed, with a focus on mushrooms. I weaned myself off of antidepressants so that I could begin my journey with psilocybin, and in the summer of 2020 took a week off to go on a solo road trip, exploring the natural wonders of Utah. I visited Zion, Bryce, Escalante, Capitol Reef, Arches, and Kanab, all while microdosing mushrooms.

I remember being in complete awe at the beauty of this Earth; it was like stepping into a dreamscape. On my first night, I saw a rainbow over towering red rock formations and knew that I was on the right path. I noticed a shift in my presence, faith, and habits. I felt a connection to all things. I started to care more for myself, becoming more conscious of what I was putting into my body and how I felt. This was when another divine lesson started to present itself. The more authentically in tune I was with myself, the more my energy synchronized with my surroundings.

As these changes were happening, I also witnessed changes happening with my dad. His health was deteriorating, and in 2020, he was diagnosed with cancer. Soon, I started to see just how precious life truly is and realized that I was spending my life in ways that were no longer serving me. It was during this time that I began waking up to the realization that I was destined for greater things.

In November of 2021, I hired a facilitator to guide me on a private psilocybin journey. It would become one of the most pivotal moments of my life. The person who guided me turned out to be a guardian angel who changed my life for the better in so many ways. The journey allowed me to tap into a deep, meditative place where I felt calm and peace beyond what I had known. Less than two weeks later, he invited me to a kambo and bufo ceremony, telling me very little in advance. All I knew was that purging may be involved.

I remember it like it was yesterday: being terrified, showing up alone, and not knowing anyone, immediately before having one of the most profound experiences of my life. Once the kambo had deeply cleared my system, the bufo blasted me into another dimension, beyond space and time. It was like what you might imagine experiencing right before death, filled with white light and scenes from current and past lives. I saw deities, Ganesha, Jesus, and colors and heard numerous voices telling me to surrender. "When are you going to learn how to surrender?" they asked. It was a day that would forever change my life, giving me a glimpse into the infinite, showing me that we are all one and this existence is all about love.

At the time, I was on a leave of absence from work, urgently seeking my higher calling. While I had always felt a burning desire to put my heart and soul into something, few things had allowed me to truly feel my soul's passion, until then. So it was that within a few weeks of my kambo and bufo experience, I found myself in the orbit of Grandmother Ayahuasca.

I have this rule: If the universe shows me something three times, I take the guidance as a sign that I need to do it. So, Grandmother came knocking, and it was more than three times. And by January of 2022, I found a beautiful, loving container to hold me in what would become my most life-changing experience yet.

Plant Medicine And Surrendering

Ayahuasca is often referred to as Grandmother to convey her guidance, care, and wisdom. Still, I wasn't entirely certain what to expect. This turned out to be a blessing, as my experience was far beyond all expectations. It felt like a divine appointment to be at that ceremony and witness the unfolding of my reality. The journey was both loving and firm, revealing areas in my life in need of change. I went into the ceremony with a list of intentions, one of them being to learn what my first tattoo would be. As I began to connect with the medicine, I saw the word "surrender" pulsating in vibrant hues while hearing voices from my past urging me to release. It was then that I knew what my inaugural tattoo would be.

Ayahuasca showed me that my purpose was to heal people with natural remedies. I was presented with my path and shown hundreds of people I was meant to help. Grandmother revealed how my corporate job was harming our planet and how it would ultimately harm me if I stayed. She revealed my family's ancestral trauma and how it manifested within me. I saw my partner at the time, depicted as a dark wolf with red eyes, feeding on my life force energy. I also gained insights into how social media and the entertainment industry manipulate people.

Though it's commonly advised not to make drastic changes immediately after a ceremony, the next day, I deleted all my social media accounts, ended my relationship, and seriously began looking for a way out of my corporate job. Though the seed had been planted, it took three months before I left my corporate job, with no clear plan, and began to trust and surrender.

Silence Is Golden

A few months prior, three people had shared that a vipassana meditation retreat was one of the most important things they had done for their growth. So, I applied my rule of three, went to the website, and saw that it was completely booked out. I had no idea that being in silence for ten days with no devices, reading, exercise, speaking, or eye contact would be so popular! Yet after applying to lots of retreat centers around the world, within two months I somehow got myself into the closest one, near Joshua Tree. After leaving the corporate world, with its constant external focus, it was time to go inward.

Vipassana, at its core, is a meditation technique for observing things as they are. It teaches how to compassionately train one's mind to become more aware and to liberate oneself from mental reactivity. One of my favorite moments of the retreat was on day six, when I was still struggling with my chattering thoughts, having trouble dropping into the morning meditation. Amid the flurry of my thinking, I caught a glimpse of my tattoo and realized that I could fully embody what it meant. I then dropped into the deepest meditative state of my life. It reminded me of Paramahansa Yogananda's description of cosmic consciousness: a beautiful, divine void of interconnectedness.

After the retreat, while driving through Joshua Tree, I experienced a big emotional release, feeling elated, blessed, and overjoyed. I got to breathe in one of my favorite national parks and felt the presence of my late grandfather, as I often do when I'm adventuring in nature. He was there with me celebrating. My heart was bursting with gratitude.

It's rather amusing that I was able to make a new friend while at a silent meditation retreat. Yet Natalie and I seemed to have a similar vibe, evident energetically through the silence. Afterward, I shared with her that I had just left my corporate job and a relationship, surrendering fully to the divine flow, unsure of what was next. She responded with an invitation to join her, her boyfriend, and some friends on a trip to Europe, set to happen in a few weeks. My intuition accepted the invitation with a full-body "yes."

Time To See The World

Our journey brought us to Barcelona and San Sebastian in Spain, as well as the beauty of Lisbon, Cascias, and Sintra in Portugal. Afterward, I ventured alone to the historic landscapes of Croatia and Montenegro. While traveling, the dots on my arm from my kambo experiences were clearly visible, and I found myself in lengthy conversations, explaining the medicine and how it works to cleanse the body and spirit. I saw frogs everywhere. I even found myself in front of the Froggyland Museum. Yet as I went to take a picture to send to a friend, my intuition whispered, "This isn't for them; this is for you."

After attending Burning Man that year, I felt called to continue working with kambo and Grandmother. Every time I did, it felt like a new layer was being shed, allowing me to step into myself more authentically. I was guided to start serving kambo and a week after buying the camper van of my dreams, my teacher offered a kambo training program in Oregon. It had been a lifelong dream to see all the national parks and on my way to the training, I got to visit two more, bringing my total to twenty-six national parks in three years.

My path to serving kambo unfolded quickly. I traveled to Iquitos, Peru to train with the Matses tribe. I was able to experience the strongest and most potent medicine, fresh from the frog. They also introduced a new method involving powdered kambo mixed with hapé, administered through the nose, resulting in the most intense experience of my life. Leaving Peru, I felt a newfound clarity, fearlessness, and confidence.

Saying Goodbye

During my kambo initiation, my father was diagnosed with cancer again, this time in his prostate. Within a month and a half, he was treated with forty rounds of radiation, and his health declined rapidly;

he lost more than a quarter of his weight and started to lose the will to care for himself. Even simple tasks became too much for him. When I visited, he took the opportunity to apologize for what had happened during my childhood. We knew it would soon be our final goodbye. A week prior to his stroke, he told my mom that he wasn't afraid of dying anymore.

I got the call on the morning of September 9; my brother asked me if I was sitting down. Our father had had a stroke, tried to get up to tell someone, and fell, hitting his head. He was rushed to the hospital and kept on life support. I arrived in Las Vegas to say goodbye to him at 3:33 p.m. We listened to his favorite Beatles songs while I told him that I forgave him for everything that had happened. Tears streamed down his face as I spoke. I promised him that I would honor his legacy by striving for world peace, as it was what he had always requested for Christmas and his birthday. I know now that the peace I create within myself is the peace I am able to spread to the world.

Surrender to the divinity in it all; that was the gift I received from my father's passing. I was so grateful for all my inner work and my medicine work enabling me to feel at peace, knowing that he was no longer suffering and that he is always with me in spirit. I see the signs all the time.

My journey of healing and transformation, guided by natural remedies and community support, reflects the resilience and growth that emerged from life's challenges. From childhood transitions to personal struggles, each obstacle has fueled my journey of self-discovery. I now surrender to embrace all life's divine gifts on this journey with gratitude, and wisdom. I am humbled to share my story of healing and transformation with you.

JAMES COLASURDO

Get Out Of Your Mind And Into Your Life

Unlike some of my colleagues who are writing chapters in this book on resilience, I did not survive a series of biblical plagues. I did not endure frightening threats to my life and career.

Well ... maybe a little. Yet I wasn't driven out of business on a stake, or even a steak. I was not ravaged by disease, destruction, or life-threatening maladies. Some of the good folks writing in this book survived severe crises that would have destroyed lesser men and women. Most of these folks survived a dangerous conflict, a direct grade-A calamity, physical challenges, or a good old-fashioned shitstorm. The metaphors for their situations can be quite dramatic: anything from a superhero facing a cosmic strike from the heavens with a Captain America shield to a person robbed in a sailor's raincoat as shit rains down from every angle.

The visual image for my struggles and challenges to my resilience are much more prosaic: a man, emerging Monty Python-style from his own brain. Or just as likely, a stately schooner or large boat lost at sea, traveling in an ever-widening circle to nowhere. It wasn't disease, despair, trauma, or spectacular bad luck that hobbled me. Quite simply, it was me. Or more precisely, my brain. That gray, messy glob of tissue that calls the shots for all of us from within our own heads. I was trapped in my brain to my continual self-sabotage. And I expect I was not, and am not, alone.

My Words Are My Weapon And My Shield

First, a quick history of my life to bring this concept into focus: As I write this, I am sixty-eight years of age. I am a successful clinical psychologist, based in Brooklyn, New York. I have resided in New York City for forty-eight years. (I have resided in my brain for considerably longer.) When I was young and growing up in New Rochelle, New York with a large, active family of five siblings and my youngish parents, I learned that I had a weapon which could guide me through any crisis. That weapon would be my mouth. I discovered I could quickly hold off my pesky brothers and sisters with my verbal ripostes and attacks. My younger brother would yell at me that I was "dumb." I would reply, "You don't even know how to spell IQ." My sister would make fun of my acne-ridden face. I would tell her she had a good face for radio. My mother attacked my laziness for resisting chores, and I would tell her I was merely intellectualizing the problem to come up with new solutions. My father would rail about my poor grades, and I would recite Einstein's reportedly poor grades. Didn't make sense, but it got me through.

When the tough guys I grew up with threatened to beat me up, I made them laugh. It got me out of many potentially dangerous situations. When the nuns at grammar school smacked me with a ruler and threatened me with eternal damnation, my quips would even make their habits shake with laughter, and they would forget about me. Some of the time, anyway.

And thus, my crisis management style was born. Basically, it was this: Glide through life, think your way glibly and quickly through your problems, come up with a funny quip or riposte, and survive until the next threat. In terms of survival, surprisingly, it actually did work. I viewed myself as a traveling jazzman or even a rocker, improvising funny riffs in real time, making people laugh, and surviving. In terms of reaching my potential, actually learning what was being taught in high school and a series of colleges, this philosophy proved a miserable failure. But I didn't care, so long as I could keep everything moving, avoid real intimacy, somehow stumble into jobs that would keep me alive, experience sensual and hedonistic pleasure, and not get too analytic and think about what I was actually doing.

As an example of the fast-moving yet misdirected and often self-sabotaging nature of what was going on, I was selected along with several other students to attend the Blair Summer School of Journalism on a scholarship basis in 1972. It was an attempt to identify supposedly bright students who had writing talent on the East Coast and give them the opportunity to explore journalism in many aspects, including field trips to Washington and press conferences every week with some major government figures (including Nixon's press secretary at the time, Ron Ziegler, and a younger Ted Kennedy). A couple of local editors in my area were interested in my writing and urged me to contact them. The problem was I wasn't that interested in my writing, since I had little discipline and no clear direction. What did I do? Basically glided through my senior year, buoyed by cold beer and wine, marijuana (a new love), and various psychedelics. Although I did become the editor of my high school newspaper, I filled the paper with pictures of myself and my friends, created tortured "in-jokes" about various teachers, mocked virtually all the cliques in the school, and in retrospect offered nothing either original or vaguely literate. I never did get back to those editors.

But in my mind, I must have been doing great. Made editor of the paper. Was very popular with my fellow students. Got high with my friends. And fruitlessly searched for a girlfriend. Although deep down, I knew I would not know what to do with said girlfriend if I ever found one, this certainly didn't stop me from looking. And it was another addition to the evolving (or devolving) persona I was exhibiting to the world: that of a "loose man." Always up for a drink or a smoke, a good time, a pleasant physical sensation, and never forget the snappy verbal badinage. I was promiscuous, searching for quick physical fun with a woman and the idea of always leaving them laughing, even with my clothes on. Again, what I *wasn't* displaying was any deep substance, true ambition, spirituality, or true empathy for others, although it was in me somewhere. I did read a lot, especially from the classic writers—Dickens, Thomas Wolfe, Hemingway, Thomas Hardy, James Joyce, among many others—over the years. I read newspapers voraciously, especially my daily *New York Daily News*, *Post*, and the godly *New York Times*. I particularly favored the columnists Tom Wicker, Pete Hamill, Jimmy Breslin, Red Smith, and Murray Kempton. I didn't hang out with people who wanted to meaningfully discuss any intellectual ideas, but they laughed at my jokes and bought their share of rounds at the bar. That is all that seemed to matter to me. My family and friends encouraged me to become a journalist. In my head, I liked the idea. In my life, I did very little to further this idea.

When I landed at a mediocre Connecticut college, chasing and "scoring" sex with women became my most ardent activity. I didn't know who I was competing with (I think I do now), but the idea was to bed as many women as I could while living on my parents' dime in college. I once again became the editor of the campus paper and actually got some positive attention for some articles I wrote. But when a campus advisor invited me to work closely with him to see just how good I could be, I ghosted him. I didn't want to know how good I could be, because there was the possibility I would have to work hard. And I could be exposed as the fraud I secretly believed I probably was. One positive development on the campus was when I met the man who was destined to become my best friend: Mark Schneider. He is a contributing author in this book. His hijinks, absurd sense of humor, similar interests, and general creativity would form the backbone of a lifelong male friendship . . . even when we were inadvertently separated by time and circumstances for twenty-five years. The other positive development was running for and winning the title of Homecoming Queen on the campus as a personal goof on society and another excuse for a party.

Hedonism, Catholic School And Distorted Reality

College life became repetitive, if hedonistic and occasionally fun, on three different campuses. My mother sent me to a private Catholic school in upstate New York, to "straighten [me] out" from my hedonistic, sexually obsessed, and self-defeating ways (My grades were below sea level). This, of course, only made things worse, and at the threat of being kicked out of the school on charges of general immorality, I somehow managed to land at George Washington University in Washington, D.C., an actually respectable school.

Of course, the same self-defeating behaviors that had gotten me this far continued to manifest. I managed somehow to graduate GW after many memorable adventures, including heckling Jimmy Carter with my fellow students and watching many ambassadors and politicians give speeches, although none inspired me enough to get me to volunteer to work with them. I yearned to get back to New York, with its bright lights and promise of surface hedonism and fun. Once again, no thought was really given to a serious career, career goals, or settling down with a woman. I did continue to enjoy settling down with a drink, however, and telling jokes, in between what was called "dating" in the '70s. Without getting into details, this conception of dating is considerably different than what it resembles today.

September 1977 was a tumultuous and meaningful time, as I arrived in Manhattan with the proverbial seventy-five cents in my pocket. Okay, it was about $150. I settled in with another dear college friend who had eternal patience, calm, and an ability to tolerate a roommate who dripped water from the shower all over the apartment, tossed dirty clothes everywhere, and proved amazingly undisciplined and incapable of cooking anything but spaghetti and burnt tomato sauce. By now, partying, as in drinking, smoking pot, and experimenting with select drugs seemed to manifest over everything else. Chasing concerts and albums, and sitting in famous sports stadiums, I pursued a lifelong love of professional sports, jazz, rock and roll and blues. Transcending all was the "chase" of available women. And of course, partying with whoever showed up or was available. I suppose I knew I wasn't really a member of the Rolling Stones. It didn't stop the daily movies and tunes in my head. I was beginning to see how a fantasy life, focused on hedonism, "sex, drugs and rock n roll" and even fame was zapping most of my energy. I suspected this, but didn't really care because it was a damn good fantasy film, and I always had a front row seat. And it certainly beat reality.

Almost immediately, I secured a job as a "copy boy" at the *New York Daily News* for about $125 per week (my rent was $125 a month). Like the chimney sweep and lamplighter, this job no longer exists in our digital world. Yet there I was, in a proverbial dream job with the guys I idolized from afar right in front of me: Jimmy Breslin and Pete Hamill. Mike Lupica and great sports writers were also in residence. I even got to go out with city-side reporters at night and cover the occasional crime or murder. But something happened. Or rather, didn't happen. It just didn't matter to me. I was hanging out in comedy clubs, drinking, and chasing women. This led to two not-so-good attempts to tell jokes on stage (I kind of "bombed") and an actual paying job to do stand-up in front of senior citizens. This was actually a fun job I somewhat enjoyed. A friend told me I was "*Saturday Night Live*" even if the audience was "Wednesday-afternoon dead." Often overheard in the audience was "What did he say?"

From SNL To LA

The loose pursuit of comedy led me to abruptly give up the journalism "dream" and head out to Los Angeles for a year to stay with yet another old friend. In that year, I drank prodigiously, chased women endlessly, and came back to New York enervated and insecure. Living chiefly in my head, I wrote a couple of pilot scripts, which went nowhere. Back in New York, I first worked in a public relations office because it was a job that I thought I could do, with literally no experience. When the boss caught a glimpse of a fake funny memo I wrote about free bathroom privileges we could all be grateful for, he asked me to write a book for him, which he would publish and I'd get a writing credit on. It was called *A Guide to College Alumni Publications,* and it sold three and a half copies in 1980.

The aforementioned Mark Schneider, my best friend, had become successful as a rising young copywriter in an ad agency in New York. He seemed to be making "the big bucks." He appeared to enjoy the company of a lot of smart, good-looking women. I thought "Why not advertising?", again, with literally no experience. Mark was heading out to his agency's Los Angeles office. He made a very successful pitch to me—because he knew I hated public relations—to join him in L.A., where he would help me push an ad portfolio at various agencies. As before, I would stay with my friends in a commune-style residence in West Los Angeles. And like that, I left New York again, a windblown man in search of good times, but now increasingly thinking about a career. Guess I knew I needed to eat on a consistent basis.

After a tough struggle for a few months, leavened with the usual good times in L.A. bars and restaurants and fun nights with fun women, I finally landed the golden amulet: A full-time copywriting job at N.W. Ayer, Los Angeles. A real job with a real salary. I became a "made man" in a business seemingly made for fun, good times, creativity, parties, and perhaps a lasting career. Either way, I had so much fun, there were so many parties, fun nights, transient times of pleasure, and I lived in three different neighborhoods including the Hollywood Hills with a very rich lady friend. I barely thought about what I'd be doing or where I would be living next. Mark went back to New York City, which I was learning (and should have known) was the real "Mecca of Advertising." So I gave up my little Mazda sports car and my steady married girlfriend and bid a teary goodbye to my small group of friends and flew, almost impulsively, back to New York. The only problem was I did not have a job.

No Job, No Money No Ride

I subsequently suffered perhaps the biggest challenge in my life thus far. I did not have a job, I had little money, was living with my parents about fifty miles from the city, and had no girlfriend. But by simply expending shoe leather pounding the pavement and hustling my portfolio throughout midtown Manhattan, I finally got a bona fide job offer in about two to three months, amid much anxiety. I was set in New York City in the right business. A fairly well compensated Mad Man copywriter, although on Second Avenue. And so began a fifteen-year career with many highs, a few significant lows, and finally the brief insightful breakthroughs that would significantly change my life and teach me some real lessons about resilience.

Those early years remain somewhat of a blur. Alcohol and cocaine seemed to rule in advertising society. I did my share, but thankfully did not really enjoy the cocaine "buzz," as it amplified my already significant anxiety and made my heart beat like an old bass drum. The end of the coke years came when two close friends in the business passed away in their late thirties from abusing the stuff. My end came when I found myself in my ramshackle apartment with a beautiful woman who I had ardently pursued. The problem wasn't that we were having sex. The problem was that we weren't, as I had taken to lecturing her about the history of Vietnam while she sat, bored, at the edge of the bed, and finally had the good sense to leave around 3 a.m. Such was the come-what-may nature of my frenetic social life.

The Eighties

I was a "hot copywriter" on the way up, and slowly the salary began to jump. But my next test of resilience came when I suddenly found myself beleaguered with night sweats and an amazing loss of energy. I felt like I was in a movie theater watching my life go by. At that time in the early '80s, AIDS was the talk of the town, and people in our circle were either sick or dying. I was straight but had been with several women who were quite liberal with their favors, and so I naturally assumed I had AIDS, for which there was no cure. I figure I had six months to live. This was of course ridiculous, although not totally impossible. In the plush theater of my mind, with my own personal seat, I replayed dreadful future scenarios over and over. This was when I first perceived the benefit of therapy, opening myself up to a therapist about my fears and having a safe forum to ventilate fully—tears, fears, and all. Unfortunately, it took quite a while to make therapy a habit due to my deeply distorted image of myself.

I'd discovered I contracted what was called "non-A, non-B hepatitis" which today is simply hepatitis C. I realized I would live after all, but my pace notably slowed. For the first time, I seriously questioned my lifestyle of booze, drugs and promiscuity. I checked my behavior quite a bit and took about six months off from the bars and the ladies of New York City. But a trip to Jamaica in January seemed to revive me, and soon I was back in Manhattan as a somewhat reduced version of myself. I was still the hot copywriter, and I began my relentless search for the best and highest-paying job. Firmly ensconced in my head, I never got a chance to see just how selfish and self-involved I was, fruitlessly searching for pleasure to blot out my encroaching depression and increased anxiety. I've come to learn that many men do the same when overcome with depression and anxiety. I create what many men create, a "false self." Mine was based on Jack Nicholson, a rebellious, self-assured, witty, and fun-loving icon always in search of a good drink, a good time, a good opportunity for badinage. And that image held in my mind for a very long time.

The Charmed Life?

Around this time, I was fortunate enough to meet Diane, my first wife. She was a high-IQ, highly successful part-owner of a music studio in Midtown and lived in a beautiful apartment off of Central Park West. Diane's humor, generosity of finances, and good will was infectious. We were married for seventeen years. We traveled the world, and New York City, together. We brought out the best in each other, engaged in witty repartee, and discussed intellectual ideas on a daily basis for about the first five years. Unburdened by children, we used our considerable combined salaries to buy an amazing new apartment on West Seventy-Ninth Street. We had a wide group of interesting, sophisticated friends. We seemed to be the prototype of a successful, charming New York couple, savoring the best that the city and the world had to offer.

And that's when the devil struck again. The briefly repressed inner voice, full of hedonistic and self-sabotaging desires roared back. I entered into a series of meaningless, sexually focused affairs, seemingly wanting to be confronted and caught. Because Diane was no fool, she caught me easily, and the trust between us was indelibly shattered. I did work hard to win back her affection and approval. I managed to pull this off shakily, but the old devil's whispering continued. Then I hit the most challenging test of my resilience. I had become utterly bored by the advertising business. My work had won both business and awards. But in my endless quest for more, I switched agencies about five times, always at a higher compensation. But I landed at an agency whose name betrayed the style of their advertising: Grey. It began to feel that, like the athletes I used to worship, I was heading for the scrap heap.

And I had become a high-priced appliance in an agency of uninspiring folks, including me: all of us hanging on to high salaries to make our mortgages and our expenses. But the drudgery and low quality of our creative output virtually ensured we would be stuck in this agency at the agency's whim. I could not abide this situation. The old false self began to crumble. I had to search for something to do. A dinner with a neighbor, who was a successful clinical psychologist, whetted a long-suppressed interest in psychology. I began to study and read voraciously anything with a psychological bent: Adler, Jung, CBT, Carl Rogers, and of course, the master, Sigmund Freud. Freud mesmerized me with his artful writing and compelling case histories. I spoke to my wife, told her of my desire to go back to school, and she pledged to continue working to help support me, as my income had been much larger than hers in the preceding years.

Despite my selfish, addictive need to pursue extramarital affairs, my first wife hung in with me throughout graduate school. It was selfless, noble, and extremely supportive. I will be eternally grateful for and to her. I couldn't have become a clinical psychologist without her.

The Scariest Day Of My Life

The scariest day of my life was the day I walked out of Grey Advertising, and soon began classes at the John Jay College of Criminal Justice. I wanted initially to be a forensic psychologist because I thought it was a different take, and *Silence of the Lambs* had just come out. After completing my master's and working in a prison as an intern, the scales fell from my eyes. I saw that criminal psychology is more of an assessment game, not an opportunity to offer empathy and treatment to a group which, in the overwhelming number of cases, for many chiefly socioeconomic reasons, is not looking to truly change from within. After achieving my master's, I focused on getting into a doctoral program to truly try and help everyone, myself included.

Mostly not working outside of intermittent freelance during my doctoral years was tough. But anyone who's achieved a doctoral degree will tell you it's a full-time job. My proudest day was in early 2004, when I finally completed my thesis and became a New York State Licensed Clinical Psychologist. At around the same time, the weight of my bad behavior on my marriage became too much for my wife and me. We divorced in 2003, and I moved to Brooklyn. This somewhat dented my finances, as my wife's career had hit hard times as well, and she had to protect her future. Gone for me was the fancy apartment I mostly owned on Seventy-Ninth Street. And the good amount of savings I had built up.

The Next Phase

The next phase of my life began with a serious need to earn money, pay rent, and figure out how to help people and myself. I was still in a somewhat false-self mode as I worked in nursing homes, clinics, hospitals, and even a Mobile Crisis Team, all to get the experience needed to truly find a way to improve the lives of everyone I met. A somewhat grandiose dream, perhaps. But it was what drove me. I had also figured out that the Freudian, psychoanalytic way was not a good fit for me. It is based on the past and has serious problems in today's world. But as helpful as psychoanalytic thought was formerly, I still had not found, for me, a theory and practicality that worked for me. That was to come later.

After a couple of disastrous love affairs, I was lucky enough to meet my current wife, Tracy. We do struggle at times with some aftershocks of my former behavior, but we are going forward in the best way that we can. I was lucky to meet her.

In the meantime, I was still cowed by the enormous challenge of starting a private practice. It seemed daunting, it seemed impossible, it was incredibly threatening to my sense of self. I had been working in nursing homes, as existential a form of psychology as one could ever attempt. I was dealing with lonely, largely depressed, and anxious men and women who were suffering from dementia. Psychoanalytic therapy was virtually useless in this world, and I was largely relying on Cognitive Behavioral Therapy. As effective as it was, I still felt something was missing, but I could not put my finger on what it was.

That opportunity was presented to me as I walked through a Barnes & Noble one day. My current wife picked up a copy of Eckhart

Tolle's *Power of Now* and handed it to me. And there it was: the noble, empathic philosophy of Buddha, distilled through Tolle's brilliant synthesis of Buddhist, Christian, and Taoist philosophy amongst others. It brought the power of these vital Eastern ideas once again to the West. I personally experienced this power as I meditated alone and in a group. I saw the effect of my disastrous, anxiety- and negativity-laden thoughts and how they limited me. I truly saw mindfulness as the key to unlocking my true potential as a therapist, but more importantly, as myself, the authentic me. Actually living without the haze of alcohol, drugs, promiscuity, grandiosity, and self-delusion. I shut down the theater in my head and decided to live in the now, the only time we live. I saw what Tolle promised: that when we fix ourselves on the inside, the outside usually follows. I voraciously read through a lot of the stable of mindfulness authors like Thich Nhat Hanh, Mark Epstein, Joseph Goldstein, Sharon Salzberg, and many others.

I meditate daily, have meditated for well over five hundred hours, discovering pleasant and unpleasant truths about myself, but I have finally become my genuine self. I offer this genuine self to everyone I encounter. My practice has grown, expanded, and prospered. My philosophy has been disseminated by many folks of all types who come to me in need. And yes, it can help you as well.

When I got out of my mind and into my life, I felt the freedom that anyone can feel when they realize that their depression and anxiety may be reality-based but they are amplified by a distortive mind building up negative thoughts like clouds to a brilliant blue sky. As in nature, the clouds will drift away, and the joy shining underneath is accessible to anyone who is willing to be mindful. I have been so joyous since getting out of my mind. I invite you to join me and experience the joy of living an authentic life, as your authentic self. It's never too late to start.

I close with this thought from my website:

> "A Zen Master is nothing more than someone who
> has repeatedly screwed up and eventually learned
> something. We can do the same."
> —Mark van Buren

MIKE ALDEN

Finding Wicked Happiness

Fed Up

We've all had moments in life when we're simply fed up. When we've had enough. An inflection point when a line has been drawn, and there is no going back. For me, one of these "linchpin moments" was when I woke up after a night of heavy drinking. It was a night with my best friend, Kevin, that was not dissimilar from so many nights we'd shared out at the bar before. I wasn't an alcoholic. I didn't drink every day or even yearn for a drink. But when I did drink, I drank too much. That morning, I woke up and told myself, "I'm done drinking." At forty-five years old, I just decided I'd had enough with alcohol. I'd had enough of feeling hungover, wondering what I'd said the night before, and of the "hangziety", the crushing tidal wave of anxiety that would crash over me following a night out.

That morning, I made a decision to quit. There was no big declaration. I didn't announce my decision on social media. I didn't tell my partner or mention anything to Kevin. I just stopped. One day without alcohol turned into one week. Then, one week turned into one month. One month turned into one year, and one year turned into two years. Now it's been nearly five years since I've had a drink.

Removing alcohol from my life allowed me to see my unhappiness more clearly. My businesses were generating tens of millions of dollars annually, which afforded me all of the accompaniments of wealth including a big house in a private New England neighborhood, expensive cars and watches, and the freedom to do what I wanted whenever I wanted. Life was abundant, but far from easy. Despite the amount of money my businesses were generating, it was still a constant struggle to "make it", with one crisis after the next.

Back then, I was in a committed long-term relationship. It wasn't that I didn't love her. There was something I couldn't ignore nagging at me that she was not my life partner. It's not that there was anything wrong per se. She took care of me, put up with my entrepreneurial bullshit, and seemed to "get me" in a way I'd longed to be understood. Even so, if I'm being honest, the proverbial relationship door was always. I wasn't fully invested. There were times when I saw an impossibly beautiful woman, and I'd turn to a friend, half joking and say, "I'd drop everything for her." Despite our connection, I couldn't shake a gnawing sensation that there was something else that could fill a void within my soul.

Soon after I'd decided to stop drinking, before I had developed a new suite of coping mechanisms that did not include the escapism of alcohol, some significant issues emerged with my former wife, and I found myself in a harrowing custody battle for my then fourteen-year-old daughter. That experience was the straw on top of everything else that almost broke me, and I knew I needed to seek professional help. I'm a big believer in therapy. For most of my life, off and on, I have worked with a therapist. Knowing when I've needed help and having the courage to seek help have been some of the most defining moments in my transformation. Initially, I sought support for the custody issue with my daughter, but I quickly realized that the issue was much bigger: I needed help finding myself and my own happiness.

Money Doesn't Buy Happiness

Money doesn't buy happiness, but it's not the whole truth. Money certainly helps with happiness. There is a lot of research about this topic, and many studies show that there is a money threshold that does increase happiness when people have enough resources to pay their bills, get out of debt, and live a sustainable financial life. Beyond that money threshold, more money does not equal more happiness. I hadn't yet gotten the memo because I was chasing money not only for happiness, but because I felt I had something to prove. I was a kid from the projects who had grown up surrounded with drugs, violence, and crime. Now, having "made it," I felt that everyone needed to know. I felt I needed to prove my own worthiness. Since I didn't feel inherently worthy internally, the need to prove myself constantly only exacerbated my own insecurities and fears. Pretty soon I was going to learn that constantly hustling for the money and my own worthiness was eroding my own internal happiness.

Coronado Island

During one of my business trips, I reserved a two-room villa at the famous Del Hotel on Coronado Island in San Diego, CA, a hotel and location that are the definition of opulence. Nestled right on the beach, in one of the most exclusive areas in California, the nightly room rate was more than most Americans' mortgage. I hadn't stopped drinking yet, and over a few beverages, I turned to my business partner, Jason, and confessed how unhappy I was. He didn't get it. He gave me the typical response you'd expect, "Mike, look at where we are and all that you have. How can you not be happy?" Jason missed the memo on money not buying happiness too. At the time, all I could articulate in response was, "I hate my life. And I just wanna be wicked happy." Like me, Jason was looking at the external factors in my life like wealth, the hotel, location, etc., and wondering how it was that I could possibly be anything but elated with my life.

Not only can you not buy happiness, happiness is an inside job. I needed to address my own lack of inner peace and worthiness, stemming from the incessant need to prove myself and learn to love myself before I could learn to love anyone else.

Sometimes It Takes Years, But It Doesn't Have To

At the time, I wouldn't have told you I was going on a healing journey. I didn't even know I was consciously trying to heal. I didn't know I was wounded. When working with my therapist, my lack of self-love was a "glowing" indicator that I had a lot of work to do in this area. I wanted to love who I was, who I had been, who I had become, and most importantly, who I was becoming. Once I became aware of the power and fulfillment that came with my own self-love and acceptance, the money and material things, along with the need to prove to the world that I was worthy fell away. For the very first time in my own life, I became my own priority. Most of my life, even as a child, I was taking care of others. Now, as a CEO, father, and caretaker everything and everyone in my life, prioritizing myself was a real breakthrough. Being generous and considering others' needs is important, but when we care for others to the exclusion of our own internal happiness, it isn't good for anyone.

Only You Can Do It

Three years after I quit alcohol, I made the decision to really get physically healthy. I've always been a "big guy". Having been an athlete most of my life, with football being the sport that got me into college, I've gone to the gym and exercised since I was thirteen. the game changed, and in my forties, being a big guy wasn't serving me anymore. The scale read 257 pounds, and like quitting alcohol, once again, I told myself that I'd had enough of being overweight. Once again, I didn't tell anyone or announce it to the world. I just started. I knew I was tired of just being a big guy, and for the first time in my life, I wanted to get ripped. At forty-eight years of age, I knew that this would be a daunting task.

I did reach out to some friends who were bodybuilders and fitness experts for advice on how to go about getting fit. Even with their advice, I realized that only I could do it. They weren't going to lift weights for me; they weren't going to get on the stair climber for me; they weren't going to diet for me. I also wanted to do it naturally. Getting assistance from performance-enhancing drugs is polarizing, but for me, I didn't want to do it, which made it even harder. So the journey began. Day by day, hour by hour, I made strides. In the beginning, it was very difficult. I tracked my body fat and my weight each week. After about twelve weeks of training hard and my third body scan it hit me hard. I had lost about fifteen pounds of pure fat, but what really hit me was the visceral fat. Visceral fat is the bad fat that is responsible for things like strokes, heart disease, cancer, and a whole host of other diseases. I cut my visceral fat by several percentage points which ultimately increased my life span. Sitting in the gym comparing my scans, I realized that even though I had had advice and some help with the diet plan, the only person really responsible for this change was me. At that moment, I felt a sense of pride and joy that I had never felt before. I was actually proud of myself. All of my other accomplishments in business and my professional career never gave me this feeling. The only other time I felt this was when I was sworn in as an attorney and I signed my name in the same book as John Quincy Adams in Boston, Massachusetts, but that was over seventeen years ago. Sitting in the gym locker room looking at that body scan, I fell in love with myself, and it felt amazing. That moment also changed everything for me.

Endings

Right around the time when I decided to commit to my physical health, my long-term partner and I unexpectedly ended our relationship. To be honest, it caught me off guard, and it wasn't ideal. We had just sold the house we were living in and were living in our condominium, which was a much smaller environment. I didn't have a plan or even a thought about leaving. However, I did know that long-term, we would not be together anymore. When working on myself with my therapist, I discussed what I was looking for in a partner, and she wasn't it. It didn't make her a bad person; I just knew that if I wanted to transform and grow, I needed someone who was aligned with my goals and desires. Almost fifteen years ended abruptly. It hurt, but it was very far from a surprise as we'd both felt it was coming.

From Helping A Friend To Unexpected Love

Several months later, a friend who'd been a New York Times best-selling author reached out to see if I could help a friend of his with her book launch. I of course obliged. What I didn't know was that my life was going to change forever. That phone call was going to give me everything I was looking for: love, happiness, acceptance, encouragement, drive, and a new outlook on life. When I got on the call with this author, I instantly felt something. I didn't know what it was. I had never felt it before. I didn't know what she looked like. I also didn't know much about her. But something was different. I have worked with hundreds of authors, heard their stories, and had been on similar calls more times than I could count. But this was different. In fact, it was so different that I interrupted her telling me her story and said this: "This may seem weird, and I don't know why I'm about to say what I'm about to say, but I have this overwhelming connection and attraction to you, and I feel like I just have to tell you." Now, this was a business phone call. Not a Zoom call. I didn't know anything about her. But something overcame me, and I just said it.

She paused. And as the consummate professional said, "That's great to hear. Let's talk about my book that is launching in 76 days."

I said, "Of course", and we continued to talk about her book and how I could help her. We talked for about an hour, and I think both of us felt something more than just the business connection. Something just clicked. That was February 13, 2023. After the phone call, I texted her and told her how amazing I thought she was, but I still didn't know much about her. One thing I didn't know during our first conversation was how beautiful she was. After we spoke, I Googled her, and her beauty was breathtaking. The type of beauty that is once in a lifetime. There are plenty of beautiful women on this planet. Then there's her beauty. She's on a whole different level of beauty. What really I fell in love with first were her voice and her words. I fell in love fast. Two days after our initial conversation, I told our mutual friend that I thought I was in love. "Seriously? In love after a couple days and just a phone call?", he said. I told him, there was more than just a phone call.

This woman is not only objectively beautiful, she's also brilliant. She has a doctorate in neuropsychology, but she's not just book smart. She's witty, funny, and super fit, along with being the kindest and the most charismatic person I have ever met. Just over thirty days later, on March 17th, I dropped everything and moved to Philadelphia to be with her and her two sons. That woman Dr. Taryn Marie Stejskal is now my fiancée and the reason why this book has become a reality.

I've Been Transformed

As you know, businesses have generated hundreds of millions. I've personally made a lot of money in my life. I've also lost a lot, and when we met, I was in a valley financially. Even without the finances I was accustomed to having, today I am the happiest I've ever been. Together, Taryn and I have already built a nine-figure business. Without her brilliance, it wouldn't have happened. I've watched her change people's lives on stages, and she is changing people's lives right now with this book.

It is a privilege and an honor just to know her. But to be able to wake up beside her every day is almost like a dream. To watch her be a mother to my bonus sons, Samson and Sawyer, and now a bonus mother to my daughter, Morgan, is beautiful. I'm in complete awe of her every day. Being with a woman like Taryn would not be possible without me making the decision to transform my body, mind, and spirit, which ultimately transformed my life. It turns out that there aren't any shortcuts you can take to reach transformation and happiness. It's an inside job.

MARK SCHNEIDER

Became The Shitstorm Savant And Learning That Every Storm Cloud Has A Silver Lining.

A Tale Of Two Centuries

Never in my wildest dreams could I have envisioned building a legacy as a Shitstorm Savant. But life is funnier and often freakier than fiction. My story may seem tragic and my writing style may seem unorthodox, but bear with me as I take you along my wild journeys of ups and downs, through catastrophic health challenges, falling off financial cliffs, mental health challenges, and relationship roulette.

For decades, I enjoyed a storybook advertising career in which good luck and fortune landed in my lap. On the surface, I lived what we call "the good life" with all of the trappings of a wife, two kids, two dogs, good friends, a loving family, and a dream job leading to early retirement. Then in the summer of 1999, cracks in my life's foundation widened to reveal an ill-fated marriage, an ethical battle with my not-so-sweet C-suite colleagues, and a series of severe health challenges that stretched into a series of shitstorms that lasted for years.

My life took a turn for the worse five hours before the turn of the century. Just before the stroke of midnight on New Years Eve, as we turned the page to 2000, a mysterious illness invaded my body. I was bedridden with a 102° fever, and as my family celebrated the arrival of the twenty-first century, I was accompanied only by my faithful dog Bo. Rather than a feeling that this illness was just passing through, I had a premonition that this sickness was just the beginning of significant change on the horizon for me.

The lessons I learned since then have been transformative, despite the fact that my own life story could be a plot for a Coen Brothers dark comedy. No one wants to go through their own shitstorms in life. I've found that life is like boarding a bus, and that bus of life will take twists and turns, even take you off course, at times, breaking down, and even crashing into a ditch. Having the courage and perseverance to stay on the bus of life, to keep going, even amidst the shitstorms have been some of the greatest challenges and the greatest teachers of my life.

Early in my life, like many of us, I enjoyed a Midas Touch where everything in my life seemingly turned to gold without much effort. But then, my fortune changed, and my Midas Touch turned to rust. It came to feel more like Murphy's Law ruled my life in the sense that what could go wrong always did. As a result, I proudly overcame six shitstorms that I would like to share with you. These tales are meant to uplift you and encourage you, and perhaps you can even relate as I'm sure you too have weathered many a shitstorm.

Texas Sized Shitstorm #1

In 1994, I recognized an opportunity of a lifetime. My career path has been shaped by embracing new marketing research trends ahead of the mainstream. At this time, database marketing was in its infancy, and I was chosen to launch the creative division for an innovative database marketing firm, they were the market leader in database marketing. The only catch was we would have to move to the Lonestar state of Texas.

Moving to Texas was a big decision. It scared me politically. My family didn't want to move until they witnessed the Texas mansion lifestyle. What sealed the deal? Promising my daughter red cowboy boots.

Surrounded by brilliant researchers and technologists, business boomed. My division grew to sixty people in six years. Early retirement was sitting on Easy Street.

Everything changed in 1999 it all happened so fast. The ad conglomerates circled the building to acquire our company which caused anxiety for me and everyone else. The stress was relentless. I got sick again, this time, almost falling into a coma before I was ordered to rest.

When I returned, without understanding why, I was put on probation. Months later, I was told to engage in unethical activities related to the sale. When I refused, I was vocal about my feelings and was fired.

On my last day, I said goodbye to Sam, the gentle giant security guard—and my late-night shoot-the-shit buddy that I loved just chatting with. We used to just chat about anything that came up and I felt like we were friends. Or at least, friendly.

As I reached out to shake his hand, he leapt backward saying to me, "I feel intense bad vibes. You're on the rollercoaster ride of your life, my friend." The next day, my masseuse, Jeanelle, reacted similarly to physical touch. Those encounters haunted me. Why they treated me like this I will never know, maybe they thought I was the bad guy.

Key Lesson Learned: Every shitstorm teaches invaluable lessons. This one taught me to bite my tongue when I engaged in controversial conversations that could harm me and recognized that my moral and ethical compass are worth more than a paycheck. While also showing me that those who seem like "friends" really reveal their true colors when the proverbial shit hits the fan.

Monster Mistakes: Shitstorm #2

After leaving the database marketing company my qualifications delivered numerous job offers. Unfortunately, my lack of emotional intelligence prevailed, vowing never to sell my soul to corporate devils again.

I was a rebel with a cause, investing three years and hundreds of thousands into a series of questionable startups, most notably NoName Co.

The people we surround ourselves with greatly influence our lives. If you aren't careful, the company you keep could destroy your life. Upon meeting the slick NoName Co. founders, my gut sounded an alarm: These are ugly conmen. You're their filet mignon. Say NO!

I didn't listen. Driven to live on my terms, I assembled a killer team: a world-renowned restaurateur, a top-five sales leader from GE, and the grandson of a Kansas utility icon.

On September 10, 2001, we celebrated an uber-successful launch party. My revenue forecast was $50,000 per month. My celebration was short-lived as 911 arrived the next day. Defiantly, I continued the venture for two years, before eventually losing a fortune.

This King-Kong-shitstorm was a reminder to listen loudly to my gut. It also taught me a vital quitting lesson. When starting anew, define your exit strategy from the get-go. It's not about the fall but how we rise and learn from it that truly matters.

Three Strikes, I'm Out: Shitstorm # 3:

I retracted my anti-corporate vow and started pursuing jobs. Simultaneously, I fell into a dark depression.

Strike 1: Amid it all, a rare opportunity surfaced in California. I was determined to make the most of it. I was forewarned it was a notorious workplace, but the mountain views and supersized salary won out.

Despite not sleeping for eight days, I dug deep into my soul and aced the interview. My 1500-mile journey was a joy ride... until I discovered the black clouds had followed me West.

Major car problems ensued the entire trip. Moreover, day one was so harrowing that I called my wife: "Don't pack; this job won't last." She informed me that our beloved dog, Bo, passed away. Three months later, I was gone from what I thought was sunshine, paradise and financial security.

Before departing, a staff member and TV psychic offered me a free psychic session as a goodbye gift. I went from a skeptic to a jaw-dropping believer.

He predicted I'd receive two offers in Pennsylvania. He cautioned me to tread lightly during interview day due to black ice.

He was spot-on, including the black ice. The same day, I landed a dream job with a large publishing company and a national Six Sigma company. For those who don't know, a Six Sigma company is a business that uses a quality control methodology to improve its processes and reduce defects. Heading back east was a gift, as my father was seriously ill. It was a fresh start filled with promise.

Strike 2: The publishing company was rated one of the top places to work in the U.S. Lucky me perhaps? Oh, contraire. As the long-timers pointed out, it went from heaven to hell after the founder's death and the takeover by a notorious former record executive.

After two weeks on the job; the morning I purchased a house; my boss informed me he was fired and I wouldn't last. The pressure was intense. I had to resign from my Six Sigma consulting gig to laser focus.

Boo! As you probably could see, like my psychic friend from my previous employer, I was fired on Halloween and had a major panic attack. I desperately needed an anti-anxiety pill but couldn't get one. If you have ever had an anxiety attack it is crippling and you will do almost anything to get out of the pain you are in. You feel paralyzed in your own body and you just want it to stop.

I received horrible advice from a family member who was actually in healthcare: "Go to the emergency room and say you're contemplating suicide." Say what?

Wracked with anxiety, I agreed and was outfitted in a straitjacket (I kiddingly requested a smoking jacket) and sent to a psych ward for the weekend. It was insane(pun intended), but I journaled about the weekend experience to get me through a very difficult time. Journalling, I would highly recommend it as it helps us express our feelings and work through the darkest of moments. Harnessing, you guessed it, our resilience.

Livid from the bad advice I had gotten, I contacted my headhunter, who explained that finding a commutable job would be a long shot. Two weeks later, I landed a job to co-launch a new division for an established firm. Things could only go up from here. Right?

Strike 3: Guess what? On day one, I discovered that my new boss had resigned due to a commission dispute. I never got along with her replacement, and six months later, I was forced out. You have to ask yourself, did I do something wrong in a previous life?

Simultaneously, my marriage continued to go south. In what was one of the hardest decisions of my life, I asked for a divorce. As if I had not had enough difficulty in my life. Why not throw in a divorce too?

Strike three, does that mean I'm out? In the game of life, just like baseball you get more chances at bat and as you will see I didn't knock it out of the park; but one key takeaway. I was still in the game.

Key Lesson Learned: When nothing seems right, channel your inner detective. Once you've cracked the code, don your metaphorical cape and make a daring move and as I said above. Stay in the game.

My New Life

Learning from prior mistakes, I took a step back to assess my options.

My wife and I began mediation, which is certainly less painful than a nasty drawn out divorce.

Welcomed back by my Six Sigma client, we developed a campaign that increased leads by 900%. Since my contract included significant performance bonuses, I was confident 2008 would be a banner year.

I started dating and was having the time of my life. Until you guessed it, another shitstorm of epic biblical proportions was about to wreak havoc on my life.

Category 5 Shitstorm #4

I had my own meltdown during the 2008 financial meltdown, as Murphy's Law ruled my life for a year. Here is a bullet point synopsis of 2008 for you.

- My daughter fell seriously ill
- My Dad died
- My dog died
- I reluctantly accepted a job at a financial firm rife with corruption. When my dog died, the owner barked, "It's a f'ing dog. Get back to work." I quit.
- My car died
- My divorce escalated into a legal battle
- I lost $117,000 when my contact at Six Sigma quit over a disagreement with a notorious President who refused to pay his bill

- My girlfriend and daughter were at odds. I found myself stuck in the middle.
- The housing market crashed, and we sold the home at a significant loss.

Key Lesson Learned: One lesson in particular stood out: Forming a relationship with a woman who didn't get along with my daughter was the biggest mistake of my life. When you enter into a relationship with kids, you are a package deal. As a couple, you navigate the storms of life together, and ensuring my significant other had a meaningful bond with my daughter would not be something I would overlook again.

Stranger Than Fiction: Shitstorm #5

Knowing it was time to play it safe, I decided to focus on consulting. But I soon learned there was no such thing as a place that was completely shielded from challenge. Here's what I mean:

- An opportunity arose to join a new healthcare venture with a well-established client base and partners I trusted. While finalizing our deal, the founder died of a heart attack at thirty-eight.
- I launched a coaching venture with a well-connected associate. Doors were opening. Then her mother died, and so did the partnership.
- I went west to pursue a special project with an Outdoor Channel investor. He had a heart attack the morning I arrived.

It didn't just feel like someone was raining on my parade. It was a shitstorm on my parade. Good things happened amid all my shitstorms. For example, I met a remarkable woman and moved in with her. But even that had a comical twist. While moving in, my sweatpants got tangled on a branch, and I flew into a wall of poison ivy. At the time, it was amusing, but looking back, I wondered if it had been a sign of things to come in our relationship.

Over time, my health plummeted. Every day was a struggle. I was exhausted and just felt horrible. My doctor pointed out the obvious: My life had been filled with stress and poor diet. I'd thought I could be "resilient" by simply pushing my physical and mental health to their limits. Not only did I misunderstand resilience, I was wrong about pushing my limits.

I kept on trucking until collapsing three times at the movies. Turns out, I had been poisoned by the medication I was taking for an enlarged prostate. My injured brain was a (technical term) mess, and the stress of it all spelled the end of the relationship with the woman with whom I was living. I definitely didn't "bounce back". In fact, it took three years for my brain to recover from all of the stress and medical issues.

The Longest Shitstorm # 6

Being an early adopter—haha— I contracted COVID in February of 2020. During this time I had launched a memoir business. It sprung up when a friend was diagnosed with cancer and I wanted to help chronicle his life story. Unfortunately, COVID transformed into long COVID, and I had to put the memoir venture on pause.

In May, I had cataract surgery. New physical complications arose, and fraudulent insurance errors ensued. It was exhausting. But I made an important decision that has served me to this day: I was determined to keep showing up, even in this brutal contact sport of life.

My long COVID symptoms classified me as a "silent sufferer." Many dropped hints that I was depressed, not ill with long COVID. These comments were hurtful and made me feel alone. Maybe it was a little bit of both. COVID and depression. At this stage of my story you must be saying, how much more can this guy handle? Well, I'm glad you asked. I got a lucky break(not), rupturing my Achilles and developing severe Uveitis. Suddenly, everyone believed me. Hallelujah!

I acquired a new nickname: The Black Cloud. It was funny initially, but the moniker wound up angering me. Could you blame people for coming up with this? Doesn't it seem like there was a black cloud? I was committed to turning my black cloud life sunny-side up. I was determined to win the game of life!

The Winds Of Cha-Cha Change

When my birthday arrived, I wished for sunnier days ahead; said the genie, "Your wish is granted."

I moved into a carriage house flooded with exquisite light that ignited my creativity.

Two weeks later, I received notice that I had to move out because the owners needed to sell. "I'm mad as hell and can't take it anymore," I screamed. The universe heard my message. Was my genie defective?!?!

Asking for help has always been challenging. Desperate, I shared my tale of woe with my bro. He and his wife just purchased a new house and invited me to live with them. "Yabba dabba doo."

By July, it was time to move on. Another stroke of good luck: I found a charming loft in a former 1700s post office with a pond.

I was on a roll as my doctor enrolled me in a long COVID clinic, where I received extraordinary care. Their advice? You are disabled. Embrace your condition. Although it was highly challenging and still is, it ultimately changed my life for the better, forever.

To celebrate my birthday, I started dating. I kiddingly called insurance, attempting to classify dating as PT, claiming relationships and sex improve health. I was rebuffed. What I've learned is that not taking things too seriously and adding some comedy to life makes the difficult things a little easier.

Dating was fun but took up too much time. My doctor ordered me to cut back, but I didn't heed her advice.

One woman stood out. She loved classic rock and jazz, strolling the city arm in arm—and anchovy pizza! Moreover, she attended the same college, CCNY, as my Dad and was a dancer, like my Mom.

One problem. We lived 137 miles apart, and the weekend commute pushed me beyond my limits. Long COVID pushed back hard. Then one fateful Sunday, she witnessed my SF-style brain fog and yet another relationship ended. My doctor's words rang out: "You need to heal before dealing with life." I committed to taking my recovery into sixth gear. How am I still hanging on, you ask? I love life, it is a gift. Is my ability to weather these constant shit storms a sign of resilience? I'm not sure, but we only got one shot here on this planet and I was determined to make the best of it.

The Storm Before The Calm

My recovery was brutal. I contracted COVID for the 4th time, igniting severe exhaustion, brain fog, a lung infection, and countless weeks in bed. I intuitively knew it was time for radical life change.

My New Lens On Life

Getting knocked down as often as an aged prizefighter, one develops Hulk-like resiliency. It was time to take control of my life.

I established a new routine that embraced my long COVID. I slept 10+ hours daily, added rigor to my diet, and invested in cryotherapy and red light therapy, instead of pharmaceuticals.

I began intensive visualization and forest bathing to design my new path.

I developed a pre-sleep ritual where my mind, body, and gut engaged in soulful, comedic conversations to ensure my entire being was in sync.

Treating my body as a temple began paying extraordinary dividends. I was ready to turn lemons into anti-inflammatory lemonade.

Sweet revenge! I began righting my wrongs, bad habits, and twisted thinking that contributed to my demise. Revelations abounded.

With my newfound lease on life. It was time to select and focus on a passion project that would awaken my lust for life and revive my career.

Which way do I go? Consulting? Memoirs? A meaningless job? I had no clue.

It Only Takes One

As I said in the very beginning of this chapter, life is funny. One event or person can change one's life: preparation creates opportunity.

One fateful day I received an email from Dr. Taryn Marie, a renowned expert in resiliency, and an exceptional, empathetic communicator. Her words caught my attention. Dr. Taryn was launching a resiliency compilation book and was seeking contributors.

A 10,000-watt light bulb illuminated my mind. Resiliency, resiliency... resiliency is my calling! My friends and family praised my resilience. It's been an integral part of my life, but I never connected the dots until that moment." Making it this far in life with all of my difficulties. How did I do it? Resilience!!!

Having a resiliency project in place, I was ecstatic.

Re-Energized

Backing up a moment, in 2020, I started writing a humorous book about my black cloud journeys, "When Shit Hits the Man™.

When I shared the idea with others, it received overwhelmingly positive feedback. Many expressed interest in sharing their stories for the book and podcast. I felt I was on to something big.

Unfortunately, my long COVID was peaking, and *When Shit Hits the Man* moved into the future projects pile... until this fortuitous project revived it. This very book you are reading, my chapter has changed the course of my life and hopefully yours. Those black clouds all have a silver lining, even COVID.

Committed

On May 17, 2024, I committed to the project of contributing to *Triumphs of Transformation* and reignited my work on When Shit Hits the Man Club.

The timing was perfect. In a world quivering with uncertainty, more people are in a world of hurt, and shitstorms are on the rise, I knew that my stories and past trauma could help others. Not only others, but this book has also changed my life.

The familiar feeling of "this is it" returned after lying dormant for decades, leaving me more energized, alive, and optimistic about life.

I even reconnected with my college roommate after decades. He's now part of the project, and our renewed friendship is a gift from god. All of these negative things have ultimately led me to this opportunity that will change the trajectory of so many people's lives.

Finally, I would live my dream of making significant contributions to the greater good. All of my difficulties, all of my pain, all of my misfortune have brought me and now you here. We are all resilient, we all can make a difference. My stories actually aren't that unique. They are my stories, but you too have been through shit storms. Reading this book is a testament to your resilience and your transformation.

When The Shit Hits The Man™ Club: An Introduction

Born out of need for my own life, When Shit Hits the Man™Club is the first oasis uniting fellow shitstormers. It is my trials and now transformation that has inspired me to build a community that features a blog, podcast, books, and events.

The truth is, no one should navigate a personal shitstorm alone. Yet, we have been navigating alone because there was no alternative... until now.

Having worked with many nonprofits, I know that it takes a village of kindred spirits to create an environment where resiliency flourishes and "you get me" conversations bring collective sighs of relief.

Shitstorm misery loves storytelling company. Humor is our medicine. We ignite resilience, raise spirits, and always have each other's backs.

What Doesn't Kill You Makes You Stronger, Wiser, Happier!

Hardship has its silver lining, imparting invaluable life lessons. What did I learn?

- Family, friends, and health always come first
- I'm disabled and empowered by knowing my strengths and embracing my weaknesses and limitations
- I eat better, sleep much longer, and find joy in every day— even the sucky ones
- Making a difference in people's lives is paramount

- Chemistry and common values define who I hang with and walk away from
- I rarely sweat the big stuff
- I finally understand the power of now

Long COVID was my tornado-siren wake-up call. It forced me to evaluate my life and make significant corrections to how I live. It's funny; maybe my shitstorms were worthwhile after all.

Why do people experience excessively lousy luck? According to my doctors, that question remains unanswered. Life's a game of chance; some would say there are winners, and others lose. But staying in the game is critical. How we define winning is our decision. We decide what we call our wins. Whether it is making it through that horrible work experience, or successfully navigating a medical set back. Coming out the other side and still being here is a win.

I—we—have the power to minimize damage and overcome shitstorms by addressing harmful habits, personality flaws and fearlessly examining our biggest mistakes. Acknowledging what has happened in my life has not been easy but has made me stronger. Laughing at near death experiences and horrible professional defeats has been my way of making it through. This may not work for everyone, but we all can decide to look at life through a different lens.

Why did I write this chapter? I have a dream: Put some of my story way out there—a monumental Babe Ruth Homer. Then help others by giving them a forum, a platform to share their story. Just like what my fellow authors have done in this book. As I conclude this chapter, I'm humbled and happy. My nest egg is sparser, but my life is richer. You're next. Staying in this difficult yet beautiful game of life has brought me to where I've always been destined to be. You too are here and it's time for your win.

ADLEY KINSMEN

A Voice You Didn't Know You Had

You know when you just got your soul *rocked* by a God whisper? It was like that.

I was fresh out of college, newly transplanted in Nashville, with the ink drying on my first record deal, living in the liminal space between knowing my life was on the precipice of completely changing before it actually had. Each day was filled with the quiet anticipation a person feels in the rare moments they know everything is about to shift, just before the big reveal.

Up until this moment, I had planned to work at a nonprofit, to speak, encourage, and inspire people to make real change in the world. Now, my life was rapidly transforming into a series of experiences I didn't recognize, let alone imagined were possible. I doubted myself and wondered if I was equipped for what was about to happen next. So, at the gym, feeling alone and uncertain, I laid on a yoga mat and prayed to God for guidance and reassurance saying things like, "How did I end up with the size of this blessing." And "You've got the wrong girl."

God Whispers

That's when I heard HIS voice as audibly as I'd heard any voice in my life, and HE said to me, "Ad, I just gave you a stage, a microphone, and a voice you didn't know you had. What do you think you're supposed to do with it? Go speak, go encourage, go inspire people. That IS what you're supposed to do. I just gave you a way bigger platform than you were giving yourself."

More than I could have hoped for was being handed to me, and I wanted to make sure God knew how grateful I was for what he was doing in my life, so I made an agreement with Him right there, "Okay," I said, "you just gave me such a leg up. I will earn everything else. Thank you for the platform. Thank you for this opportunity. I'll earn the rest."

I Dare You

Although so much was changing, it was only a few months before I laid on that yoga mat that I'd accepted the dare that set everything into motion. I was a senior at Oklahoma State and on Wednesday nights, in Stillwater Oklahoma, if we got enough Miller lights in us, my sorority sisters and I would sing karaoke at a local bar on campus. I had a love of music, playing guitar and burning CDs, but it had really only been a hobby for me. That is, until, a sorority sister and I saw an article online. She half-jokingly dared me to try out for a new television show where singers auditioned for well-known musical artists and were chosen by the artists to compete. The show was called The Voice.

I accepted the dare and drove across the country, through the night, chugging energy drinks between stops for gas to arrive in time for an 8 a.m. audition with all of the bravado that comes with a person who has not slept and has significantly elevated caffeine levels coursing through their blood steam. I wasn't prepared. I wasn't even nervous because I was just making good on my sorority sisters' dare. I would audition and drive home. That was the plan. I didn't expect to make it on the show, let alone win the entire second season of The Voice, which was the number one show in America at that time.

A Raw Deal

My life did change, but once again, not in the ways I anticipated. The "record deal" I signed prior to being on the show, offered by a "family friend" in Nashville, forced me to hand over commercial rights to my name for the rest of my life. As a "good, Christian man," I trusted him. And I genuinely don't think he knew the damage he was doing with this contract, or how unconscionable it was. But I was completely owned, and it forced me into bankruptcy to have a shot at moving forward in entertainment. I couldn't use my own name commercially during this time, which was the only leverage I had after the show. I was not in a healthy relationship with my boyfriend at the time and my dad was dying of alcoholism. What was supposed to be the summit of a lifetime had turned out to be the lowest point of my lifetime. I had imagined feeling an immense amount of joy, and instead, I was feeling intense hurt and pain.

That was the moment I realized I had a choice. I could choose to believe that I was a victim and give up, believing that God had "got the wrong girl." Or, I could choose to believe that there would be a testimony in this experience, that this difficulty would ultimately serve me and be one hell of a redemption story some day. As Lisa Nichols taught me, "You either let your pain be your fortress for all the reasons why you can't. Or you let your pain be your fuel and be all the reasons why you have to."

Pain = Power

I decided to use my pain as fuel.

I reconnected with the core of the person I wanted to be, the person who inspires, encourages, and makes a positive difference. I found that the quickest way to pull myself out of my own pain was to help other people win. Under a fake name, I started consulting an app development company (which I had ZERO experience in) and I would stay up all night researching how to help them achieve their goals.

I saw families who lost their homes in tornadoes in Moore, Oklahoma, and I thought I could help them in their moment of need. I wrote a proposal for Nissan where I would get them publicity if they would give a car away to a family who had just lost their home in the tornadoes. Then I said, I'm going to steal a country music star's car, and long story short, I ended up stealing Joe Diffie's car and driving it across three states, bringing TV and radio to every single Nissan dealership along the way. Then we gave away this car to a family that had lost their home. Focusing on how I could help others: helping Nissan win publicity, helping Joe Diffie and myself promote our new music, and giving a family who had lost everything a new car, pulled me out of the gutter.

Fast forward to today and, just like music, helping brands win more attention on social media started out as something fun. I realized I was wired to help and entertain, so I didn't care if anybody watched. Unlike the music industry, I figured out I could share my content directly with followers instead of waiting to get permission from some suit behind a desk. At first, I made no money from videos whatsoever. I was vlogging for maybe 13 people. This was 10 years ago. Nobody watched, not until 2019. And then in 2020, we began averaging over 1 billion organic views a month. My life was changed forever. And I knew that everything I had learned about "attention hacking" on social media was not for me. Yes, I figured it out along the way thanks to some great mentors and many years of persistence. But it was not for me to feel cool, or superior, or famous. It was for me to pass along and show others what is possible when you keep yourself in the game.

I couldn't have imagined the business that I would create by learning how to tell stories online that break through, get attention, and help brands build visibility. Now, I get to be in service by entertaining, doing the work I love, because we've developed a systematic formula to help videos go viral consistently and predictably. God gave me the initial platform, stage, and microphone that was larger than anything I could have envisioned. Since then, I stayed true to my promise, and even in the lowest moments, I work to "earn the rest."

I think anytime you make a deal with God, the way I did that day on the yoga mat, God has this little way of challenging you. "Oh, really?" he says. And he throws a massive obstacle your way almost immediately as if to say, "Do you really want this? Do you really want your dream? Or did you just say yes expecting that it would be easy?"

JESSE ABSHIRE

Betting On Myself: How Adversity Shaped My Path To Fulfillment

The tale of my transformation begins in my formative years, growing up in a quaint California town alongside my grandfather, grandmother, and mother. My grandfather, a World War II veteran and a natural-born hustler, emerged as my primary male role model. His life lessons on resilience, self-belief, and the notion that our only limits are those we impose on ourselves profoundly shaped my outlook. As I matured, seeking his approval became increasingly important to me, underscoring his significant influence on my life.

Early Growth

This journey toward personal growth and education started at a very young age. I recall an encounter with the principal of a one-room schoolhouse, where students from kindergarten to eighth grade shared a single space. At around four years old, he challenged me to learn the alphabet, doubting my capability. Determined, I mastered it forward and backward in less than two weeks. Despite my accomplishments, he still deemed me too young for school, which was a crushing blow. Yet my grandfather pointed out the value of what I had achieved, teaching me a crucial lesson about finding success in the face of failure—a lesson that would become a cornerstone of my philosophy.

Inspired by my grandfather, I joined the military and became an army mountaineer, a decision influenced by vivid childhood memories of playing soldier on his land and an underlying desire to provide for my son, born when I was very young. Although I had an opportunity to pursue college football, the military offered a more secure path for supporting my family, with benefits like a signing bonus, comprehensive medical care, and housing. My service was a complex journey filled with profound friendships, loss, and invaluable leadership lessons. It taught me that even in the toughest times, a slight shift in perspective can make all the difference.

Relentless Forward Motion Makes The Impossible Possible

Reflecting on these experiences, my story is one of overcoming adversity, guided by the lessons of my grandfather. It's a narrative about the transformative power of resilience, the importance of failure in learning, and the continuous pursuit of personal growth. The heart of resilience lies in the weaving of hope into the fabric of your soul, creating a tapestry of perseverance that is unbreakable in life's trials.

My time in the military allowed me to overcome obstacles that I once considered insurmountable. The experience taught me the breadth of my capabilities, surpassing my wildest imagination. A pivotal moment unfolded during a grueling twenty-five-mile march clad in full battle gear, a rucksack on my back. Conquering that challenge felt like a triumph over the world itself, marking a significant turning point in my young adulthood. It instilled a profound lesson: relentless forward motion makes the impossible possible.

However, my military journey wasn't without its trials. I sustained injuries leading to digestive problems, necessitating a series of surgeries. One particular surgery aimed to ease defecation, but it came with a significant drawback: difficulty controlling bowel movements, forcing me to rely on a leakage pad. This stark contrast between my identity as a formidable soldier—capable of navigating rugged terrains and hitting a target from a thousand feet—and the vulnerability of not making it down a hallway without an accident was humbling. It ushered in what I perceived as the most challenging phase of my life, confronting me with a reality that tested not just my physical strength, but my mental resilience and identity as well. Beneath the armor of resilience beats a heart that has learned to sing in the rain and dance in the shadows.

A Period Of Transition

The subsequent phase of my journey was marked by extensive medical treatments and my reassignment away from active duty into a medical health company, signaling the beginning of my transition out of the military. This shift brought unexpected challenges, including hazing from peers who saw me as different now. The realization that I was on the path to being medically discharged was daunting, compounded by the bureaucracy and extensive paperwork required to complete the process. Those nine months were arduous, yet they were transformative, introducing me to the world of medicine while I worked for the division surgeon of the 10th Division in Fort Drum, New York.

This experience ignited a passion for medicine and the profound impact of helping others with my knowledge. It offered me a glimpse into the gratification of contributing to the betterment of others, steering me toward a healthcare career. Despite finishing a bachelor's degree in business and finance—funded by the army but not my passion—I recognized my calling in medicine. However, my academic background lacked the necessary science credits for medical school admission.

Determined, I pursued a master of science to bridge this gap, ultimately attending the Medical University of Sofia, Bulgaria. As an institution recognized by the American Medical Association, it allowed me to transfer my credentials back to the United States. The decision to study in a foreign country, with a rich history but unfamiliar to me, was akin to the entrepreneurial leap of building a plane on the way down. Without knowledge of the language, never having been to Europe, and leaving my young children behind, I embarked on this journey. It was a gamble with immense potential to secure a better future for my family. The internal dialogues I had during this period were crucial, framing my mindset to endure the sacrifices and seize this opportunity for growth and achievement.

Embarking on medical school in Bulgaria presented a steep learning curve, not just in the medical sciences but also in mastering a new language. The initial years blended pre-med coursework with intensive Bulgarian language studies, aiming for fluency to communicate effectively with patients during clinical rotations. With patient interactions and European credentialing exams conducted in Bulgarian—and sometimes Russian for older patients—learning the language was crucial. This endeavor was my first serious attempt at learning a language other than English, a significant departure from my half-hearted high school attempts at Spanish.

An Insurmountable Hurdle

Navigating through my journey, I encountered one of the most challenging obstacles yet: a battle with severe panic attacks, which, at their onset, felt like an insurmountable hurdle. Initially, I suspected a medical anomaly—specifically, a pheochromocytoma, a rare tumor of the adrenal gland known to mimic the symptoms of panic attacks. This hypothesis was a testament to the medical student in me, searching for a tangible cause behind the terrifying episodes that left me feeling utterly powerless.

An MRI revealed some abnormalities in my adrenal gland but nothing conclusive enough to explain the severity of my symptoms. This led me to a reluctant acceptance that the root of my struggle might not be purely physical. The panic attacks were debilitating, striking with such intensity that I found myself incapacitated, lying on the ground in public spaces, fighting to regain control over my body and mind.

This experience was a stark departure from my identity as a strong soldier; I was now confronting internal adversaries without the familiarity of external tools or strategies, apart from medications that alienated me from my sense of self. The journey toward recognizing that the panic might be originating from within was daunting. Admitting that the turmoil was, in fact, psychological, felt like acknowledging a war within my own body, a civil conflict between the mind and flesh.

However, it was this acknowledgment that paved the way for genuine healing and growth. Accepting the internal nature of my struggles marked the beginning of resilience. I learned that true strength is not about denying vulnerability but about embracing it and using it as a foundation to build a stronger self. The process of overcoming my panic attacks, of learning to coexist with them and eventually gain the upper hand, taught me a profound lesson in resilience. It reshaped my perspective on adversity, making other challenges seem less insurmountable by comparison. This transformation underscored a powerful truth: We can harness our most difficult experiences as catalysts for growth, turning the very waves that seek to break us into the ones that lift us higher.

Navigating Rough Waters

As I navigated this new linguistic landscape, I encountered challenges that transformed into opportunities for growth. Despite the initial perception of speaking in a "word salad," this linguistic journey enabled me to conduct basic medical histories and physicals, enrich my experience in the city, and forge friendships, even if my initial attempts at speaking Bulgarian were met with amusement

In parallel to my academic and linguistic endeavors, I explored a lifelong passion for golf, receiving a sponsorship to play on the European professional development tour. This experience allowed me to travel and compete in a sport I loved, a dream that traced back to makeshift putt-putt courses in my grandfather's yard and imaginary golf tournaments under a streetlight. These childhood memories of golfing with my grandfather and self-competition underlined the importance of imagination and escapism in shaping my aspirations.

Throughout these transitions, the role of family, particularly my relationship with my younger brother, remained a constant source of support and challenge. From navigating the complexities of sibling dynamics to facing life's adversities, including divorces and temporary homelessness, my brother's unwavering support was instrumental. These trials brought us closer, fostering a deep bond that provided stability during tumultuous times.

My career path post-medical school took unexpected turns, from directing a preschool and mental health treatment center to working in vocational rehabilitation and ultimately training at an adult mental health hospital for the state. Despite professional achievements and material success, including purchasing a condo with amenities, a lingering sense of unfulfillment persisted, prompting reflection on my true happiness and life's direction. This narrative underscores the interplay between professional aspirations, personal growth, and the enduring value of family support in navigating life's challenges and triumphs.

Finding Fulfillment Beyond Tangible Objects

This period represented a pivotal shift in my career trajectory and the discovery of my true passion. As I matured, I realized that fulfillment in work transcends financial gain; it's about engaging in activities that bring genuine joy and satisfaction. This insight resonated with me, especially as I began to feel a disconnect from my medical career, noticing a growing preference for being anywhere but the hospital. This internal shift coincided with the onset of COVID-19, prompting me to explore new business ventures. I obtained my financial service professional license and founded Abshire Family Financial and Abshire Capital Management, marking a new chapter in my professional life.

However, this journey was not without its challenges. A back injury from my military service severely impaired my mobility and quality of life, culminating in a period where I weighed over 373 pounds and struggled immensely with my physical and mental health. Questions about depression at doctor's visits starkly reminded me of my struggles, yet the thought of leaving my children without a father kept me determined to find a solution.

After numerous consultations, a pain management doctor introduced me to treatments that alleviated some of my discomfort, significantly improving my life. Despite these advancements, my weight remained a barrier to further treatments for a degenerative disc in my back. Caught in a catch-22, unable to lose weight due to physical limitations but needing to for medical treatment, I was referred to a weight-loss surgeon.

The decision to undergo weight-loss surgery was transformative, resulting in a loss of over 120 pounds. Although I continue to face challenges related to nerve damage and other health issues, the surgery granted me mobility that had been long forgotten, enabling me to focus on aspirations beyond mere survival.

Reflecting on my educational and professional achievements, I recognized that the completion of my degrees signified not just the end of an educational journey but the realization that the pursuit itself is what's most important. This realization underscored the belief that the timing of one's start is irrelevant compared to the determination to achieve and finish one's goals. This lesson has been a guiding principle in my life, emphasizing the value of perseverance and the pursuit of passion, regardless of when one begins.

I discovered a profound satisfaction in helping others and sharing knowledge, which for me functions like a self-fulfilling prophecy. My interests extend beyond creating tangible objects, like a shelf in the garage, to designing business structures, driven by an innate love for mathematics and numbers. Their definitive nature appeals to me—their outcomes are either right or wrong, a simplicity I deeply appreciate.

Building A Fence

Now I share my passion for financial literacy by teaching across the country. My business, which holds licenses in sixteen states, is a testament to a gamble I took on myself and my unique vision—a vision I realized doesn't always need validation or understanding from others. This journey underscored the value of pursuing my internal blueprint for success, even when I'm the sole believer in its potential.

In guiding my team, I liken the process to building a fence: You place the first post at the beginning and another at the far end, marking the start and finish. The challenge and essence of vision lie in connecting these points, embodying the journey from where you are to where you aspire to be. I've come to see the beauty in this journey, including the failures along the way, as they're instrumental to learning and growth. Failures in business, lapses in parenting, and moments of personal shortfall have all been invaluable teachers. Each day offers a new opportunity to be better than the last. Although I sometimes fall short, the lessons learned from these failures are vital components of personal development and growth.

Bet On Yourself

Throughout this narrative, I've chosen to highlight pivotal moments that shaped my journey, providing an overview of the transformative experiences that led me to where I am today. Ultimately, I decided to bet on myself, choosing entrepreneurship over the security of a conventional nine-to-five job. This choice was not about rejecting the notion of working for someone else but about embracing the challenge of realizing my dreams, despite the risks involved.

My journey has taught me that perceived obstacles are often only daunting until we confront and overcome them. I use this philosophy to inspire my staff, illustrating those financial goals, while they may seem unreachable at first—whether it's earning $10,000, $30,000, or even $100,000 a month—become attainable through persistence and hard work. This mindset reinforces my belief in the boundlessness of our potential.

My unwavering optimism is rooted in a belief that the boundaries of our potential are only as constrictive as we allow them to be. It's a conviction that the trials we endure serve a greater purpose, acting as the anvil on which our determination is forged and sharpening our capacity for gratitude when triumph emerges from tribulation. This philosophy underpins a fundamental message: the importance of investing in oneself. To bet on yourself is to embrace the entirety of your capabilities, acknowledging that the path to achievement is often paved with uncertainties and challenges.

Choosing to take a leap of faith in one's abilities can be daunting. The fear of failure looms large, a specter that can dissuade even the most steadfast heart. Yet it is in the act of overcoming this fear that we unlock the truest expression of our potential. The alternative—a life of wondering, "What if?"—is a sentence to a half-lived existence, shackled by the regret of unexplored possibilities.

When we commit to betting on ourselves, we open the doors to infinite possibilities. Each decision to pursue our passions, to follow our curiosities, and to challenge our limitations, is a step toward a life rich in achievement and fulfillment. This commitment is not a guarantee of success in every endeavor, but rather a promise that the journey itself will be replete with learning, growth, and the kind of satisfaction that comes only from having dared greatly.

In every moment of doubt, every period of struggle, there lies a pivotal opportunity for growth. It is in these moments that we are called to remember our resilience, to recall the strength that resides within us, and to push forward with renewed vigor. For it is through hardship that we gain perspective, through struggle that we learn the value of perseverance, and through challenges that we discover our true capacity for greatness.

Therefore, I advocate for a life led by the courage to bet on oneself, to take the risks that frighten us, and to pursue the dreams that inspire us. In doing so, we not only elevate our existence, but also inspire those around us to consider the boundless potential that lies within their grasp. This is the essence of optimism—not a blind faith that everything will be easy, but a steadfast belief in our ability to navigate the complexities of life and emerge not just unscathed, but stronger, wiser, and more fulfilled than ever before.

JOSHUA BURKE

Forging Strength Through Crisis And Change*

The very embodiment of *American Psycho*. Untamable fury arose within. Crimson-faced, my veins bulged, and my eyes shot lasers of viscera at those in the room unwilling to bend to my will. In an uncontrollable reaction that would alter the course of my life, I lost it.

Spiffed up in a bespoke suit and hand-folded tie. Hair coiffed to perfection. Focused. Determined. Professional. Prestigious. Powerful. An exceptionally busy day, like every day, I was asked to squeeze in yet another appointment. Though annoyed at the audacity of such a request, I relented. Clearly, they didn't understand how important my work was and by extension, how important I was. Didn't they understand that I had better things to do than to attend my daughter's annual checkup?

Accompanied by my wife and baby girl, our oldest daughter had recently turned five and came to the med unit for a checkup and a series of shots. My attitude and body language clearly said, "Listen kid, the clock is ticking, so let's get this over with quick. I have a hard stop at the top of the hour, and the big boss needs something by the end of the day. Got it?" I gave her the compulsory hug, faint support, and inauthentic praise for her braveness. "You're a big girl. You've got this. It's just a shot. And Daddy's really busy—so come on and hurry up."

With a voice and volume that could wake the banshees from the deep, my daughter A. once had a meltdown so intense, she literally gave herself a nosebleed. No wineglass was safe when she let it out. She's always been a strong and often stubborn girl—I'm not sure where that comes from. To my aggravation and enragement, my five-year-old girl did not want a long needle stuck in her arm, and she let the entire embassy know about it. Her screams were so violent that everyone in the room was shaken. Except me. I was triggered.

At that moment, my every deeply buried wound and childhood trauma erupted. With embassy nurses, my wife, and our daughters present, I had my own meltdown. It was an explosive episode that I can only describe as an emotional rock bottom. In an outburst of unstoppable rage, I lifted a stool and repeatedly, violently, slammed it on the floor—with so much force that the wheels shattered and shrapnel engulfed the room. My foreboding voice silenced everyone. Frozen with fear, they were terrified and traumatized. By me.

This was not the kind of anger taught by Aristotle. Not a controlled, tempered, this-is-just-an-act-to-teach-you-a-lesson sort of anger. It was the fiery red Anger character from the movie *Inside Out*. Reactionary, loud, abrasive, eruptive. Blind fury.

When incidents like this happen, especially in such a prestigious institution, paperwork follows. The government I served for nearly a decade nearly accused me of childhood endangerment and destruction of government property. Justifiably. Despite the undeniable gravity of the situation, I initially looked for excuses outside of myself. If only she had not screamed so loud. If only she had taken her shot quickly like I asked. If only my work schedule wasn't so busy. If only we were back home in the U.S. If only, if only, if only. . .

Fear and uncertainty clouded my judgment, and the thought of facing my demons head-on seemed overwhelming. Yet in that vulnerability, I found a glimmer of hope, and I accepted the opportunity to seek treatment. Within a few days' time, I was medically evacuated from post and began the longest, toughest journey of my life. This was a journey to prove if Rumi was right when he said, "The wound is the place where the light enters you." Little did I know, this wound was not the end but the beginning of a journey toward resiliency, toward triumph over adversity, and toward personal transformation.

The Journey Within

"But how did this happen? How did I get here? What in my life led me to this point?" I repeatedly asked myself on that painfully long flight back to D.C. Where did this anger come from? When I was about thirteen months old, my parents divorced and often struggled financially. I was fortunate that growing up, I had three loving parents. My dad had remarried, and all my parents were in my life and always present at major birthdays, school events, etc. I became the middle kid of a mixed, five-child household, and I struggled to find my place and to get the attention I thought I needed. Big feelings occasionally came out, though were mostly suppressed.

Often fidgety and hyper in thoughts and deeds, I have occasionally been described as having the attention span of a hunting dog in a squirrel park. Eventually I found swimming to be an outlet to bring some needed balance—and my parents felt that I no longer needed therapy. Bless their hearts.

Peace For Others Not So Much For Me

A few years after college, in the wake of 9/11, managerial metrics and year-on-year sales quotas seemed insufficient and shallow. So I left that world behind and joined the Peace Corps. From climbing mountains to spelunking in caves, I faced highs and lows both literally and emotionally while volunteering overseas. While such emotional fluctuations happen to many of us at home, they seem to happen with greater intensity and frequency when living in an unfamiliar environment. An incorrect pronunciation or seemingly innocent hand gesture can land one in a humiliating and embarrassing situation abroad. After an intense day, getting scolded by the local shopkeeper can often be the last straw that emotionally fatigues so many of us. PTSD, alcoholism, and other unhealthy addictions appear often in expat communities.

After my two-year assignment, I remained abroad to explore business opportunities and to nurture a budding relationship. Two daughters and nearly two decades later, our relationship is as strong as ever; we jokingly remind ourselves that pressure makes diamonds. I'm eternally grateful to Anca for supporting me through this journey of life. She and I both attended a great MBA program, and our path toward superficial successes was mapped out. My best friend and business partner, we've been blessed to create successful side hustles. I've struggled financially many times, and I found the accompanying anxiety especially crippling. Both of us grew up broke, so a certain degree of financial abundance has been a welcome shift in our lives. Yet as we all have seen, prosperity alone does not resolve deeply rooted issues.

A few years after business school and seemingly from nowhere, a mentor appeared in my life. She had recently returned from an assignment in the same country where I had served as a volunteer years before. She urged me to consider joining the diplomatic corps. In time, I was accepted and left behind the strategy consultant profession. Once again, I answered the call to serve.

We were preparing for our first overseas assignment when a family tragedy struck. In a period of less than two months, my mother almost died twice. Getting her to a stable environment was paramount, and to survive this ordeal, I had to bottle all my emotions deep down. When the situation became more balanced at home, we moved to Türkiye. Shortly after we unpacked, there were multiple incidents of bombings over the course of several months. More trauma. More deeply buried. At this time, Anca was pregnant with our second daughter, the perpetually innocent G., who brings so much joy into our lives. The first weeks and months of parenthood are so very challenging, especially when overseas, especially with terrorist attacks happening regularly. As diplomats we are trained to conceal—not to feel—not to let it show. More suppressed emotions. I now recognize that I had been living in a perpetual state of fear for years, the fight or flight part of my brain was overstimulated. Yet relief was in sight; we were assigned to my dream assignment, my wife's homeland. Then, more family tragedy.

Shortly after arriving at the next overseas assignment, my stepbrother died. I was serving in the Peace Corps during the worst of his schizophrenia and was a bit removed from the daily challenges that my family faced. Eventually, he was able to find medicine which kept him mostly balanced and that helped to keep him alive for another fifteen years. Yet as is common with many medicines, there were side effects, and he died of a heart attack at thirty-five years old. My father, reflecting on the most challenging times of Matt's illness, shared at his funeral a comment that has always stayed with me: "The exact time when a person is most difficult to love is the exact time that they are in the most need of love."

So how did the incident happen in the med unit? In a period of less than thirty months, we miscarried, my mom almost died twice, we moved overseas, our second daughter was born, we endured multiple terrorist attacks, we fought legal threats to our business, we launched an international charity, we moved overseas *again*, and my brother died. And I, trying to keep calm and carry on, stored it all inside and bought a bespoke suit.

On that infinitely long plane ride to D.C., soaked in shame and riveted with regret, I stared blankly out the window. Only later did I learn the Wayne Dyer saying: "Just as if you squeeze an orange, orange juice will come out; when we are squeezed, whatever is inside of us will come out." If I was to salvage my relationship with my family and whatever was left of my career, I needed to enter the cave of my psyche and clean out decades worth of emotional toxicity within.

Eager to pass this test with dignity and diligence, over the next several weeks I read, reflected, fasted, journaled, exercised, wept, studied, and completed dozens of hours of cognitive behavioral therapy. Dr. David Burns's book *Feeling Good* was required reading and remains an immensely helpful resource. Yet no amount of head knowledge was going to work without deeper internal reflection.

The time and space to sit with my actions was profoundly difficult. I had flashbacks of the cave scene in *The Empire Strikes Back*. Luke goes into the cave with his weapons and faces his worst enemy—Darth Vader. But after defeating his worst enemy, Vader turns out to be Luke himself. At some point in our lives, we must all fight our own Vader. We all must battle our fears and our inner dark side. This painful process required me to dismantle and examine the foundations of my previous lifestyle and belief systems. It involved questioning the very essence of who I was and who I wanted to be.

As diplomats we are almost always reacting to outside stimuli. Global crisis—reaction. Boss needs something immediately—reaction. Colleague disagrees with you— reaction. We're always on; it's literally codified in our manuals that we are considered on duty 24/7. Constant, perpetual reactions can be stimulating, addictive, and occasionally dangerous. Emotional and mental health challenges are widely experienced, yet not widely understood. COVID-19 caused further devastating damage across the globe and has highlighted the importance of emotional wellness. Since the pandemic, it's estimated that mental-health-related medical evacuations for diplomats have nearly tripled.

More recently, in developing leadership courses for U.S. diplomats, I share Viktor Frankl's famous quote, "Between stimulus and response there is a space. In that space is our power to choose our response. In our response lies our growth and our freedom." But years before I could teach that quote, I had to find a way to live it. How exactly could I find the space between stimulus and response? What tools could I find and use to help me shift from being reactive to being responsive?

We are currently living in a time of unprecedented distractions and stimuli. While I am deeply grateful for modern technology and medicine, my preferred path leans toward ancient remedies. Since that fateful time in D.C., I have continued to study and practice both modern and ancient natural techniques that are helpful in bringing balance to the mind and nervous system.

Mental Health Crisis

There is no question that our society is facing a mental health crisis. Yet I have come to agree with many experts that this may be more an issue of mental fitness. That small distinction, in my view, empowers us as individuals to take greater ownership of our own well-being. James Clear in *Atomic Habits* says, "You do not rise to the level of your goals. You fall to the level of your systems." With hundreds of small shifts, I have developed personal practices and systems which have improved my overall fitness and regulation of my nervous system. I've learned firsthand how important our physiology is to our psychology. Healthier eating, less and better caffeine and alcohol, more time in nature and with community, family time, daily exercise, boundaries, self-care, discipline, etc., have all helped me tremendously.

While ancient wellness methods and biohacking trends have unquestionably helped my mental fitness, to truly find emotional healing, I needed to dig deeper. "One does not become enlightened by imagining figures of light," Carl Jung reminds us, "but by making the darkness conscious." I needed to go deeper into my cave and confront my darkest shadows.

In the bleakest part of my ordeal while in deep meditation, I uncovered a painful realization. For nearly four decades, I had been continuously blaming myself for my parents' divorce. I was living my life with deep-rooted shame, guilt, and rejection. For most of my life, I didn't believe that what I did or said mattered because, at my innermost core, I didn't believe that I mattered. All that I had buried so deep inside is the juice that came out when life squeezed.

I have come to accept that my emotional state can fluctuate more than most. With family history and environmental factors playing a role, my psyche can be especially sensitive, and without appropriate awareness and action, my moods can fluctuate ferociously. On the never-ending path of emotional healing, after acceptance comes forgiveness. Despite initial resistance and with help from a dear friend, I eventually learned to forgive myself.

I had been carrying a heavy load for a long time, yet awareness, acceptance, and forgiveness have helped me to release the burden and to drop the millstone from my heart. Expressing gratitude for everything that comes my way has also been tremendously helpful. I finally realized that since I invited myself to the pity party of my own creation, I was able to leave at any time. I emerged from my desolate den of despair lighter, brighter, happier, and healthier. Taking massive accountability for my actions—accepting all I've done and said—has been an excruciatingly painful yet strengthening exercise. "Life is just 10 percent of what happens to you," John Maxwell says, "and 90 percent of how you respond." By taking ownership for my actions and refusing to be a victim of my circumstances and external events, I felt emotionally strong enough to reenter the world.

Since my time in D.C., I have mostly maintained my wellness practices and have found additional tools to support my wellbeing. I have competed in triathlons, completed yoga teacher training in India, and most importantly, I have regained love and respect from my children. To earn their forgiveness and to celebrate the special bond between fathers and daughters, I also helped to organize a daddy-daughter charity ball.

While a portion of my journey is shared here, the story of transformation is one that never truly ends. Each day brings new challenges, insights, and opportunities for growth. It's often said that you can't stop the waves, but you can learn to surf. Like many of us, I have faced some challenging waves. Since the events in this story, I have experienced a few more tidal waves, and I've certainly fallen off my board. Yet whatever storms may appear on the horizon, I now know that I have the tools, the friends, and the family to help me rise yet again. For the true triumph of transformation lies not in reaching a destination but in the continual process of becoming. Having lived in Türkiye, I am quite fond of Rumi, and I'll close with another of his quotes: "Yesterday I was clever, so I wanted to change the world. Today I am wise, so I am changing myself."

Out for a recent stroll amid the bounty of beauty ornamenting the National Mall, I found myself in a deeply reflective state. The beloved cherry blossoms were on full display. These moments are fleeting, as the blossoms peak for only about one week a year. It's the visual equivalent of catching a snowflake on your tongue. It lasts just a moment. Then it's gone.

Nearly four thousand trees flirtingly flaunt their blooms each year. The story of these cherry trees dates back to 1912, when they were presented as a gift from the People of Japan, but it goes much deeper—deeper into the soil, that is. The first trees donated by Japan had trouble taking root in U.S. soil. Many immigrants can appreciate such a challenge, I imagine. With some time and help from skilled horticulturalists, a method was found to allow these trees to thrive. By grafting one type of cherry onto the rootstock of another, the trees were able to survive, thrive, and inspire.

Blanketed by the blossoms below, an obelisk of immense proportions, the monument to our first president stands as a sentinel keeping watch over the crowds, the capital, and the country. The cornerstone of the Washington Monument was laid in 1848, but construction soon stalled. After the Civil War, the monument was left unfinished and was considered an embarrassing eyesore.

Looking closely at the monument, one now can see the variation of the hue about one-third up from the base. During the twenty-year construction stoppage, the original quarry closed, and another source of marble had to be found. If you will forgive the poetic license, I like to think that new marble was grafted to the rootstock of the original base. What initially had trouble thriving, needed some help to reach the highest heights. With patience and dedication, the monument was completed in 1884 and, soaring to 555 feet, remains the tallest stone structure on the planet.

Like so many of us, there are times that I have felt uprooted; times that I've struggled to find fertile soil to thrive. So many moments that I felt my foundation crumbling, uncertain of how I would rise to heights of my potential. I'm grateful for this poetic reminder—the whispered words of wisdom from flower and stone—that with persistence, resiliency, and with a little help from our friends, we too shall rise, we too shall blossom.

*The views expressed in this chapter are those of the author alone, and in no way reflect the views, opinions, or policy of the U.S. Government or those of the American Foreign Service Association.

JULIE LANCASTER

Riding The Lightning: A Journey Of Inner Bravery And Resilience

"You've got five minutes to pack and say goodbye. Starting now."

The sudden urgency reverberated through my tiny tin-roofed house. BBC News had been crackling through the hand-crank radio for weeks. Political unrest was keeping the country on edge; it was the top news story now at my doorstep. I sprang into action. This wasn't a drill. Post-election unrest and whispers of a possible coup had escalated to a point of no return. South Africa's intervention in Lesotho was imminent; it was time to flee the storm brewing on the horizon. Shit was getting real.

Thankfully, I had a note taped inside the front door of my eighty-square-foot house. *In case of emergency, pack the following: passport, money belt, toothbrush, camera, sleeping bag, water bottle, Lonely Planet Africa book, clothes. If possible, pillow.* I had no idea what to prepare for, but the list also included *mofau*, Sesotho for "travel food," for which there is no English translation, along with my Basotho blanket, the traditional garb.

I Have To Go

With my Gregory backpack brimming with essentials, I made my way to my host family's house, where M'e Malucia, the matriarch, awaited with wide eyes and a heart heavy with the weight of this sudden farewell.

"Ke tlameha ho tsamaea. Kea u rata," I whispered, the words heavy with love and urgency. *I have to go. I love you.* Her embrace enveloped me, a bittersweet refuge in the face of uncertainty.

Next, I sought out my host brother, Ntate Neo, my closest confidant in a land of unfamiliarity. Fluent in both Sesotho and English because he was a teacher, I was able to communicate with ease. "I am sorry," I murmured, emotions and memories catching in my throat. "They are taking me to the capital, and I don't know if I'll be back. Thank you for everything."

And just like that, I was swept away, leaving behind echoes of my African name, Nthabiseng, reverberating through the village. After seventeen months living in this African kingdom in the sky, as it's affectionately known, this chapter of my life closed in an instant.

It might seem scary, but to me at the time, it was exhilarating.

Once we left the rural mountains, our vehicle joined a convoy consisting of two passenger vehicles followed by a tank. This pattern repeated as far as I could see. We were escorted by military tanks all the way to Maseru. The capital was a distant cry from the familiar vibrant taxi music and lively food vendors. The chaos was palpable; the buildings and their thatched roofs were smoldering. The seventy of us, now gathered, had been plucked from all corners of the country. We each had just one bag of possessions.

Somehow, amid the chaos, a bus miraculously appeared, as if summoned by the sheer desperation of our situation. We piled in, our hearts racing with equal parts adrenaline and disbelief. Six hours later, we arrived in our South African destination, greeted by jacaranda trees and bird of paradise flowers.

As we pulled into the manicured Holiday Inn in Pretoria, I couldn't help but feel like I had stepped into an alternate universe. Just moments ago, I was living by candlelight, and I owned more chickens than I did pairs of socks. And now, here I was, staring at a McDonald's across the street, surrounded by the tantalizing aromas of bagels, margaritas, and the promise of a swimming pool. Talk about culture shock.

I was sad, but also in heaven. We indulged in all the big-city delights and waited for things to simmer down.

A Bold Decision

After a few blissful yet wildly confusing weeks, it was time to say goodbye to our hotel home. Choices needed to be made. To complicate matters, I had just started dating another American from Tucson, Arizona.

Some of us were allowed to return to our mountain towns, and others were not. Mark and I were offered plane tickets to our respective homes. My Pittsburgh, Pennsylvania home was quite a way from his southwest desert. Our three months of courting had been short but powerful. One thing was clear: I wasn't ready to say goodbye. A second option presented itself: Take the money for the tickets and run.

We got creative. Meeting with a travel agent, we learned that we could buy round-the-world plane tickets for almost the same price as just going home! We immediately crafted an itinerary that had us circling the globe for the next six months.

Our journey would begin with a bold move—traveling overland from South Africa to Kenya, a trek of three thousand one hundred miles fueled by nothing but our backpacks and our love. Along the way, we would traverse the diverse landscapes of East Africa, from the sandy shores of Mozambique to the lush greenery of Malawi and the sprawling plains of Tanzania. We'd ride in the back of pickup trucks, squeeze into crowded buses, and even find ourselves washing our armpits in tiny train sinks.

Upon reaching Nairobi, we'd fly back to South Africa, then Australia, New Zealand, Hawaii, and home.

We were riding the lightning, following the energy and inspiration wherever it led us. Exploration became our compass. We were swimming with dolphins, volunteering on farms, and hiking in downpours. With infrequent shower options, we became intimately familiar with each other's scents—a closeness that bordered on comical at times. We grew accustomed to buying hard boiled eggs laid by backyard chickens spanning the continent. Vendors knocked on our bus windows, passing the eggs and a two-inch square of newspaper, carefully cinched, holding enough salt to dip our eggs in. Each day was filled with special small moments that added up to something big and spectacular.

New Heights

In those moments, I felt untethered from the constraints of ordinary life, embracing the freedom to be bold and unrestrained. I was alive, truly alive, and nothing could stand in the way of our unstoppable journey.

During our travels, we would look at options in the next country and dream up possibilities. Reflecting on the exhilarating summiting of Mt. Kenya four years prior during a college study-abroad program, I had an idea. "How about Mt. Kilimanjaro in Tanzania? Could be fun, right?" Without missing a beat, he replied, "Sure." And just like that, we decided to tackle the tallest mountain on a continent boasting fifty-four countries.

We headed to Moshi at the base of the towering mountain. Along the way, someone gave us the name of a Peace Corps volunteer who worked at a school there, and we felt confident that we could find him. Foreigners stuck out. As became the norm, we were welcomed with open arms. He outfitted us with fleeces and parkas for our climb. It was seventy degrees Fahrenheit in Moshi with an expected zero degrees on Uhuru Peak.

We grabbed some Diamox at a local pharmacy to ward off altitude sickness. Since it was merely recommended and not mandatory, I opted out. "I don't need a crutch," I confidently told myself.

With nearly seventeen thousand feet of elevation to gain, we began. Traveling on a shoestring, we chose a faster route with tent camping, as opposed to the cost of staying in huts and adding on days. Additionally, this Machame Route seemed interesting, as it wasn't an out and back; we'd descend on the Mweka Route.

This mountain starts trekkers in the rainforest and goes up to the arctic summit. Some equate the journey to walking from the equator to the North Pole due to the five ecological zones passed through. We joined the thirty thousand annual hikers.

A licensed guide is required for any excursion on the mountain. Frankly, this felt like luxury. We didn't risk getting lost, and porters would lug our food and gear. We handed over our packs with delight and ease.

Up we went. Hiking boots with a fresh coat of wax, wool socks for wicking and warmth, quick-drying pants. Feeling invincible, we were striding along at a brisk pace despite the mud slicks turning the trail into a slip-and-slide. Our trekking squad included Mary and Magnus, our new Swedish pals.

Suddenly, our porters zoomed past us in flip-flops and jeans. They danced across tree roots like it was a casual Tuesday stroll, not even breaking a sweat. To boot, each of them adorned our backpacks, but not as expected. They balanced our state-of-the-art, expedition-sized, weight-distributing mountaineering packs...on their heads. Meanwhile, we struggled to keep our balance, looking like amateur contestants on a bad reality show.

What's more, they had other bags on their backs that included things like tea kettles and cantaloupe. I like to think of myself as rugged, but now I was feeling a bit like a prima donna who might be expecting a manicure and silk sheets at camp.

The second surprise was the display of "toilet paper flowers" as we neared the first camp. There was an unpleasant amount of poop in crevices in which previous trekkers had relieved themselves. It was gross. But arriving at camp for a picnic dinner with tents set up for us had me quickly forgetting the fecal cairns.

The next day, we continued to climb. Anyone who knows me will willingly say that I walk obnoxiously fast. At this point, I tried to be our trailing caboose. Unpredictable waves of bowel spasms led me to panic-dash toward those crevices. I wasn't acclimatizing as planned.

Arriving at camp the second night, now above ten thousand feet, we were greeted by an outhouse, much to my delight. That delight quickly left upon approach, seeing that the deposits were towering above the rim of the seat. It was clear that I was not the only one with an excited colon. But we slept, and woke, and carried on again. My appetite was minimal, a headache was lurking, but all seemed well enough.

The Bravest Thing You Could Do Right Now Is. . . ..

On the third night, I discovered a whole new level of vulnerability. Just as Mark and I were getting cozy in the tent, ready to hunker down for some much-needed sleep, I felt it. I shot up, but not fast enough. The tent stayed zipped, but my dignity did not—I exploded right into my long johns. Right beside him. Sometimes humility is not a pretty sight.

Now at Barafu Camp, we were told to sleep until 11 p.m. At that time, we'd wake up and prep for the summit. The final push! Just four thousand feet to go. Crawling out of the tent, we were greeted by the comforting aroma of tea being brewed. Despite feeling less than ideal, my bossy inner voice chimed in, "Mind over matter. I'm fine," I tried to convince myself. But my mental fog made it confusing as to what to believe.

Warming my hands with the mug, I took my first sip of tea and immediately knew something was wrong. I quickly turned away from the group and unleashed a spectacular display of projectile vomit. Trying to regain my composure and not completely terrify everyone, I wiped my mouth and declared, "Let's do this!" with a maniacal enthusiasm that left my team unsure if they should feel motivated or very, very concerned.

On we went. Every step felt like a seismic effort. On the cindered slope, it was like two steps forward and one step back. Each step made me want to collapse, and one by one, others passed me by.

My brother always says I could sell sand in the desert. I don't see myself as particularly persuasive, but I tried to lean into influencing the group. "Hey, let's all take a break; what's the rush?" But they weren't buying it. At this point, it was just the three of us: Mark, one guide, and me.

The moon and stars should have been breathtaking, but I couldn't muster up any gratitude. The physical fatigue was debilitating, and my mental faculties only let me think, "Pick up your left foot, put it down. Pick up your right foot, put it down."

After twenty minutes of my grueling pace, Mark turned to me with concern in his eyes. "Julie, you aren't thinking straight and you're sick. I see how hard you're trying. But listen to me. The bravest thing you could do right now is. . . turn around."

His words hit me hard. I looked at him, knowing I trusted him completely. I knew he was right—I wasn't thinking clearly, and I was sick. He had my best interest at heart. With a heavy heart, I turned around. Defeated.

I went back to camp and waited for what felt like forever. I felt the darkness. I heard the silence.

Am I Brave?

As I waited, the negative self-talk crept in. It told me that I was an imposter. I thought, "Until now, my identity was this: I am brave. I persevere. I am someone who isn't stopped by fear. Now, I finally recognize what I have been blind to all this time; I am not as strong as I thought I was." So now, here I was, feeling that my entire identity was a joke. Was I not cut out for real risk-taking? Who was I to think I was brave? I was clearly not the same caliber as the folks I was with up there. With shame, I thought, "I'm a fraud." Then I asked myself: "What evidence do I even have that I have ever been brave?"

This question gave me pause; it was a record-scratcher for me. When I changed the tone a little and asked in a curious way, it landed differently. It challenged my critical, all-knowing black-cloud self-talk. Could I find some evidence?

In that stillness, a flicker of clarity emerged. It dawned on me that my identity was not defined by this singular day. My inner turmoil also revealed something profound: Bravery isn't just about scaling mountains or facing physical challenges. It's about the courage to confront our own doubts and fears, to question our assumptions, and to define who we are.

By this time, dawn was arriving, and I felt the light creeping into my mind as well. *I guess it's brave to be traveling in Africa; lots of people I know aren't doing that. I guess it's brave to have chosen to climb this mountain, not knowing what really to expect. I trusted Mark, and I believe that trusting people is brave. It's brave to listen to my body and not pretend that it's fine.*

Through the darkness, a glimmer of understanding emerged. I realized that my journey was not a failure, but a lesson in resilience and self-discovery. It was a humbling reminder that bravery is not always about conquering external obstacles, but about embracing our internal struggles with courage and grace.

Victorious, the summited group returned to camp, unapologetically enchanted with standing atop the tallest freestanding mountain in the world. All 19,341 feet of it. I joined in the celebration. They did not see me as a failure, and in this moment, I truly understood how important it is to challenge what we tell ourselves. I was grateful for them, for the mountain, and for this lesson. We were victorious.

As we started to descend into warmth and higher levels of oxygen availability, I got a pep in my step. My stomach settled. My mind cleared. The altitude sickness was gone, just like that.

A Lasting Journey

My perspective-taking journey started this day but lasted for years. I now see bravery and resilience as the power couple that I always have access to. Whether it's a country evacuation, the climbing of a mountain, parenting, or work. When I am saying "yes," I make it a "hell yes." Then I go for it and do my best to let go of the outcome. Paradigm shifted.

For me, the real challenge was internal. My life was forever changed when I realized that even while ascending, I can confront the condescending within. Now I know that if I continue to put one foot in front of the other, the path will be revealed. On the mountain, in life, and in business. There will be opportunities, and then I will make choices. I am brave and resilient. I am now better skilled at recognizing and questioning self-doubt. I also know that comfort zones look different to everyone, and so does bravery. I more easily give grace, as I can never truly know others' internal struggles. I will keep paying attention and learning and making choices again and again. I will keep riding the lightning.

Asking questions has now become the lifeblood of my career. I serve clients through coaching, retreats, and leadership academies to bond, teach, and transform. I help people to challenge self-limiting beliefs and assumptions and to shine an examining flashlight onto what lurks in dark corners of their minds. But I know it starts with me. Can I fine-tune my mental antennae to spot internal judgment, name it, and kick it to the curb like an unwanted houseguest? Can I continue to be intentional in the moments I am given? Can I practice fierce curiosity and radical self-acceptance?

The mountain left me forever changed. And next time, maybe I will take the Diamox.

KATHLEEN CAMERON

From Heights To Healing:
My Journey Through Lung Crisis

In 2020, I found myself at the pinnacle of my business career. The numbers spoke for themselves: I had earned $3.3 million that year. By 2021, that figure had soared to an astounding $12 million per year. My life was a whirlwind of success and recognition. *Forbes* featured my story, and I appeared on the television show *The Doctors*. *Business Insider* praised my entrepreneurial achievements. Everywhere I turned, there were signs of triumph and accolades.

I was traveling the globe, hosting retreats, and guiding others on their paths to manifestation and personal growth. I felt unstoppable, riding high on the wave of my accomplishments. My days were filled with meetings, events, and the relentless pursuit of more success, impact, and growth.

Ignoring The Whispered Warning Signs

Yet amid this feverish pace, I began to ignore subtle whispers from my body. Fatigue crept in more frequently, and the vibrant energy I once thrived on started to wane. I brushed it off, attributing it to the demands of my busy schedule. Little did I know these whispers would soon become deafening screams.

Everything changed leading up to my first retreat in the Bahamas. My life had taken some turns in the preceding months; a separation of my marriage and family and a group of my team leaving together to start a business on their own felt like normal parts of life I could certainly handle. Or could I?

Surrounded by eager participants and the serene backdrop of a luxury resort, I had been fighting a walking pneumonia. Still, I felt inspired and motivated to teach and made sure I would make it there, and I did. The air was thick with anticipation as I prepared to lead another session. But instead of the usual excitement, I felt an overwhelming wave of exhaustion wash over me. My breaths became shallow, and a searing pain gripped my chest. The pain was almost unbearable, and I fought to get through each lesson. My mother made the decision to get me a plane out of the Bahamas and take me to Mount Sinai Medical Center in Miami, Florida. Even though I had pretended everything was fine, she knew otherwise.

In an instant, my world came crashing down. What I initially dismissed as taking on too much was something more sinister. I had been diagnosed with pneumonia a couple of weeks earlier, which now turned into fluid in the lungs and four pockets that trapped my right lung into the size of a coin, a severe case that left me gasping for air and battling an invisible enemy within my own body.

Suddenly, the woman who had been invincible in the face of every challenge was now confined to a hospital bed, tethered to machines and struggling to breathe. The once vibrant life I had meticulously built seemed to slip through my fingers as I grappled with the reality of my condition.

It Gets Worse

As if pneumonia itself wasn't enough, my medical team delivered another blow: I needed lung surgery. The pneumonia had caused a severe infection that led to fluid accumulating around my lungs. This fluid was pressing against my lungs, making breathing nearly impossible. The only solution was to undergo a lung decortication, a major surgical procedure to drain the fluid and prevent further complications.

The prospect of surgery was terrifying. It felt like a cruel twist of fate that, at the height of my success, I was now facing a life-threatening condition and an invasive procedure. Yet amid the fear and uncertainty, I made a promise to myself and to my vessel—the body that had carried me through every triumph and trial. I vowed that I would have a miraculous recovery. This wasn't merely a hope but a declaration of faith and resilience.

The day of the surgery arrived with a mix of emotions. As I lay on the operating table, surrounded by the sterile white walls and the hum of medical equipment, I closed my eyes and focused on my breath. Each inhale felt like a small victory, a testament to my body's fight to survive and heal. I whispered a silent prayer, reaffirming my promise to emerge from this stronger and more resilient than ever. Moments before I went into surgery, a dear friend sent me a video of me on the beach in the Bahamas during our releasing fire ceremony. I was surrounded by a green light, looking like wings, an angel to remind me of my healing energy. I knew at that moment I would be just fine.

Waking up in the recovery room, groggy and disoriented, I felt a sharp pain in my chest, a reminder of the battle I had just endured. The road to recovery stretched out before me, daunting and uncertain. But with each passing day, I regained my strength, one breath at a time.

An Inward Journey

In those long, solitary hours in the hospital, I was forced to confront aspects of myself I had long ignored. My illness and surgery stripped away the layers of success and external validation, leaving me face-to-face with my own vulnerability. In this raw state, I began to understand the true essence of resilience.

I realized resilience wasn't about pushing through pain or ignoring the signals from my body and mind. It was about honoring those signals and giving myself permission to be human. For so long, I had equated strength with unyielding perseverance, with an almost robotic drive to achieve. But in the quiet moments of my recovery, I discovered that true strength lies in the ability to listen—to ourselves, our needs, and the wisdom within.

I began to practice emotional regulation, a profound shift from my previous mode of operation. The spiritual significance or meaning of pneumonia is linked to grief, an emotion I never allowed myself to feel post-separation. Instead of suppressing my emotions, I allowed myself to feel them fully. I cried, laughed, cursed, and embraced the full spectrum of my humanity. This journey into the depths of my emotions was both terrifying and liberating. It taught me that experiencing the fullness of our human existence is not a sign of weakness but a testament to our resilience.

As I navigated the path to recovery, I learned to give my human—my physical and emotional self—a voice. For too long, I had silenced that voice in pursuit of external achievements. Now, I listened intently to its whispers, cries, and joys. I allowed myself to rest, heal, and rebuild my body and my entire being.

The process could have been quicker and easier. There were days when the weight of my situation felt unbearable and the road to recovery seemed endless. But with each small step forward, I reclaimed a part of myself. I learned to celebrate the little victories—the first breath of fresh air without pain, the gentle return of my strength, the moments of clarity and peace.

A New Path Forward

In the aftermath of my illness, I emerged with a renewed sense of purpose and a deeper understanding of what it means to be truly resilient. My business continued to thrive, but now it was fueled by a different kind of energy—a grounded, mindful approach that honored my ambitions and well-being. Two years later, I am the healthiest I have ever been, I exercise daily, fuel my body nutritiously, and have released over one hundred pounds of weight (trapped emotions). I recently ran a 10K race, and while challenging, it showed me what I could really do.

I began to integrate the lessons I had learned into my work, teaching others the importance of balancing their drive with self-care and emotional awareness. I shared my story as a tale of overcoming illness and a testament to the power of embracing our humanity in all its forms.

This experience taught me that resilience is not a destination but a journey. It's the ongoing practice of honoring our physical, emotional, and spiritual selves. It's the courage to pause, to listen, and to heal. And it's the unwavering belief that no matter how impossible the challenges we face, we have the strength to rise, transform, and thrive.

Reflecting on my journey from the heights of success to the depths of illness and back again, I am filled with gratitude. I am grateful for the lessons learned, the support of loved ones, and the resilience that carried me through. My story is not just one of triumph over adversity but of transformation—of finding more profound meaning and purpose in the face of life's greatest challenges.

As I continue to navigate the ever evolving landscape of my life and business, I carry with me the profound wisdom gained from my experience. I am reminded that true success is not measured by the accolades we receive or the wealth we accumulate but by the depth of our connection to ourselves and the world around us. It is in this connection that we find the strength to heal, grow, and transform.

In sharing this chapter of my life, I hope to inspire others to embrace their journeys of resilience. May we all find the courage to listen to our bodies, honor our emotions, and believe in the miraculous power of our healing. In these moments of transformation, we discover the true essence of our humanity and the boundless potential that lies within us.

MAURICE WILLIAMS

From Court To Community: How Basketball Shaped My Path And Purpose

Basketball has been a defining force in my life, shaping my journey from an at-risk youth to a community leader and mentor. This sport, more than just a game, has been my refuge, my connection to others, and my platform for positive change. My story is one of personal trials, transformation, and triumphs, all intricately woven through the love of basketball, mentorship, and purpose.

My First Love

I was introduced to basketball at a young age, at a time when my life could have easily taken a different, more perilous path. Growing up in a rough neighborhood and attending arguably the worst middle school in Philadelphia, it was all too easy to get caught up in the wrong crowd. Students fighting each other, students fighting teachers, and classroom disruptions due to poor behavior and lack of interest were common themes. Trouble was never far away, and I often found myself on the brink of making poor decisions that could have had long-lasting consequences. I joke with my wife all the time that "basketball was my first love." It found me at a time when I needed something to take my attention, time, and energy away from doing the wrong things. There were plenty of opportunities to do more wrong than right. Our environments have the power to shape our outcomes without notice or approval. It just happens, and we are left with figuring out how we got to where we are, forcing us to look at the people around us and the decisions we've made. We tend to become what and who we are around. It's almost inevitable. I always say our decisions can lead us to our destiny or our destruction. The decision to commit to basketball saved my life. I don't know where I would be without it.

The Basketball Connection

Basketball became more than just a personal refuge; it became a bridge to others. As I grew older, my relationship with basketball deepened. It was no longer just a means to stay out of trouble or build friendships; it became a way to connect with people on a deeper level. I realized the profound impact the game had on my life and wanted to share that with others. Basketball had given me so much—discipline, focus, resilience and I wanted to pass those lessons on.

I started volunteering at the neighborhood schools, and it was during these sessions that I truly understood the transformative power of basketball. I saw kids who were shy and withdrawn come out of their shells, youth who learned the value of teamwork and cooperation, and children who lacked direction find purpose and passion. Through basketball, these kids were learning life skills that would serve them well beyond the court.

That Ball Has Purpose

With a growing desire to make a lasting impact, I founded Ball With Purpose, a year-round basketball school that develops leaders on and off the court. This program isn't just about teaching the fundamentals of the game; it's about using basketball as a tool for personal development and community building. We focus on leadership, communication, and goal-setting, ensuring that the lessons learned on the court translate into real-life skills.

The program is flourishing, attracting kids from all walks of life. It is a safe haven, a place where they learn, grow, and thrive. Through this program, I have witnessed countless transformations. Kids who were once deemed "at risk" become leaders and role models just like me. They learn the value of hard work, perseverance, and teamwork. They develop goals and aspirations, understanding that with dedication and effort, they can achieve anything they set their minds to. Kids come to Ball With Purpose to get better. Families stay in Ball With Purpose because they believe in the mission and see their children thriving.

I remember one player in particular, Terrence. He was a talented athlete but struggled with discipline and focus. He often got into trouble at school and had a hard time staying out of fights. But he loved basketball, and I saw potential in him.

I took Terrence under my wing, spending extra time with him after practice, talking to him about his goals and aspirations, and helping him develop a plan for his future. It wasn't easy—there were setbacks and challenges along the way—but slowly but surely, Terrence began to change. He started to take his schoolwork more seriously, stayed out of trouble, and became a leader on and off the court.

Seeing Terrence graduate from high school, go on to college, and succeed both academically and athletically was one of the proudest moments of my life. It reinforced for me the power of mentorship through basketball. Having a caring individual who can see you for who you are and who you desire to be can help to keep you on the right path.

Having Vision Leads To Success

There were a few key basketball themes that I used to help Terrence find his footing on and off the court. The first was that in basketball, it's important to keep your head up to see the floor, your teammates, and the defense. Having good court vision makes players successful, as they are able to avoid defensive strategies and attack offensive opportunities. Likewise, off the court, the ability to see into the future—to the person I desired to be, the program I hoped to have, the business I intended to build—is equally important. Vision saves lives. Vision influences decisions. Vision protects purpose. Vision empowers us to stay true to the plan! Let us continue to be reminded of the vision that we have for our lives. A clear vision provides a sense of purpose and direction, enabling you to make choices that align with your values and ambitions.

Terrence was a talented basketball player who was able to do magical things on the court. He was a natural athlete. I would remind Terrence that while you're naturally gifted, how you practice and how often you practice matter for your next level. Off the court, we all have natural abilities, talents, and gifts, but without a quality work ethic, we may miss the best version of ourselves, thus giving away success that is rightfully ours. Growth is found in a set of choices. Growth, while available to everyone, is only achieved through consistent effort, self-reflection, and a willingness to embrace challenges. The spirit of our work ethic has to be unwavering and high in good character. Our work that becomes everlasting and full of impact is from the essence that drives our actions. A pure spirit continues to bear fruit! Good character is undefeated and is a currency that never goes outdated.

Don't Try To Do It By Yourself

"Pass the ball, Terrence. You're not out there by yourself. Use your teammates!" Terrance had a hard time understanding the power of good teammates. He thought he could win games all by himself. No championship is won by just an individual. It takes a team to win big. My wife has been the *support* that I needed when I didn't want to continue on. She supports me when my vision gets blurry with doubt, fear, and unworthiness. She keeps me rooted and grounded in purpose. We have to seek and stay in environments (or build teams around us) that keep us moving in the direction that we desire to go. She challenges me, holds me accountable, and understands the dream. It is important to have a solid team around that understands the goals you've set and is able to help with those achievements (or championships).

Basketball Gave Me Purpose

Through basketball, I found my purpose and my voice. I became a mentor, a leader, and a positive force in my community. I've taken my coaching on the court to coaching on stages, both in person and virtually. I've taken my passion for winning, training, and development on the court to help me deliver countless speeches, workshops, and more. My experiences have made me an engaging and empowering storyteller and motivational speaker who inspires audiences around the world. The lessons that I've learned through basketball have given me the ability to connect with people from all different types of backgrounds and ages, inspiring them to live purposeful and fulfilling lives.

Transformation is pressed out of the decisions we make and the environments we live in. The principles of basketball continue to evolve me, helping me to be the best CEO, mentor, speaker, coach, and family man I can be. My commitment to basketball was actually a commitment to being better than yesterday, and although I did not play professionally, the championships I've won in life with major achievements and my business have been deeply fulfilling and rewarding. Each victory off the court is a testament to the lessons learned on the court, driving me to continually strive for excellence and inspire those around me.

DR. MELISSA SASSI

Turning My Worst Nightmare Into My Superpower: A True Story Of Resilience, Transformation, And Triumph

I've scouted and developed 290 tech CEOs in eighty countries over the last six years that have gone on to raise more than $500 million in investment capital to build and scale their up-and-coming ventures. Their companies now have a collective valuation of $2.7 billion. I chaired the team that created the world's first digital skills and readiness standard that was endorsed by the OECD and World Economic Forum. It became a global standard of the IEEE—the world's largest engineering organization with 400,000 members in 2021. Vint Cerf, one of the Fathers of the Internet, once called me a digital trailblazer.

I'm A Wild Duck

People often ask how I came to be, what inspired my passion for technology and innovation, and if I've always been so resilient. As I was awarded IBM's prestigious Blue Core Award, a recognition given to the top 1 percent of IBMers worldwide, Ross Mauri, General Manager of IBM Z and LinuxONE, called me a Wild Duck. In IBM terms, this is reserved for people known for their insatiable desire to innovate, create, make, and do. I'm known for inspiring others to find comfort in vulnerability and ways to unapologetically show up with authenticity and transparency.

Taken...My Children

Despite having stood on five hundred stages in sixty-two countries in venues with the United Nations, the World Bank, Microsoft, IBM, and more, I still struggle finding the right words to tell my story. My children—Zahra, Zahran, and Youmna—were three, five, and seven when they were picked up from elementary school and taken to Tunisia, a small North African country that's sandwiched between Algeria and Libya. We're victims of parental kidnapping. Despite knowing where they were, influencing their return home was impossible. I heard things like "this is a civil issue, ma'am," from local law enforcement, "we have no jurisdiction in Tunisia;" "now you can focus on your career;" or "why didn't you hide the passports?"

At the time, Tunisia was ranked 144 out of 167 by *The Economist* in its 2010 Democracy Index, and Zine El Abidine Ben Ali ruled Tunisia with an iron fist. His dictatorship would last for a total of twenty-three years and fall with the Jasmine Revolution and serve as a spark to the Arab Spring. His authoritarian family and their regime were known for rampant human rights abuses, corruption, bureaucracy, and repression. There was a general lack of trust in public entities, people, and systems.

It took me three years to develop the strength and courage to visit. Despite having visited many times prior, I no longer had a support network to rely upon if something were to go wrong. I did not speak Tunisian Arabic, my French was subpar, and there were no hotels and no tourism industry in the town where they lived. Factory smoke from its steel industry was always my clue that I was arriving to Menzel Bourguiba. Untreated household waste and toxic chemicals from the town's heavy iron, steel, cement, and tire industry could often be found in the lagoon on the outskirts of town.

Despite the challenges and the resilience required, knowing where they were provided some level of comfort compared to others with similar histories. Agreeing to legally give up custody to my children, I was able to visit and spend time with them; however, many years would pass before I could bring them to the capital without an escort from the family. I was so naive at the time and felt powerless.

A Mothers Fight

After years of evaluating our circumstances, I realized I had to regain our voice to fight for my right to be the kind of mother I knew I was and could be for them, but this could only come through having local influence, power, and connections, and I had none. I knew the first step to having a voice would come from learning the local language, and power, influence, and connections would have to come from business and social impact.

I was living in New York City at the time, working for a Wall Street firm, and finally met someone who would spark my language transition—Dino. He probably has no idea how much he changed our lives by teaching me the basics of Tunisian Arabic. I am good with languages and learned quickly. As I continued making Tunisian friends over the years and transitioned from asset management and investment banking into big tech in Seattle, I stumbled upon an organization founded by Mark Horowitz called Moving Worlds. Mark inspired me to take on a volunteer role within a large NGO and work remotely for the summer in Tunisia's capital, Tunis. I managed my U.S. responsibilities at night, volunteered during the day, gave periodic talks for youth and early-stage tech entrepreneurs at local meetups, and spent time with the children on the weekends. I made friends, met public officials, and soon started to feel at home.

Despite volunteering and having some connections, it wasn't enough to have alone time with Zahra, Zahran, and Youmna. Let's fast forward a bit. I was working in big tech, and one day, my daughter said to me, "mommy, mommy, I'm learning Microsoft"—my employer. I realized she was learning Microsoft Word in her classroom, yet she had no access to a computer lab. Imagine hundreds of kids in school learning to prepare for the future without access to their own computers, a scenario far too many youths today experience globally. There were thirty or more students sharing one computer. How is that preparing young people for the future of work? It's preparing them to be left behind, where the world truly becomes the haves versus the have nots.

My children were kidnapped, lived through the Arab Spring, watched the downfall of a dictator who later died in exile, and now, their futures would be without opportunity? I knew there were a lot of things I could not change about this world, but I worked in tech, and one thing I could solve was access to computers for her classroom. I set out on a mission that led to bringing four hundred laptops to twenty schools across the country.

But what good is a laptop and an internet connection without skills? I recruited engineering students from a local tech club, took some time off work, and spent weeks traveling the country inspiring youth with the introductory building blocks of computer science through a program offered through code.org. We were deep in the Sahara, on the Libyan and Algerian borders. Sometimes when we arrived, the town square would welcome us with a banner, or the children would sing; the National Guard would show up, and sometimes the mayor.

Transforming Cultures Through Technology

Our trip made us see with our own eyes and experience how technology can transform the lives of everyone everywhere. It's an enabler or equalizer that transcends me, my children, and lives. It was no longer just about Zahra and her classroom, but the world. One of the most pressing issues of our time is access to technology—devices, internet connectivity, and digital skills. Despite the challenges brought about by technology in society, it brings economic independence, education, and a voice. It's our future.

We started a company and have now taught tens of thousands of young people to code in twelve countries. We've collaborated with the UN and were nominated for three different international awards. I've personally spoken at many different UN events, visited the homes of Presidents and Prime Ministers, and it shaped my career into one of enabling others through technology and innovation.

This is how I discovered my life's work and how I turned my worst nightmare into my superpower.

It gave my son a voice, and it gave my daughters their voices. It helped me spend the entire summer with my children and enabled them to see the power of technology, grit, passion, and problem-solving.

If I fast forward to where we are today, two of my children are now living in the United States with goals of big-tech careers, and one will be finishing her high school studies soon. Zahra, Zahran, and Youmna were three, five, and seven when our lives changed, and they are now seventeen, nineteen, and twenty-two, with big futures ahead of them. Who knows how our story will continue to unfold? It has always been important for me and for us to ensure our trauma was transformed into a force for good. Leaving a mark on this world that's bigger than us and our history has required resilience. This is my story of resilience, transformation, and triumph.

OSVALD BJELLAND

Origination For Life

In The Blink Of An Eye, Let Alone A Cursor

Today, with the advent of technology, the world has shrunk to the size of a cozy global village where everyone shares a social media fence and news travels instantaneously. It was not like this even 150 years ago in 1875, when my great-grandfather, at age fifteen, set sail for America, with his three older brothers, and they had little to no communication with his family in the intervening two decades. Our world is largely unrecognizable from even a half-century ago when I, like half of the world's population at the time, I still lived in a small rural village, Sandeid, alongside just five hundred people with our constant companions, the rugged fjords of western Norway. Like my great-grandfather, in high school, my world began to expand with the arrival of television, albeit with only a few channels. I couldn't have fathomed a future characterized by mobile phones, let alone the arrival of the internet.

Setting Sail

After high school, following in my great-grandfather's footsteps, I, too "set sail" to be a citizen of the world living in London, New York, and Oslo. For decades, my work would take me to Mumbai, Moscow,

Beijing, Madrid, Berlin, and countless other global capitals of culture and commerce. I continued my schooling beyond my travels, as my greatest learnings were derived from trial and failure, variation and adaptation, and most importantly, from the wisdom gifted to me by the remarkable people I had the good fortune to encounter. My travels taught me that not all learning is planned, not all innovation is born from strategy and a structured process, and often, expansion and growth emerge from need and necessity.

The Origins Of Origination

Six thousand years ago, the chili pepper was discovered by the Aztecs and Mayans in Mexico, springing up on the fertile threshold between the jungle and desert. Classified as a fruit, the chili pepper's unique flavor, a mix of sweetness and smokiness, along with its hallmark spice, is but one testament to mother nature's ingenious capacity for adaptation. This food staple first emerged, growing sustainably between two starkly different climates, a novel form of life that evolved in response to ever-changing environments.

Origination, the ability to create from the natural forces that shape life on this planet, is deeply embedded within our humanity. Like the chili pepper, humans have achieved massive progress during the past centuries, so that now, in our lifetimes, our life expectancy has increased many fold in response to the advances in fields like nutrition, sanitation, and medical care. Literacy and access to the superhighway of global communication, along with the simultaneous historic highs in multiple forms of travel means the number of people who have the privilege to experience other cultures beyond their own is ever-expanding. We have seen moral progress as well. Slavery and torture, widely practiced since the dawn of civilization, while disturbingly still occurring, are now condemned to the greatest degree in human history. Generation after generation, humans have demonstrated the ability to achieve new milestones, again and again.

A Crossroads

With the world's population having burgeoned to eight billion, where we are indeed facing what it means to be hot, flat, and crowded in the words of Thomas Friedman, as significant climate issues and social crises threaten our ability to simply exist, let alone coexist with one another. As a result, we find ourselves at a crossroads with an urgent need to invest in the well-being of people and the planet in fresh and bold ways.

We have long viewed growth as being synonymous with positive progress. In the natural world, growth symbolizes the presence of life. Yet at this critical juncture, we must reexamine this belief, as growth upon growth can compound to become too much of a good thing. This pivotal moment on our planet compels all of us to recognize that all growth is not positive, but instead to promote "good growth", defined as progress that favors the solvency of current life, our environment, and the future generations to come.

Good Growth

At the core of good growth lies a simple, yet often forgotten reminder to all humans: Each of us has the power to make a difference. We can all contribute, in ways big or small, to being the originators of good growth, to orchestrate solutions that renew hope for humanity at a time when we have an urgent need for innovative solutions to our most pressing problems.

In his 2024 letter to investors, Black Rock CEO Larry Fink, cited a sobering statistic: four out of ten Americans between twenty and thirty years of age see no hope for the future. Personally, I have sensed the despair Fink describes building for years with a reach that extends far beyond the U.S. to include our global community. The antidote to despair is hope and the treatment for hopelessness is optimism.

For those of us whose hope and optimism has flagged, you are not wrong, you're just realistic. In our lifetime, we have experienced sudden, seismic, and significant challenges that have sent shock-waves through the bedrock of our reality. Ranging from the dot-com bubble and the 9/11 attacks, followed by a financial crisis in 2008, and more recently, the COVID pandemic. The only constant for much of recent life has been the whiplash of continuous change.

Taking Back Our Control To Create

In political, journalistic, and even everyday conversations, we hear the rumblings of jealousy and fear, vows for revenge, othering of entire groups of people, and ugly language the propagates hate. This toxic symphony of volatility, promoted simply by our speech, surrounds and even supplies the soundtrack to fuel some of the world's most pressing international conflicts. Our recent global events have shown us that it's not that we've lost control, it's that we've realized how little control we have. While our lack of control holds up a reflection that is in stark contrast to what we once believed existed inside of our sphere of influence. One of the most impactful ways we can take back what is within our span of control is to be aware of and to change the tenor of our current conversational tune.

Reimaging Human Flourishing

At the heart of hope and resilience lies our ability to originate not just any progress, but good growth. Flourishing requires us to heed four timeless principles that strengthen us as individuals, promote global understanding, and support the common good:

I.   The unprecedented systemic challenges we face demand new and different approaches to how we care for our water, land, and air. We must re-originate how we work together and govern, what we build and transport, how we grow, and what we eat.

II.   Harnessing our timeless passion for progress requires optimism. We now invest in good progress to drive the next human Renaissance. With eyes fully open to the risks and hardships of our global population, not merely focused on our own gain, we must maintain an optimistic view of the road ahead.

III. Rather than merely weathering the storms of crisis and transformation, we siphon each storm's energy to drive meaningful change. This is our chance to unite, to learn from each other, and to conceive fresh ways to move us all forward.

IV.   We stand at a critical juncture where the choices we make together will determine the course of history that is yet to be written. This means that we are all authors of the future of humanity.

To secure a brighter future for all, we must address the four global transitions that are changing the world:

THE TRANSITION TO SUSTAINABILITY. Not since World War II have the global energy and capital markets faced the challenges that require bold change. As we navigate the complexities of a multipolar world, the need for sustainable growth has never been more pressing. This demands a renewed focus on renewable energy, inclusive economic development, and ESG-driven investment strategies. With ESG spending expected to double to a record of USD $16 billion in five years, the challenge is clear: how can we ensure that these investments serve our long-term interests while yielding meaningful returns?

THE GREAT WEALTH TRANSITION. There is a profound shift in generational wealth looming on the horizon. With more than one-third of the world's 2,780 billionaires now age seventy or older, the stage is set for the transfer of $5.2 trillion over the next twenty to thirty years. But as this wealth changes hands, we must ask: will it be used to address the great challenges of our time—and will it create a better world for future generations?

THE AI AND TECHNOLOGY TRANSITION. A revolution in materials science is unfolding, driven by the advances in Artificial Intelligence (AI) and supercomputing. From the development of advanced batteries and microchips to innovations in recycling and catalysis, the possibilities are vast. Furthermore, AI holds great promise in the pursuit of carbon neutrality, enabling the precise balancing of carbon emissions and offsets in key areas such as data centers, energy grids, secure communications, and sustainable food and water systems. As AI-enhanced decision-making becomes available to the smallest of organizations, the potential for a more sustainable and resilient world becomes real.

THE TRANSITION TO FRONTIER MARKETS. A profound demographic shift is underway, as the world's population becomes increasingly concentrated in developing countries. Today, 152 frontier nations are home to roughly 6.82 billion people, comprising nearly 86 percent of the global population. The five BRICS countries (Brazil, Russia, India, China, and South Africa) alone constitute 40 percent of the global total, with a combined population of more than 3.24 billion. While aging societies in China, Japan, and Europe wrestle with demographic decline, regions like Africa and India are blessed with youthful populations that will yield a demographic dividend in the decades to come.

Embracing Origination

Embracing the concept of origination and good progress calls for us to tap into our collective capacity to facilitate ideas, solutions, and partnerships at scale, unleashing the creativity and innovation for a more sustainable future. In this moment, we need a movement to achieve good progress that effectively addresses the challenges we face. The good news is that history demonstrates that we can have a profound impact when we work in concert toward a common goal.

Embracing origination means we get to collective operate alongside core competencies, ways of seeing the world and interacting with one another:

SEEK PURPOSE. Try over time to get closer to what you truly love doing. Ask yourself: what makes you happy? What makes you feel most alive? That question has led me to build one gratifying enterprise after another. I have delighted in the work I have performed with exceptional clients, policymakers, scientists, creatives, and others. They taught me so much and afforded me such joy, and along the way I have also prospered financially. I have much for which I am deeply grateful. Yes, there have been downturns, but those have served as valuable teachers.

LEARN AND GROW. Failure is a stepping stone to personal growth. Every setback is a "set up" for introspection and growth. None of us are free of defects. To move forward, you must not give in to the tyranny of perfection. Forgiveness becomes indispensable. Leadership expert Anthony Howard sees forgiveness as a "pardon", an act that breaks the handcuffs of resentment, and sets both the victim and perpetrator free. If you don't forgive yourself and you don't forgive others, you cannot progress toward positive growth.

COMMUNITY AND DISCIPLINE. The longer I live, the more I appreciate the sanctuary that a loving family, dear friends, and supportive colleagues can provide. Nurture your relationships and give the people in your inner circle the dignity, appreciation, and respect they deserve. Discipline and well-established routines provide the scaffolding upon which personal development and achievement are built. Rituals act as the lifeblood of culture, giving shape and meaning to our shared experiences. Embrace the power of structure and consistency.

Now, It's Up To You

Together, we are greater than the sum of what we could contribute individually. As a global citizen, when we invest in making ourselves, communities, and ecosystems better through good progress, we uplift all of humankind. For too long we have privileged individual pursuits over the good progress that benefits those on our planet collectively. The concept and principles of origination call for us to break the bonds of the past and adopt new ways of being that allow us to invest in an even more storied and spectacular future. We are, after all, stronger together. I look forward to originating and authoring the future of the next seven generations of humankind together. Our future begins today.

QUINTON AARON

From The Shadows To The Spotlight: My Journey To The Blind Side

My name is Quinton Aaron. I played the character Michael Oher in the 2009 blockbuster sports biography *The Blind Side* based on the true story of the former NFL Super Bowl Champion with the Baltimore Ravens. Michael, or "Big Mike" as most will say, was blessed to be able to chase his dreams when given a unique opportunity in life which ultimately led to his success. However, I am not here to talk about Michael. This story is about me, Quinton Aaron, actor, singer-songwriter, author, philanthropist, and producer. You see, I had a very unique upbringing as well, not identical to Michael's but a story of triumph nonetheless.

Entertainment Is In My Blood

I knew from a very young age that I was born to be an entertainer. Apparently, it was in my blood. I say that because I found my father a couple years ago, a month and a half before he passed away, and connected with about a dozen siblings I never knew I had. My big sister told me that my father had a voice similar to mine and was always singing, and as it turns out, my great-grandfather was a famous blues musician back in the day. My mom told me that I took to singing at an early age. She said that I hit my first note when I came out of the womb and the doctor smacked my bottom; my cry sounded like I was singing. I remember, as far back as four years old, singing all the lyrics to some of my mom's favorite songs.

In a lot of ways, music and movies were my saving grace. I'd get lost in characters on shows I loved to watch in order to escape my harsh reality, where I was constantly bullied in school and felt like nobody liked me. Looking back, I believe that I loved pretending to be other characters because it meant I didn't have to be me. I know what you're thinking: "Aw, but you were so adorable and awesome." Yeah, I was, but it took some time before I figured that for myself. Later in life, with the help of my amazing mother, I was able to get a grip and gain some new perspective on a lot of things. Life started to really make sense to me, and I knew where I was headed. Acting was going to be my career of choice. In fact, I remember kids disliking me in high school because of my decision not to pursue football any longer. I was called big for nothing, among a lot of other distasteful words that I choose not to repeat. However, I was determined without a shadow of doubt to make it in the industry, and with the help of my mom, I felt like we couldn't be stopped. God was going to continue to provide whatever we needed along the way.

Blindsided With Opportunity

October 27, 2007, I auditioned for the movie which is now a classic, "The Blind Side". My mom was my manager at the time. In fact, it was 3am when she woke me up to tell me to read a breakdown she had found online about the character. I couldn't fully open my eyes, as it was the middle of the night, and I was sleepier than a baby in his high-chair nodding off in his noodles. So, she read the breakdown to me, and I remember thinking at the time, "That sounds like something she was writing about me." Shortly afterward, I went back to sleep as I had to wake up the next morning to travel to Brooklyn. I was working on a short film called *Mr. Brooklyn*, and my mom called me around eleven o'clock that morning while I was on set. She told me to check my email when I got a chance, because I had been scheduled for an audition for the lead role in a major motion picture. Of course, I thought that she was blowing smoke. However, it turns out she was telling the truth.

So I did the very best that I could to make sure that I went into that audition fully prepared, because this was one of those once-in-a-lifetime type of moments that my mom always taught me to take full advantage of. I was determined to go in there and leave it all in the room. When I did, I was shocked by the response of the casting director and the other people in the room. For the first time ever, I had witnessed everyone in the room with tears in their eyes, crying because of my performance. The casting director, Twinkie Byrd, got up out of her seat and came over to me to give me a big hug while saying to the room, "We found our Michael." I gotta admit this was the first time that I had ever been in this situation before as an actor. I thought that it meant I got the part immediately.

When I left the audition, I was walking to the train station, and I had this overwhelming sense of joy and happiness come over me. The best way to describe how I felt was like Will Smith in *The Pursuit of Happyness* when he ran across town after getting out of jail to get that job and they gave it to him even though he thought he wasn't going to get it. When he left that office, he was walking down the street crying and clapping his hands. That emotion right there is what I felt after leaving the audition to return home. I remember thinking that I was going to try and play a trick on my mom when I got home. I pretended as if the audition went horribly, but I couldn't keep a straight face. Besides, little did I know I had already gotten a callback for the next day. For those of you who do not know, a callback is when an actor did well in his audition and they want to see him again.

So here I was, completely over the moon as I had never been up to this point in my green acting career before. Don't get me wrong, I had auditioned a ton, but never had I ever gotten a call back. I was moving up in the world. I went back to the same office the next morning for my callback, and I had a phone call with the director, John Lee Hancock. John was awesome, gave me a ton of compliments and then a couple of notes that he wanted me to apply while taping my audition again. So, like the pro that I am, I did what I was told to the best of my ability. Next thing I knew, I was being flown out to Los Angeles to meet with the director face-to-face. This was the first time that I had ever been on a plane, so needless to say, I was scared.

I was nervous sitting in first class when the pilot decided that his passengers needed to know just how high of an altitude we were going to be flying at. I remember thinking to myself, "The level of disrespect that just came out of this man's mouth right now, he should be ashamed of himself." Sitting in the first seat at the front of the aircraft, I experienced what seemed like a small panic attack. When this beautiful young flight attendant saw that I was scared, she sat next to me and held my hand through takeoff. After I calmed down and refrained from soiling myself, I did the only thing any guy in my position would have done and asked her to marry me. Unfortunately, she was dating the pilot, so I immediately changed the subject, as I figured it probably wouldn't be the best idea to piss off the person in control of my life at that time.

They Aren't Doing It Without Me

Moving on, I had all these emotions running through me, as I had never been in this position before and felt for the first time like life as

I knew it was about to change for the better, for my family and myself. The visit with the director went great. We met for almost an hour, talking and getting to know each other, and it was like I had this in the bag. When it was over and I was ready to leave, we got up and I walked out of the door of the office into the hallway, where I saw another actor get up to come in to talk with the director after me. Lo and behold, it was Omar Benson Miller. I recognized him from the movie 8 Mile, which starred Eminem. I remember immediately tucking my head between my legs and saying to myself, "Aw, shit! They're gonna give it to him. He's already fucking famous." This was December of 2007, and unfortunately due to 20th Century Fox Searchlight shelving the project for the remainder of their option agreement after Julia Roberts had turned down the role of Leigh Anne Touhy, there wasn't even a whisper of *The Blind Side* for all of 2008. Sad to say that exactly fifteen days after my twenty-fourth birthday in August, my mom passed away from a heart attack. However, one of the things she stood firm on with her beliefs was that whenever they decided to do that movie, there was no way they were going to do it without me. Those were her exact words, and I had learned long ago to stop doubting Momma. So I always kept the faith that The Blind Side was going to happen and that I was going to play Michael Oher one day.

Going back to my mom, she had been diagnosed with congestive heart failure (CHF), a disease that can cause a buildup of fluid in several parts of the body, making blood flow extremely difficult, which can lead to heart attack or stroke if not taken care of properly. Back in June 2019, I was diagnosed with congestive heart failure, too, and as you can probably imagine, when the doctor walked into the room with his white coat and said those words to me, they completely rocked my world. All I can think about was my mom. I remember sitting there on the bed in my gown, under the covers because the room was freezing, and I just tuned out everything the doctor was saying after those three words. I was waiting for him to walk out of the room. Once he did, I burst into tears and I started praying to God, telling him that I was not ready to die. Throughout that brief moment of self-pity and fear, I started to remember that God is always with me, and it made me think back to the day that my brother and I got the news that changed our lives.

The winter of 2008 was the coldest and darkest winter to my brother, Jarred, and I. I couldn't get a job anywhere; we ran out of money to pay the bills. We lost all of our utilities. I was going back and forth to court trying to delay being evicted. I was also walking to and from my aunt's house every day to pick up hot food she had prepared for my brother and me so that we wouldn't starve. At this time, we were still living in the apartment that our mom had passed away in. We had nowhere to go. Then suddenly, in late February 2009, I had booked my first job all winter. It was a security job working at SilverCup Studios, where they shot shows like *30 Rock*. I remember on the last day of filming this commercial that I was working on, I was standing outside of the door where my post was when the phone rang. It was the sheriff's department. I answered, and the sheriff told me that in seventy-two hours, my brother and I would be evicted, and everything still in the apartment at that time would be locked in and become property of the owners of the building.

So, I hung up and began to gather my thoughts. Suddenly, I saw Tina Fey walking toward me. I was freaking out because I was like, "Oh my God, oh my God, oh my God, that's Tina Fey." As she was approaching, my phone rang again. I pulled the phone out my pocket, flipped it open, and answered. It was my manager.

She said, "Quinton, guess what?"

The first thing that popped into my mind was *The Blind Side*, so I said it, and she replied, "How did you know?"

I freaked out and screamed. At this point, Tina Fey was directly in front of me, so I hung up on my manager and told Tina Fey that I had just booked the lead role in a major motion picture. Mind you, my manager never told me that, but that's how hard I was claiming it. Tina congratulated me and went on her way, and then I said, "Oh, shit!" and called my manager back. She told me that someone from production would be calling me to see if I still wanted to do the movie, so I got off the phone with her, and then it rang again.

On the other line was the line producer, Tim Bourne, who informed me of the opportunity to play Michael Oher still being on the table, and I immediately agreed to it. Tim offered to fly me down to Atlanta as soon as possible, and I asked, "Define as soon as possible? Because I can come tomorrow."

Tim replied, "No problem. I'll get you a first-class ticket to Atlanta tomorrow." I couldn't believe this was happening, although I had one more request.

"Can I please bring my brother because I have no place to leave him?"

Tim said, "Absolutely. I'll get you two first-class tickets to Atlanta, Georgia tomorrow."

Trying not to cry on the phone I said, "Thank you" and hung up.

By the time I got home, the information for our flight was in my email. I went home and said to my brother, "Jay, we got the part, and we need to pack, because we leave first thing in the morning for Georgia."

At that point, my brother fell back on the bed, yelling and shouting with joy, "Yes, we are finally gettin' the hell up out of here."

You have to understand, that was the first emotion that I saw from him since our mom had passed away. So it was pretty emotional for me, and I walked out of the room, around the corner, and started crying, much like that scene in the movie where I tell Sandra that I've never had a bed before. Yeah, I was like that; I mean, I was ugly crying. Then I snapped out of it. We packed up our things and turned a new chapter in our lives. I remember looking back in a moment of sadness because I felt we were leaving our mom behind. Then, it was like I could hear her voice saying, "Go ahead baby, make Momma proud. I told you they weren't going to do it without you."

SIMON LÜTHI

Becoming The Rocket Shaman: A Spiritual Tale Of Healing, Discovery, And Finding My Authentic Identity And Purpose

Before I saw awe in my imperfections, I had to heal myself emotionally.

Before I heard conviction in my voice, I had to heal myself spiritually.

Before I felt the pain release from my body, I had to heal myself physically.

Between ages three and five, humans begin to believe false information and stereotypes that compound into myths we live out over time.

Because I was bullied as a kid, I decided I was weird.

Because my wife didn't like how I cut the green onions when I made our favorite dish, I decided I could not live up to the expectations of love and marriage.

Because I took a medical leave of absence from work due to cancer, I decided I wasn't resilient.

For most of my life, I believed in a world I could only see through my parents' eyes.

They taught me not to question their vision of my future, so I didn't.

To be worthy of love and attention, I understood that my business card should be embossed with words that indicate I am the Chief of something or, at a minimum, President.

They showed me that if I opted for a career that proved my success instead of one that held personal significance, the world would compensate me with wealth and a partner who would love me unconditionally.

That's what I was shown, so that's what I believed.

What has to happen for us to mend this false conditioning and cure ourselves from believing there's something wrong with us so we can restore our truth?

It took *me* getting sick three times.

"How could it be back?" I said out loud angrily.

I touched my neck, swallowed a few times, and feverishly rose from the couch. Irritated by the familiar scratching sensation in the back of my throat, I walked toward the bathroom, throwing out expletives. How stupid was I to think I could finally feel a sense of contentment so soon after I beat this thing?

A few seconds prior, I indulged in a calm Sunday morning, watching the spring showers through a large window, feeling like one of those contemplative characters in the movies. Why was I thrown off course every time I felt content? I beat this thing six months ago. This lump was not supposed to come back. No, this *fucking* lump was not supposed to come back. It deserves to be addressed as a curse.

Turning on the light above the sink, it wasn't bright enough. I scrambled back to the kitchen, rushing past the candles I had lit an hour before, when I started my awesomely predictable, protagonistic Sunday morning routine. I quickly grabbed a butter knife from the silverware drawer and my iPhone from the charging station. Walking the three-foot plank back to the bathroom, I continued to swear over

Yo Yo Ma's hopeful rendition of Bach's Cello Suite No. 1 in G Major playing in the background.

Posturing myself against the front of the sink, I turned on the flashlight on my phone. Placing the butter knife on my tongue like one of those wooden sticks doctors use before they have you say, "Ahhh," I moved my head around to find the perfect position to see the back of my throat through the mirror. My mouth was wide open, and my fingers tensely wrapped around the butter knife.

It Is Back

Yep, there it was again—a round growth the size of a marble jutting out from the red soft tissue in the back of my throat behind my uvula (that teardrop-shaped, dangling thing). It wasn't strep. It wasn't a regrown tonsil. That's what the doctors speculated it was the last time it showed up before the tests finally produced a correct diagnosis.

"You have non-Hodgkin's lymphoma." I was first told I had cancer at the start of a global pandemic. Thankfully, after spending months locked in a barren corporate apartment, I had just moved into my new home that I appropriately named my adult treehouse. I was forced to isolate myself from my friends and family, but at least I was home, nestled in a corner lot surrounded by towering Tulip Poplars and Oak Trees.

At my kids' insistence, I reluctantly followed the doctors' full treatment plan that included chemotherapy and radiation despite my PTSD from previous healthcare experiences. To complement this, I also turned to familiar alternative healing practices to support me through chemo.

Letting the knife drop to the floor in defeat and walking back to the living room, I considered that this thing had come back to take my life.

While it wasn't the first time I had faced adversity, getting cancer was the first time I became conscious of my mortality.

Life-threatening moments showed up when I least expected them, and I always survived. When I was three, my parents rushed me to the emergency room, blue in the face with constricted airways. Our family car was totaled after being hit by a drunk driver when I was ten. Eight years later, I hit a patch of black ice on my motorcycle and flew headfirst into a field. Boom, boom, boom, one after another, the challenges came and went.

It wasn't until the first time I got sick with the sudden onset of a mystery illness in 2015 that I realized that none of the incidents were life-*threatening*. They *were* life-*altering*. I recognized that I had to consider the illness that ravaged my body with piercing chronic pain, for which Western medicine had no name and no cure as a guidepost. I define guideposts as pivotal moments that spur change, ranging from subtle to profound. If we notice them, they are an opportunity to get to the core of what we need to heal.

The Alternatives

Fed up with the nasty side effects of the medication I had been prescribed for the ghostly condition that plagued me, I decided to cut ties with Western medicine and explore alternatives. Given that my wife was a nurse, I knew she would be unhappy with my decision. For the first time in my life, I felt mentally and intuitively strong enough to say no to what others were imposing upon me. Being from Switzerland, I started by researching technologies and medicinal practices in Europe.

While on a business trip to Paris, I visited a clinic in Switzerland specializing in auto-immune therapies. Their medical team diagnosed me with heavy metal toxicity, environmental toxins, and a food allergy. They recommended a treatment widely accepted in Europe to remove metals from my body. Facing challenges accessing the therapy in the U.S., I traveled to Germany for two rounds of treatment.

A year later, the symptoms of my mystery illness had gone away, but my sage smudging and newfound existential explorations *freaked my wife out.* The person I was becoming, which I would later identify as *myself,* felt banned from our home. From liver cleanses to full-moon rituals, as I grew, our marriage fell apart. We decided to divorce.

After moving out, I reserved Sundays for rest and recovery, representing the upside of living alone and respiting from work stress. On the seventh day of the week, I would wake up, light candles, turn on classical music, and press the button on my European espresso machine before turning on CBS News Sunday Morning.

Not Happening To Me, But For Me

Now, the lump was back, threatening my progress on the day of the week I looked forward to the most. I noticed the light pitter-patter of the rain beating down on the roof. The tempo quickened and became more powerful, pulsating like the drums they would play in the Shamanic healing circles I would attend. The sky bawled for me, creating space for me to get madder. I worked hard to get healthy, get back to work, and find contentment. Now the lump shows up *again* out of nowhere?

I had learned if I could allow my anger to move through me, I would find peace on the other side. In one pivotal second, after the drums quieted, I heard only my breath and felt a subtle vibration in my hands. A physical indication I had previously identified as a sign from above during the Reiki Master certification training I had completed. Learning to differentiate between my intuition and gut reactions influenced by negative experiences and past conditioning meant that I had to become attuned to bodily sensations serving as reliable indicators. Fear and anxiety made me tremble, and intuition made me buzz. If I stopped and turned inward to pay attention, a wave of questions would beg me for answers. This time was no different.

What if this lump was not coming out of *nowhere*?

What if it was reminding me that my life was still not the life I was meant to live?

I heard the guideposts screaming for me to take a different path.

What if I stopped treating them like strokes of bad luck I could conquer and ignore?

What if I've been put in a box by everyone around me that I never wanted to be a part of?

What if the addiction to getting to the C-level was an unhealthy cover-up of my insecurities from the definitions of success I adopted from my parents?

Why was this happening to me?

No, wait. I knew better and believed in the power of affirmative language. I reframed the question.

Why was this happening for me?

Yes, that's right. I was reminded of the healing power of words I had experienced in the past.

After my divorce, a good friend suggested I check out Louise Hay's book "You Can Heal Your Life". I was actively trying new modalities to feel worthy of love. I quickly took her advice.

"I love myself. I approve of myself." For sixty days straight, I practiced my first affirmation. "I love myself. I approve of myself." I parked a five-minute walk away from my office door so I could use the time to say my affirmations out loud or in my mind's eye between thirty and sixty times each day. On day sixty-one of using these affirmations, a sudden feeling of bliss washed over me. I felt an overwhelming sense of unconditional love for myself. This whole affirmation thing was working.

That wasn't the only time I had used words to heal myself.

After the doctors told me that I had non-Hodgkin's lymphoma, unable to accept myself as a sick cancer patient, I knew that the side effects of the chemotherapy treatments could threaten my mental strength. I had to do something to keep myself strong and engaged. Given the positive impact affirmations had on me in the past, I decided to do the Louise Hay Mirror Challenge, a beautiful self-love exercise. "I love you. I love you. I love you," I would tell myself as I looked into the mirror every day for twenty-one days. Staring back at me was a fifty-year-old man with no hair on my head, no eyebrows, and no beard, swollen from water retention. I looked like my ex-girlfriend's naked pet guinea pig.

"I love you. I love you. I love you." While admiring yourself in a mirror might sound simple or even ridiculous, embracing my reflection was one of the hardest and most important things I have ever done.

And here I was, facing what I saw in the mirror again.

What was this lump trying to show me by returning a second time?

Why was this happening *for* me?

My life was not yet congruent. A deceptive office in the C-suite defined my likeness as a corporate executive. Posing as spacious, it was an isolating, standardized, and uninspiring facade. Yes, I had accomplished a lot, but I was now in a position to renegotiate contracts I had made with myself so I could get off of this roller coaster of dis-ease and choose my experiences while I still had a spot here on earth.

For fear of being understood as a wimpy wacko, I was still afraid of coming forward as all of who I had discovered I was: a Palo Santo-burning, pottery-making, karmic, truth-seeking businessman and big-hearted father who happened to love green juice *and* fine wine.

But how *wacko* was it that taking time off to heal in corporate America meant they would consider me too weak to resume my position? How *wacko* was it that a colleague of mine had been praised as resilient for not taking any time off as she underwent treatment for not one but two bouts of cancer? How *wacko* was it that I didn't defend myself when I returned to a stripped-down role and a deadbeat assignment? Before I left, I had launched one of the most innovative business transformations the company had seen in its entire history. How *wacko* was it that I allowed them to take that away from me because I had *cancer*?

I had let everyone around me bully me, and in turn, I became as sick and intolerant as they all were. I focused more on excelling in corporate evaluations than empathizing with my team, fearing for my job. I appeased superiors and ignored signs of stress in colleagues, mirroring this behavior at home by withholding my true feelings when my wife raised her voice.

The lump revisiting me, staring it down in the mirror that day, would be the last time I would see my life through the eyes of anyone but me.

There wasn't a goodbye party or a slew of messages of gratitude exchanged on my last day in corporate America. While I had to move through a lot of grief and sadness, I knew that leaving was not only the death of the role I played at work. My ego was slain, and it was the best thing that ever happened to me.

I decided to make it impossible for this lump to survive, enlisting help from all of the logical and illogical places I could find, including psychics, intuitive and mediums. I had to go all out to solve the riddle to find the root cause of what it was trying to show me.

As I continued exploring what I believed had made me sick, I kept returning to the words that had made me well: "I love myself. I accept myself. I love you. I love you. I love you. I love you." The words of affirmation I had used in the past saw me through some of the worst times in my life. To get that lump out of my throat, I would once again use language to heal.

"I live a long and healthy life. I am healthy." I practiced this affirmation relentlessly for ten days. On the eleventh day, the lump disappeared. I confirmed it was gone using the same butter knife-to-tongue method I used that rainy Sunday morning. I asked myself a new question.

"You get to live this healthy life. *Now, what are you going to do with it?*"

Looking around my treehouse, I see material representations of everything I had created for myself after the end of my marriage to today: the melted candles, the music playing, the oracle cards on the table, and a photo from the finish line of a thousand-kilometer cycling expedition I finished only three months after I got that lump out of my throat for good.

Our lives could be over in seconds, or they can begin again.

What Else Would I Do With This Long And Healthy Life I Get To Live?

While I have been fortunate to see the rain fall many times since that morning when the lump returned, and I still love my Zen-like Sunday ritual, doing what it took to continue to heal myself has reshaped my entire existence. Like the air I breathe that I cannot see, the deep work I did to heal myself cannot be understood through the things adorning my home. What's possible, like the gift of inhaling and exhaling, exists in the energy we exchange with life's guidepost moments and what we choose to see in them.

Because I decided I was weird, I decided to study neo-Shamanism and energy medicine.

Because I decided there was no way I could live up to the expectations of love and marriage, I decided to stop having them.

Because I decided I wasn't resilient, I was shown that I am.

Neo-Shamanism, or Modern Shamanism, is a term more widely used for those of us from the Western world trained by Indigenous people. Watching my healing journey progress into my work to help others, my brother jokingly called me *The Rocket Shaman*. The moniker summed up the speed at which I move through adversity. It had a genuine ring to it, allowing me to be a title representative of all aspects of my identity.

I will ask questions of everything, especially of myself, for the rest of my life. To restore my health, I had to listen intently to my answers. Since leaving corporate America, I have launched a wellness company with my son, and I have to admit that my title is Chief Wellness Officer. Hey, Mom and Dad, I finally earned it.

Does our cellular structure change when we speak and act affirmatively on behalf of our authentic identity? I believe, without a doubt, that it does. Healing opens new spaces to turn our truth up a notch and take it to the next level. I'm signing up as the guy who hikes through extraordinary scenery, rides his bike around the world, and launches a rocket fueled by all I am made of.

"I don't know what you are doing, but keep on doing what you are doing." My oncologist says this to me every time I go in for a check-up. Accepting that I would never know exactly what treatments and modalities ultimately cured me, I knew one thing for sure: I healed myself. And if a guy like me can heal himself, I believe anyone can.

There's always room to learn, love, and heal, even when you are a *Rocket Shaman*—or maybe even more so when you are a *Rocket Shaman*. Are you with me?

TY SCHMIDT

Don't Just Survive The Storm
Become The Storm

"They whispered to her 'you can't withstand the storm.' She whispered back, 'I am the storm.'"

What's In A Name?

Hi! My name is Ty, and I learned something recently about why I'd like to be in your life. I will explain more about that later. But first, I want to tell you about my journey from surviving the storms of life to becoming the storm in my own life.

More formally, my name is Tyler Schmidt. I'm 39 years old, and until recently, all I knew about my name was that my mom chose Tyler for the sole purpose of calling me Ty because she thought that would look good in print one day. (Hey look, mom, I made it!)

Beyond my Mom's aesthetically-driven decision to choose my name, I recently went deeper into the origins of my name and uncovered that Tyler means "house builder" or "bricklayer", to build or to construct. On a deeper level, Tyler means to make whole, to add value.

Although I didn't think that learning about the meaning of my name would ever have any meaning to me, it's been one of the most powerful things I've discovered about myself. The truth is, aside from looking fabulous in print, my name exemplifies who I truly am: I am a builder. I am a thoughtful constructor...of relationships. Of family members. Of business enterprises. Of my life. Of the life I am still dreaming of creating.

Navigating Less Than Perfect Storms

Despite my name being about a person who is a creator, until recently, I'd seen my circumstances as being more destroying, rather than building. I've been knocked down and beaten up more times than I can count by the high winds and pounding rains of my life experience. I've been a victim of consecutive storms happening back to back, and at times, those storms have made landfall in my life simultaneously, think two tornadoes merging into one big twister.

I have lived through countless storms. Here's a high-level overview of a few of them:

My father's sudden death when I was 23. That loss, and the upheaval that followed, broke me in ways I'm still recovering from today.

A career that's had twists and turns (despite having advanced degrees and accompanying student loans that I will be paying off until retirement). I didn't think I was capable of finishing my Master's Degree in Clinical Psychology after dad died. But I did, and I have used that degree in more ways than I can count.

Struggling to make ends meet and providing financial stability for my family as a freelance writer during a global pandemic. I had $7.34 in my bank account the day I convinced my biggest client to take a chance on me. I'm still working very hard on getting more financially secure, but I can say with both pride and gratitude that I have more than that in my bank account today.

Not all of the storms happened to me. Some of the storms have been self-inflicted. Maybe you can relate. My struggles with alcohol have resulted in two extended stays in the transplant ICU since 2020. There was an inflection point in that storm where I had to choose me or alcohol. I chose me, and I am proud to say that I continue to make that choice every single day.

Navigating substantial storms isn't meant to imply that I haven't received blessings and opportunities. While I do have so much to be grateful for, the fact is, I have weathered more than my "fair share" of storms.

My immediate family's tragedies are an unfathomable storm and read almost like a Shonda Rimes series, including the recent passing of my own grandmother. Compounded by an unspeakable series of tragic losses of friends, colleagues, coworkers, and lifelong confidants, the litany of deaths surrounding me have felt like trying to walk through gale-force winds and would blow anyone's mind.

You would not believe the amount of calamity in deaths, setbacks, tragedies, and depressing circumstances that have seemed to surround my life, fortunately, mostly at arm's length as my patient husband and two rambunctious boys are, at the present moment, thankfully safe, healthy, and protected from these all-consuming storms.

Becoming The Storm

It's no mystery why I'd always thought of my life as living in the storm. As you can see, there's many good reasons for my perspective. Now, I have a different point of view: We can either define ourselves as a dingy being tossed around in the storm of life, unable to navigate, anchor, or moor ourselves to a purpose, mission, or calling. Or, more to the point of this chapter, we can choose to flip the script. Instead of believing we are at the mercy of the storm, we can choose to see ourselves as the storm itself.

What does it mean to become the storm? It means to become Powerful. Unyielding. Unstoppable. A storm is the author of its own experience. Like a storm, we get to shore up our own resilience, tenacity, and endurance to be the creator of our lives, rather than reacting to the direction the winds of our life blow.

Instead of being a victim in the storm of life, I choose to see myself as the storm. Not a storm causing havoc or chaos in the lives of others, but as a powerful force of nature bringing clarity and renewal.

When the storms of life come (and they will), you rebuild. You reconstruct. You gather. You rally. You help each other. You share. You hunker down. You know there is going to be a fresh dawn. It could happen minutes later, hours later, months later, or years later, but the storm will clear.

Not all storms destroy. Some storms cleanse. Others forge a new path bringing in new life. Some may leave debris while others offer hope for a rebuild. A reunification. A renewal and even a resurgence.

A resurgence of confidence. Of conviction. Of purpose. Of clarity.

The STORM Framework

My offer to you in this chapter is to summon the courage and resolve in your own life to turn a storm that may have happened *to* you, or is currently happening to you, into a storm that happens *for* you. Or further, that you take control of the storm by digging deep into your reservoir of strength, indomitable spirit, and force of perseverance for good, betterment, and a new view that was unseeable before the storm made a clearance.

Here is my STORM framework that has become the lens through which I now view the storms in my life, in hopes that it may be helpful to you.

Self Love

In my journey toward my sobriety, I also come to love myself more as a result.

I don't love myself and my sobriety in spite of my struggles with alcohol, I love myself because of my struggles. I conquered that demon, and have found a new healthy addiction called *Supernatural,* a virtual reality workout game (though I hate calling it that) available on VR headsets anywhere and everywhere. My little sister sold me on trying it and for that I will be forever grateful. I'm not overselling it when I say this: *Supernatural* has completely changed my life.

The coaches speak to my soul every single time. I've always hated working out, but this never feels like a workout—it is a moving meditation with health benefits. Thanks to *Supernatural,* I am more active now than I've been in my adult life. The non-scale victories are many, but perhaps most importantly, *Supernatural* has helped empower me to believe I can do impossible things.

Seemingly impossible things include loving myself and believing with my whole heart that I am worthy of greatness. So are you. Because you are the storm. A storm of self-love.

Tenacity

"You need me in your life and here's why." I once wrote those exact words, entirely unsolicited, to a Wall Street Journal bestselling author when I thought I had no business doing so. Why? Because it's always a no unless you ask. At that point, I was a self-employed media consultant with $7.34 in my bank account, and I had nothing to lose.

And guess what? I got a yes. A yes to what has now become a multi-year consulting career. A yes that has provided me access to hundreds of the world's most renowned thought leaders, business titans, and celebrities. A yes that has validated my skill set and how I build meaningful relationships, experiences, and businesses.

Part of becoming the storm ourselves means we get to learn to navigate the storm of emotions that erupt in our brains when we're nervous, uncertain, or fearful. Every emotion is a coin with two sides. We can choose which side of the coin we want to focus on. When you feel nervous, you can choose the opposing emotion of excitement instead. When you feel uncertain, you can choose adventure, and when you feel fearful, you can simply do a mental coin toss and choose excitement. Recognizing that you can choose your emotional response gives you the mental bandwidth to engage in tenacity, when you are pushing yourself outside of your comfort zone.

Optimism

If you look for things to be grateful for, you will find things to be grateful for. I know that sounds obvious, but sometimes the most obvious lessons are staring us in the face and we still don't see them. The truth is, it can feel impossible to find things to be grateful for when you're in the thick of the storm.

Optimism and gratitude are choices we can make, even on our last day on earth. Recently, I was with my grandmother as she was transitioning from this life. Toward the end of her time here, she was spiraling into a very sad place. I grabbed her hands, made her look me in the eyes, and I said "What can we be grateful for?" I saw her eyes light up as she turned to look at the bouquet of flowers I had brought her a few days prior. Even in the moments leading up to her last breath, facing down the end of her life, she was able to shift her perspective. I am so grateful I got to share that moment with her.

I believe gratitude often paves the way for optimism. We find what we're looking for, and when we look for gratitude, reminding ourselves what is going right with the world can lead to believing that more things are likely to go right in the world. Like gratitude, optimism is a choice. At times, it is an absurd, ridiculous, or unrealistic choice. Choose it anyway. Always. Because what do you have to lose by believing in a more positive future ahead?

Relationships

No connection I have made in life is without meaning. I've made many connections with people from all walks of life. Some of them may not have seemed valuable or reciprocal in the moment, but over time with an open mind, I've found value in learning a lesson from every person I've met.

Believing we are alone is one of the greatest lies that has ever been told. Storms don't travel alone, so you shouldn't either. Storms require constant companions: wind, rain, lightning, and thunder. Sure, you can have just a windstorm or a rainstorm, but the really epic storms? They bring all of their friends together and put on a show.

Despite what people may tell you, forging and fostering enduring relationships is one of the hardest parts of being human. Like storms, some of the best relationships are those where people bring skills, strengths, and experiences to the table that are very different from my own. Lighting and thunder are very different, yet they pair together beautifully. Sometimes finding commonality is hard. It takes time and patience to uncover an unlikely unifying intersection. Our social networks become richer when we learn to see the value that others bring outside of what comes naturally to us.

Mindset

Your mindset controls all of your actions and most of your outcomes. Every thought you think impacts the words you use, the behaviors you exhibit, and the results you do or do not achieve. Consider a hurricane. The mighty winds and magnitude of its force are awe inspiring. Yet, the full complement of a hurricane's power revolves around the eye of the storm. Within the eye of the storm, it is not chaotic, it is calm. Despite what may be swirling around us, we can maintain a focused calm mindset.

Without clarity and perspective, we are simply reacting to our life experiences, rather than serving the ultimate creator of your experience. Storm don't forget their power. Hurricanes always stay focused.

Nothing is ever constructed without a clear set of plans. The same is true in your life. If you can think it, if you can create it. If you can envision it, you can do it. Your Creator imbued in you the genius of vision and imagination. Becoming the storm reminds us to keep our mindset calm and focused despite the awesome power we each possess at any given moment.

Why I Want To Be In Your Life

Earlier, I told you about how I reached out and told an author why he needed me in his life when I had nothing to lose. Rather than telling you why you need me in your life, I'd like to share with you why I'd like to be in yours: I want to share my experiences with whoever will listen, not because I'm special, but because I'm not. I'm just like you. I feel so passionately about connecting because I know your struggle. I know your pain. I know your heartbreak. I know your grief. I know your fears. I know your storm. Maybe not exactly, but you might be surprised at the similarity of our storms.

Because I have lived life with you, together, but apart.

A rising tide lifts all boats. This has been true for me more often than not and as my tide rises, and I believe with my whole soul that I am meant to bring others along with me. How can I help you lift your boat with my rising tide?

I'm here to remind you that you and your story matter. Especially on the days when you need a reminder. I'm here to encourage you and uplift you and sit with you if you need someone to listen.

I'm here to remind you to get out of your own way. to help you stop doubting and start doing.

I'm here to show you how to create the things you desire or rebuild after a period of demolition. At heart, I am a builder. After all, it is my namesake.

Learning to become the storm is a journey we can take on together. We can start small and build big. That's how most storms do it. Practice Self Love, strengthen your Tenacity, lean into your Optimism, learn from your Relationships, and check your Mindset.

Remember, you are the STORM.

JENNIFER BAWDEN

Poor Little Rich Girl

She was born into a top one-in-a-million wealthiest household. The descendants of royal bloodlines, both grandparents were sizable Canadian landowners and lived on large estates with horses. The world was her oyster. Heiress to money, power, and prestige. Until a violent, abusive "Step Monster" who loved her father's money and hated his children arrived. Neither of her brothers survived. Celebrity Jen Bawden retraces the abandonment, violence and bullying she and her brothers suffered as children and her miraculous journey to overcoming tragedy and rising to ski champion, best-selling author, award-winning fashion designer, tech entrepreneur, philanthropist, macroeconomic strategist, and single mom.

The Real Life Story Of A Modern Cinderella

My paternal grandfather was chairman of a top Canadian bank. My other grandfather, William Graburn, a European aristocrat, emigrated from his significant land holdings in Southern Ireland. He purchased extensive tracts of the most beautiful land in Calgary, Canada, where he built and ran a global oil and gas company. In those days, the old-money establishment was a very small world. Socializing was by class, at boarding schools, the Anglican church, country clubs, society events, and summer cottages on Canadian lakes with prominent American families. In those days, there were no more than a hundred dynasty families in Canada, known as the Frozen Chosen for their English proclivity for no public displays of affection.

When my father, an eastern private-school boy from a prominent banking family, started an oil company in Calgary, it didn't take long for him to receive an invitation to meet the three Graburn daughters. He quickly fell in love with the youngest, Judy, an Elizabeth Taylor look-alike. He flew his airplane back east, landing on her university campus in a grand entrance to propose. After a big wedding, they moved into a fairy-tale mansion on the hill in Calgary. In quick succession came myself and two brothers, David and John.

My father, Peter, built what became one of the world's largest privately owned oil drilling companies, and he pioneered new geothermal technologies globally. Until the birth of my brother John, this seemed like a perfect life. His young wife, Judy, had three children in just over three years while he explored for oil.

Tragically, my beautiful, sensitive young mother, heartbroken that he chose to stay in the oil fields for the birth of his third child, fell into severe depression. He returned home to find her in a bathtub full of blood, wrists slit. I sat for months at the window, waiting hopelessly for her return. My father, unable to build his empire tending three children, sent us to our grandparents' estate in Toronto with an English nanny, Mrs. Sloan. We saw our father on holidays and spent summers at the family cottage on Lake Muskoka.

Before The Storm

I was severely pigeon-toed and needed leather and steel braces covering both legs from toes to thigh. Mrs. Sloan adjusted this painful apparatus every week, forcing my growing bones another millimeter in the right direction. On great days, I was allowed to run, climb, and play freely without these contraptions. A happy, can-do child, I awoke every day with a sunny disposition despite being teased by a farmhand as "the little crippled girl." I was an adventurous, super-curious animal lover. I delighted in dogs, bunnies, kittens, and fish on our sizable estate, helping my dearest grandmother with her garden. Three happy years raced by and with them, the end of annoying leg braces. David, John, and I returned to our home in Calgary with our beloved nanny. I was six and starting school.

We went to our new country house on the weekend, where I first met my horse, Brownie, a beautiful chestnut filly. That afternoon, my father sat me in the saddle, showing me horse basics, getting her into a slow trot, and using my reins to turn and slow her down. At dusk, I looked at the paddock and saw Brownie at the fence. In my pajamas and bare feet, I grabbed some sugar cubes and an apple, as I had seen my father do. I climbed the white fence, swung my leg over her back, and grabbed her mane to pull myself on board to hug and pet my new friend. "I love you, Brownie," I told her, nuzzling her neck. She started to walk. I was not afraid. I trusted her. She was mine, and I was hers. I gave her a little push with my heels and made the clicking sound my father had made earlier that day. She sped up to a trot. In an instant, she was galloping. "Whoa, girl," I said, imitating my father, acutely aware of the danger, but as we moved at lightning speed, I felt the strong connection and trust that we were one she would not let me fall. I focused all my senses on moving with her as we sped around the large enclosure at full gallop. I moved when she moved, and in those exhilarating, sometimes terrifying moments, I connected with a sense of freedom I had never known. My heart raced at this new experience. "Whoa, girl," I called softly to slow her while tugging her mane housebound. She obeyed, slowed, and deposited me at the fence.

The Unveiling Of A Hidden Monster

That first winter passed happily into the following spring, with my father's ski lessons and piano and accordion nights. He taught me billiards on our regulation-size table and bestowed on me my mother's silver charm bracelet. Late summer, when I was seven, he announced someone special was coming to dinner, asking that I wear my best dress. As Mrs. Sloan and the maid were given the night off, I set the perfect dining room table with crystal glasses, silver candlesticks, heirloom silverware, our finest china, etc. The doorbell rang. A lady with dark, bobbed hair and a cropped suit arrived. My father ushered her through the foyer, stopping at the dining room, announcing, "Jenny, this is Margaret," turning then to my brothers in the living room. With the big, welcoming smile of a motherless child, I beamed and warmly said, "Hello, Margaret." She leaned down, squeezed my earlobe between her thumb and index finger, pulled my ear up to her mouth, and hissed in a perfect Wicked-Witch-of-the-West voice, "It's Mrs. Matheson to you, you snotty-nosed little brat!"

Soon a playdate was planned to meet her daughter, Valerie. I was dropped at a small apartment at the bottom of the hill. Mrs. Matheson was in a bad mood as she whisked me down a small corridor to an open door with a little girl sitting among dozens of small toys. I sat in the back of the room, picking up the nearest toy. The little girl suddenly cried and reached for the toy I chose. I gave it to her and picked up another. She immediately started to cry again, wanting that toy, too. Before I had a chance to know what was happening, Mrs. Matheson was racing through the door, screaming at the top of her lungs, "Don't touch her things! Don't touch her things, you stupid spoiled brat!" Moments later, a screeching, swearing monster was grabbing my hair with both hands and dragging me back down the hallway. As a small, tiny-boned girl, it wasn't hard for her to lift me up by my hair with both hands and slam my head over and over and over against the wall as hard as she could. I was dizzy, frightened, and feeling intense pain. She violently screamed what I would often hear over the following years; "You stupid, stupid spoiled little brat!" and "If you tell *anyone*, it will be *way* worse."

A New, Terrifying Norm

Without spending a moment getting to know me, it was clear that my father was her ticket from the small apartment of a secretary to the big mansion on the hill, and his children would be the collateral damage. Never would I have predicted a real-life Cinderella story would arise from the dreadful decade to follow. Shortly, my father happily announced, "I'm going to marry Margaret, and you will have a little sister. Isn't that great?" I looked silently into his happy eyes and realized the monster was moving in. I've often asked myself why I said nothing. If I had, perhaps my brothers would be alive today and I would have a family. That fateful day I put my father's happiness above my own. A happy family was destroyed, and Cinderella came to life. The first thing she did was fire our nanny, a devastating loss. There was never a moment again when we were safe in our home. Mrs. Matheson, a.k.a. the Step Monster, seethed with boiling rage, erupting and exploding almost daily into horrifying anger, sudden, uncontrollable, emotional, and physically violent outbursts. The new norm was walking on eggshells in a war zone. My father, once married, was not immune to her abuse and stayed away as much as possible. When elected to Parliament, he escaped to Ottawa alone.

Many children suffer from fear of an imaginary scary monster under their bed or in a closet waiting to hurt them. We had a real, live monster in our house who appeared like a fiery dragon to terrorize my little brothers and me every few days. I once counted thirty-three days in a row being physically abused. The last of these days garnered cuts from her nails digging into the skin of my upper arms as she screamed and violently shook me. "Thank you, God," I prayed after such an easy day. My brothers were rarely so lucky. She regularly left my brothers so severely beaten that they needed—and seldom received—medical attention. I crept to their beds after hearing their terrorized screams, where she regularly broke wooden spoons and forced massive strap wounds on their little bodies. Poor little John was only three when she routinely smashed his head against the sink, giving him I have no idea how many concussions. His crime? Not being tall enough to stop the tap from dripping. As I cried with him after extensive beatings and held his quivering body in my arms, he would yelp and wince, as there was no area on his body safe for me to hold or touch; he was so massively and horrifically beaten. "Go back to your room," he would whisper. "She will kill you if she catches you here." I didn't care. I stayed but knew that if I was caught consoling or helping them, I was next. My heart bled for my sweet and beautiful little brothers. I was witness to what years of evil and constant torture turned once-good boys into. I fought hard to help them. They gave me Mother's Day cards every year.

I Am Angel Jen

This existential threat uniquely shaped and solidified my morals and values. My dear grandmother prayed with me as a child. She taught me you cannot fight evil with evil. My imagination spiraled into ways to protect myself and my brothers from the monster. I thought of many things I could have done to outsmart her, hurt her, or fight back. Instead, I always touched my right cheek to remind me to "turn the other cheek." I reminded myself not to hate, fight back, or even think vengeful thoughts. As a child, I repeatedly reminded myself, "I am Angel Jen. *I am angel Jen!*" I prayed to God to help me stay strong and kind and to turn the other cheek, as I somehow knew this evil would engulf me if I did not.

Years later, I was drawn to this quote from Friedrich Nietzsche in his book *Beyond Good and Evil*: "Whoever fights monsters should see to it that he does not become a monster himself in the process. And when you gaze long into an abyss, the abyss also gazes back into you."

Drip... Drip... Drip...

The next decade consisted of constant brutal and unimaginably violent physical and jaw-dropping emotional abuse, wounding my brothers and myself irreparably. She would line us all up, including her daughter, Valerie, on the wall and ask which of us had done whatever small thing. She would release Valerie before the terrifying Spanish Inquisition began. "Who left the bathroom tap dripping?" Everyone knew it would end in a terrible, terrible beating. Soon Valerie was not invited to the party and listened from the safety of her room down the hall. I never once witnessed her being yelled at or abused. My cardinal rule was not to upset Valerie, who mostly kept to herself and did not often abuse her power.

Although she was not cut from the same cloth as her mother, she refused to help us, even when I begged. She remained a distant observer of our torture.

I tried being a perfect girl. I endlessly strategized to skirt daily beatings. My youngest brother, John, a toddler, was always front and center in the lineup. I usually passed the inquisition and got safely sent to my room to hear her screaming at the top of her lungs, seemingly forever, at my two terrified little brothers. "Which one of you left the tap dripping in the bathroom?!" Dave, a slight waif of a boy, then five or six, often peed his pants in fear before beatings began, driving her livid.

His fingernails were always bitten to bleeding from the constant stress of not knowing when she would strike. Eventually, John, still just barely four when the years of inquisitions started, realized he would always be blamed, no matter who had done the minor deed, so he confessed in return for a lesser beating before the angry monster demanded blood. When I learned to control all crying from physical torture, she upped the ante by sitting on me, cackling while hacking off my hair in clumps close to my head. None of us ever purposely provoked or deserved her rage. Years later, I came to understand we were dealing with someone with serious mental illness who enjoyed hurting innocent children, thriving on their fear.

We Knew We Might Not Survive A Bad Day

Waking one morning after a prolonged beating the night before, with many broken wooden spoons, spatulas, and other kitchen parapher-nalia that dug bleeding ribbons into my soft flesh, I couldn't move from the pain. A bloodbath the night prior had turned my white sheets red and had stuck the top sheet to my exposed flesh, making it hard to move, as the blood had dried the night before and trapped my little body between the sheets. Moving even an inch would pull the sheet and reopen my fresh wounds. The only person who watched over us and loved us was Esther, our cleaning lady. All my love went to her and my golden lab, Toby. Noticing I had not appeared for breakfast, Esther came up to check on me, afraid of what evils may have befallen. Slowly, to not reopen the ribbons of cuts and wounds, some deep enough for stitches, she gently placed hot cloths atop the blood-soaked sheets, softening them so she could pry them from my legs, bottom and back. She had dressed our wounds often. She knew hospital stitching was out of the question and used the first aid kit for our cuts as best she could. It was several weeks until I could sit without extreme pain. I had just turned eight years old, in grade three. The scars were visible for decades.

Another night, also when I was seven or eight years old, she smashed my head against the wall by my hair with such force so many times that I lost consciousness, waking the following day to my worried labrador whining and licking my face. Big chunks of my hair fell out with dried blood droplets, creating scattered bald spots. There was never one moment or day of love, compassion, or kindness from the person tasked with our authority, nor did I ever witness a drop of empathy, remorse or mercy. It was a brutal dictatorship. The power of my father's wealth and privilege corrupted her and fed her cruelty. She never helped us to do anything, go anywhere or learn anything other than how painful it was to be constantly beaten with a bat, kicked, punched, have your face smashed on the rocks, or be constantly criticized, embarrassed, and humiliated. I learned how to notice every tiny change in her personality or mood to avoid her daily intense and scary abuse. Her temper was volcanic and diabolical when activated. We knew we might not survive a bad day, as we barely had on many others. She told my brothers in front of me different ways they could commit suicide. She screamed at my six-year-old brother John that he should go to the busy street corner and run into the traffic. I was told years later that since my father was so rich and famous, adults who knew of the abuse were afraid to come forward.

She was excited and energized by negativity and delighted in shaming us publicly. The glee on the Step Monster's face earned her the nickname "Hitler Reincarnated" by my friends and brothers. Any money my father gave for our clothing went to her Ultrasuede suit fund. The two daughters she had with my father were later showered with beautiful things. My brothers had holes in their shoes and wore extra socks to be able to walk in their shoes in the winter. Meanwhile, my father flew on his Learjets. After years of unabating abuse, I begged we all be sent to boarding school. My father finally agreed.

A bright light was our family ski trips, led by my father to our ski chalet in Banff. He had forced us to ski for years, and at some point, I realized I was good at it. After training in the racing league, I started competing in freestyle. I was among the first females to find the courage to do front- and backflips from the two-story jumps the men's ski team had built. Nothing was as scary as a Step Monster, after all. I arrived home from the highly competitive provincial championships at sixteen (which I had not previously mentioned, as she would never have allowed me to go) with gold, silver, and bronze medals around my neck, earning me a spot in the nationals, which she later forbade me from attending. All the kids were eating dinner in the kitchen. She hung my awards on high cabinet knobs. "Attention everyone," she proclaimed in a loud, commanding, sarcastic voice. "Look what Jenny has done!" Lying, she said, "She's come third out of three! And look, there were only two people in this race, so she came second! And, whoops, only she showed up for this, so she got a first! One out of one! Let's all give her a big clap of applause!" Her three daughters all laughed and applauded, while John, Dave, and I sat in silent solidarity, knowing the Alberta Provincials were the most competitive of all Canada, with dozens of participants.

Unbearable Reflections

The trauma we inherited was unbearable, and I escaped. The faster I got through grade school, the faster I could leave the atrocities behind. I skipped several school years and left at sixteen to attend college in Switzerland. I won the Italian freestyle championships, came second in the Swiss championships, did stunt skiing for a Sean Connery film, and made money on ski modeling jobs. I rarely returned home after that. The greed and ruthless attacks on innocent children had stolen our childhood and robbed us of our future family, safety, and happiness. My empathy, love, and compassion for my little brothers' suffering, spiraling demise, and debilitating torture from the constant destructive abuse was not enough. In the end, neither of them made it. My younger brother, John's, very last heart-wrenching, tearful words to me, were, "The nightmares of the beatings, the screaming, the abuse just run over and over again every night in my mind."

I replied softly, "I know, sweetie, I have them, too." He added, "I don't know how you can stand them."

I tried to console him as I always did: "They will lessen with time, and everything will be okay, sweetheart."

Unable to endure the emotional suffering, tragically, he jumped out his apartment window several days later, breaking my heart. Dave was murdered just miles from the Step Monster, who lived in luxury, deprived of the funding my father had foolishly given her for his care.

From Trauma To Triumph

Traumatized from years of abuse, I was electrified and beyond happy to be in the big world, free of the monster on my back. Fortunately, I excelled at almost everything that interested me. Unafraid after what I'd survived, nothing seemed too hard. I took chances, shot forward, and didn't give up until I succeeded. After college, the Step Monster demanded my father not support me. I used my modeling money to rent an apartment in NYC and sold dresses I designed to the most prestigious department store, Bergdorf Goodman, in the same room as top designers Oscar de la Renta, Bill Blass and Yves St. Laurent. My dresses appeared on seven Cosmopolitan covers and on British royals, first families, and many celebrities, including Celine Dion and Mariah Carey. My best-selling motivational book for young women, published by Penguin Putnam, was sold in many countries and translated glob-ally. I became a noted technology entrepreneur, economist, global speaker and chaired many charity events in New York. I still mourn the early deaths of my two sweet brothers, whose lives never had a chance against such evil. But thanks to the grace of God, I've been blessed with a unique, exciting and very fulfilling life filled with lov-ing friends, though the memories are never gone.

The tragedy of my sad and terrifying childhood was the seed of my growing into a strong leader passionate about helping others and unafraid to fight for what's right. My difficult upbringing fueled a life championing and supporting others with all my heart. I inten-tionally built a family for my son, Josh, and myself from the kindest and smartest friends, wanting him to have an abundance of nurtur-ance and support. My life proves it is possible to overcome evil and live a happy life if you have the determination, willpower, and deep connection to your self-worth. I learned to tune out false messages from the insanity around me. I was certain the essence of life was love and not all the material things around me that meant noth-ing without it! I believed love would win out over evil. "Love" and "Never let the bad behavior of others change who you are!" became my mantras. My favorite quote, often attributed to Edmund Burke, is on the back of my business card: "Evil flourishes when good men do nothing!"

PRINCESS STEPHANIE DE SARACHAGA-BILBAO

Embracing My Legacy

Leaving My Legacy

Legacy is a complex tapestry woven from the threads of the collective choices, values, and experiences of the ancestors that came before us. Each of our legacies are simultaneously a poignant echo of the past, a guidepost for the present, and a signal-flare illuminating the path toward the future. Our legacy is a constant companion, incessantly seeking to be understood, the invisible thread that knits together our own identity, perspectives, and experiences while maintaining the ties to our ancestors. We can't change the past, yet we do have the power to determine how we respond to our present life circumstances. We determine how we engage with the current condition of our lives. Do we embrace it, deny it, or dance with it? Do we choose to build a top of our inheritance, disconnect from it, or even destroy it? The choice is ours.

Initially, I chose to run from my circumstances. Despite my efforts to distance myself from my past, the origins of my family tirelessly kept pace with my every move. No matter how I tried to evade my legacy in time and space, it relentlessly followed me, wearing me down and foiling my plan to live a life independent of my family's past. Legacy would not be ignored. Legacy would not take "No" for an answer. Ultimately, it was when I looked in the mirror, and I saw the woman I had become in response to every small choice I'd ever made, I understood, once and for all, that my legacy could not be severed. My ancestor's legacy was inextricably connected to every part of my being. I could not run from my legacy any more than I could escape from myself.

When Life Ended

Let me start at the place where it felt like my life ended: When my mother died. In the wake of her loss, at the age of only eleven, amid my grief, I made a small choice: I would not complain. My mother suffered from a debilitating illness for years, and she did not complain. So, I decided that in honor of her memory, no matter how difficult things were, I would not complain either.

As her life force deteriorated, so too did the life I had once known. My Basque-Mexican mother's loss meant that my connection to my loving and wonderful extended Mexican family, a place and people that were a second home to me, was severed. My father who had been honored for saving jobs and turning around companies, whose laughter was infectious, who was known for being the life of the party, when my mother died, had no life left within him. I was left with a shell of a man who has once been my father. He filled the empty void within himself with drink and violence.

He tried to push away anything that reminded him of his pain, avoiding our beautiful home by being gone for longer and longer periods of time. When absence didn't work, he tried to escape his suffering, not just by erasing the memories of the past, but by avoiding the realities of the present. He found a way to forget about taking care of things he'd once cherished, no longer paying for food, the electric bill, and even ignoring his own daughter.

Seemingly Small Choices

Our lives are the sum of the small, sometimes seemingly insignificant choices we make each day: the words we say, how we treat others, our mindset, our effort, the decision to forgive, the belief in what is possible, and the determination to persevere, instead of perishing.

I made a series of seemingly small insignificant choices:

I was going to need to rely on myself now.

I was going to trust my instincts.

I was going to survive.

I was going to take a step outside my comfort zone.

Then, I took another step outside of what was comfortable and familiar. The next step led me to the restaurant Boston Market. I stepped inside the restaurant and ordered food. Then, I gathered every fiber of my inner strength, and I applied for a job to work there.

Every day that I worked at Boston Market was a day I received a meal, and I was able to eat. I made the choice to eat half of my meal on my shift and save half for later. The small choices I made: Showing up for work, washing dishes, serving customers, and cleaning bathrooms began adding up, and soon, in addition to my shift meals, I began receiving regular paychecks. This money I earned was how I took care of myself, keeping the lights on and food in the refrigerator.

The money I was earning allowed me to take another step. This time, my steps led me to the bookstore where it was within books that I learned how to develop myself, face challenges, and be resilient. Even in the bookstore, it didn't take long for my legacy to find me. One day, as I perused the titles in the bookstore, a book by one of my family's peace initiatives and support of small nations literally fell from its position on the shelf into my arms. Once again, I was face-to-face with my legacy, the family to which I am an heir, their names written in black and white on the pages that stretched out before me. I recognized the names of my family members, Prince Alexis de Sarachaga-Bilbao and his sister, Princess Esperanza de Sarachaga-Bilbao from the teachings of my mother, Princess Katia Sarachaga-Bilbao (named after their mother) and my Abuelo, Prince Alfredo Sarachaga-Bilbao.

As a teenager, reading the names of my deceased relatives, in a book written about my family, I still made the decision to continue to run from my legacy. At that time, I felt alone in the world, like an orphan, and I still believed I could leave my past behind. Like my father, I tried to ignore the memories of the family I once knew, believing I could avoid the pain by avoiding my responsibility to my family members that had come before me.

The Past

Alexis and Esperanza's father, Prince George "Jorge", was a brave and resolute man, dedicated to his family and his community, a staunch protector of the Bilbao's legacy. He passed on these values to Alexis and Esperanza, who were profiled in the book that fell into my arms, and they embodied with a fierce sense of resilience that stemmed from a belief in hard work, an unwavering commitment to justice, and perseverance forged in an age of dictatorship and war.

Despite the darkness of war and oppression that loomed over Bilbao's history, even before the tragic bombings in 1937 and the unrelenting grip of Franco's regime, the spirit of the people never faltered. The Basque, Catalan, and Jewish nations, along with many other communities, endured the horrors of genocide with immense bravery. Even after Franco's death in 1975, the shadows of his influence lingered, as he'd strategically put loyal judges in place who carried on his totalitarian legacy through the passage of laws that forbade the discussion of history, making it illegal to acknowledge, let alone reconcile the atrocities of the past.

We Are The Ones We've Been Waiting For

As I became a young adult, grappling with my own challenges, I hadn't the faintest idea how I could be in service to a proud people and nation halfway across the world when I could barely take care of myself. At that time, I believed that the path to peace lay in forgetting, not rehashing the past. Though I cared deeply about my country and heritage, I thought leaving the leadership to others, who seemed more knowledgeable, was the wisest way to ensure the stability of our nation.

In time, I came to see my perspectives in a different light. Today I know better. I know that I am the one my family has been waiting for. I've come to understand that I cannot outsource justice, and I cannot abdicate healing. Breaking the silence enforced by the laws designed to hide the past was not a choice, it was an obligation.

When my daughter was born a decade ago, I was further emboldened to speak the truth because without knowing the reality of her family, she would never be whole. I knew that I had to confront the mistruths of our past, because if I did not, the burden of these battles would be passed down from me to her and become her legacy to fight.

As founders and leaders of Bilbao, my family members were formidable warriors. They wielded influence both on land and sea, advocating fiercely for the rights of smaller nations, striving for the freedom and autonomy that every nation deserves. This legacy inspires me to continue the fight for the rights and dignity of small nations. Even in the face of great adversities, there is unwavering strength and hope in what I do, driven by the legacy I've inherited and the values my family has upheld through generations.

Like my ancestors, I am a formidable warrior for peace and diplomacy. My series of small choices to engage with my legacy coalesced to bring me, along with my husband and small daughter, secretly across the border into the Basque Country to visit the land historically owned by my family. Though the omnipresent threat of Franco's dictatorship still existed, we were granted safe passage, guided by brave and warm people who took us to a burned-out husk of what used to be our family's home. These same people remembered seeing the bombs that fell on our majestic land from swastika-marked planes and recalled, with tears in their eyes, how my family joined arms with them to fight the Nazi's. Seeing the appreciation, the remembrance in these people's eyes incited a deeper commitment to my family's legacy. They, my family, are not gone because I am still here.

Embracing My Legacy

To this day, I now make both small and significant choices to embrace my legacy. Some of my choices are as seemingly small as reading my daughter *The Basque Dragon* by Adam Gidwitz, buying a book on Basque cooking, and sharing Basque recipes with my friends and family. I've sought out long lost relatives, forging bonds with distant relations that thought my line had been killed. When we connect and they learn that I lived, that my daughter lives, and together, we find joy in the revelation that we share much in common.

I received an email from a French newspaper asking questions about Prince Alexis de Sarachaga-Bilbao and our family's thousand-years of history. I made the choice to reply, beginning with writing one word about my ancient family. Then, I wrote another word. Soon, I wrote a sentence. Eventually, I chose to send my response to the newspaper, and in doing so, I chose to share who I was, my choices, and myself publicly for the first time.

I made a choice to no longer ignore who I was.

My legacy is made up of a series of small choices.

Today, I choose to embrace my legacy.

Gifts

This year, my cherished daughter turns ten years old. I vividly recall the profound shift from nine to ten years old during my own childhood. Age ten was the last year I was blessed with my mother's presence, before my world irrevocably changed. I am grateful that my own daughter will not experience the loss I endured.

I've given a lot of thought to the gift that I would like to give my daughter for her tenth birthday. It is not a gift that can be enclosed in a glittering package or adorned with a shiny bow. The gift I wish to give is for her to understand the profound strength that is sculpted through the continuous action of our small deliberate choices. The family, heritage, and legacy she was born into will now be her own choices to make. Although she is still a child, she stands on the precipice of learning how to make her own decisions; engaging in her own free will, choosing how she shapes and embraces the legacy passed down to her.

Remember this, my precious Mija: The essence of my legacy is woven from the strands of our ancestors that came before me. Now, you are my legacy, and through you, the story of our family continues with strength and purpose. Carry our legacy forward with grace and courage, and never underestimate, as I did initially, the power you possess to make a difference and help others along the way. Leverage your legacy to strengthen the aspects of you that make you whole and use that to make a positive and meaningful difference.

Remember that you are not defined by the imperfections of your past, but instead, by the courage to forge a better future. The trials and tribulations that come your way are opportunities for growth, learning, and to become stronger. This legacy you carry is not a shackle, it is a beacon of hope, the culmination of the unyielding spirit of all that came before you.

TARYN MARIE STEJSKAL, PH.D.

Seeking Sanctuary

Disbelief

I searched my recent memories, but I couldn't remember the last time I felt carefree, let alone happy. Yet, as I walked through Shockoe Bottom in Richmond, VA and made my way home from work at the hospital, up the steep hill on Broad Street, I felt a levity and an ease, an expansion in my chest. A smile graced my lips for the first time in a long time as I recognized the feelings I was feeling as contentment and joy.

Prior to that day, things hadn't been going well for quite a while. The last four years had been a descent into the darkness of an abusive marriage where I felt lonely, lost, and hopeless. Within the last year, I'd watched myself slipping away from myself, unable to recognize the defeated woman with pale skin and hollow eyes who stared back at me in the mirror. Where was the woman I once knew? Could I find her again? Could she be resurrected or was she gone for good? I didn't know the answer.

Within days of getting married, my new husband and I moved to Washington, DC, from my hometown of Ann Arbor, MI. It was there, in Washington, DC, a city I didn't know how to navigate, without a single friend or family member within more than a hundred miles, that the first incident occurred. We were putting up track lighting in our one-bedroom apartment, and the screws anchoring the track kept slipping from the ceiling. I could see him becoming increasingly frustrated and angry. When the track for the lighting plummeted from the ceiling once again, he picked up the pieces of metal that were meant to attach to the ceiling and hurled them across the room, with the dangling glass lights still attached, where they smashed into the wall and shattered. He was yelling something about how I wasn't listening, how I wasn't holding it steady, but I could only hear fragments of what he was screaming over my pounding heart and the blood pulsing in my ears. Had I really just seen what happened? My first inclination was to doubt my own experience. This couldn't be real. This couldn't be my life. In disbelief, my eyes scanned the room back to the mangled metal and shattered glass across the room. There was no question that this had really just happened.

Seeing the wreckage of what we'd been building together only moments before crumpled and broken flooded me with fear and desire to flee. I needed to get out. To get away. I couldn't stay there for another second. Turning toward the entryway a few feet behind me, I picked up my keys as I made my way to the door. He caught up with me quickly, grabbing my arm closest to him, but I twisted my wrist and broke free of his grip. He tried to stop me from opening the door, but got there a moment too late, and I slipped through the open crack. Outside of our building, I didn't have the faintest idea where to go. I'd gotten away, but what was I supposed to do now?

Patterns

The first time you have an experience it is an isolated incident. When an experience happens multiple times, it becomes a pattern. As it would turn out, the incident with the track lighting was not an isolated incident. His outbursts became a well-worn pattern of anger, screaming, and physical violence. At first, it was just throwing and breaking things. Then, he'd block my exit from the house or physically restrain me from leaving. He threatened me, saying he'd break or harm things that were meaningful to me if I didn't comply and limited my access to our joint finances to control me. As a critical care physician, he had access to medications, and one evening, he left a vial of a paralytic used to sedate patients on the bathroom counter as a warning.

On the last day we were together, he flew into a rage, cornered me in the bathroom, backing me into the corner and wrapping his fingers around my throat while he was accusing me of being selfish and ungrateful. I clawed at his fingers, desperately trying to release his grip from my neck, and as my peripheral vision began to blur and darken, I had another moment of disbelief, like the ones I'd experienced countless times since the track lighting incident, now four years ago. I thought, "This is how it all ends for me."

Deeper Bottoms

That's not how it all ended for me. Without warning, he relaxed his grip on my throat and stopped choking me. Then, he turned on his heels, walked out of the bathroom, and left the house, while I coughed and sputtered in his wake.

There is a saying in addiction, "Some people have deeper bottoms", and this saying is used to explain how a person who is grappling with addiction, a person who has already lost a great deal, and yet, they continue to use, undeterred, continuing their behavior despite the consequences they have already encountered. This phrase is not just true in addiction. It is true in many areas of life, and it was true for me in an abusive relationship. We all have deeper or shallower bottoms, different tolerances for loss and varied thresholds for what we can and will endure.

As you're reading this chapter, you might be wondering why I didn't leave sooner. Why didn't I pack my bags at the first sign of violence? Or hightail it out of there when a vial of a medical grade paralytic was placed next to my toothbrush? The answer is: I don't know. I had to wait till I hit my bottom.

Initially, I went through a period of believing that he would change after he apologized, hoping that it wouldn't happen again. Then, I had the quintessential period of blaming myself, believing it was somehow my fault, and I'd brought it upon myself. After that, I felt embarrassed and ashamed, and I attempted to hide the chaos of my personal life.

On that day, nearly choked to death, curled up in a fetal position, crying and frightened, I crashed full-force into the depth of my bottom. I'd had enough. That was the day I decided to leave.

New Problems

As I turned off Broad Street and made my way down 32nd street toward my new apartment, those sweet ebullient feelings evaporated as unexpectedly as they had arrived. On the corner of 32nd street, across from my apartment, where I'd been living for a few days, were several young men congregated in a circle. As I approached, they turned in my direction, some with a slight smile, looking at me, and then they made cat call noises as I walked by. I kept my head down and tried to look unmoved, while eyeing them out of the corner of my eye. I reached my porch, quickly pressed my key into the lock, and slipped inside my doorway safely out of sight.

Inside my apartment, a wave of heat and odor washed over me. Surveying the living room, Snowball, my geriatric Pekingese, had been in digestive distress. Apparently, she had not taken well to the new dog food I had purchased for her, and this had resulted in the new food swiftly exiting both ends of her body. "Gross but that didn't explain the sweltering temperature", I thought. I went to the thermostat to turn on the air conditioning. Nothing happened. It was July in Richmond, and it felt like it was a hundred degrees in the awful smelling apartment. Grateful that Snowball had not been harmed by the heat, I called my landlady about the air conditioning while I cleaned the carpet and kitchen floors.

With my phone tucked between my chin and my shoulder while I mopped, I explained the issue with the air conditioning. My landlady was not pleased. She insisted there couldn't be a problem because the unit was brand new. But I persisted. We did some trouble shooting over the phone, and nothing worked, so begrudgingly, she said she would send a handyman to inspect the problem. Before she hung up, she told me if there wasn't a real issue, if the air conditioning problem was my own user error, she would charge me $100 for the handyman's visit. I gulped at the thought of being charged $100. That would be the difference between being able to buy groceries for that week or not. I couldn't afford to be wrong about this. I took a deep breath and stood by my assessment of the situation, that there was something wrong with the unit that I had not caused as the tenet.

While I waited for the handyman to arrive, I opened the windows in the apartment for some breeze, but the stifling mid-summer heat did nothing to lower the interior temperature. "If it didn't smell so bad,

I could do hot yoga in here", I thought to myself with a laugh, trying to stay positive and elevate my mood.

I'd only lived in the neighborhood inside of a week, but this move away from Washington, DC to Richmond, VA was the culmination of months of planning. I'd carefully made secret preparations to move out, quietly anticipating the day when, while he was on call at the hospital, I could pack my things into my car and drive away without him knowing where or how to find me. In the years we were married, as my home life had deteriorated, my professional life had flourished. As part of my plan to leave, I'd applied and been chosen for a prestigious fellowship at Virginia Commonwealth Medical Center, funded by the National Institutes of Health (NIH), with a focus on treating individuals, couples, and families after one person sustained a neurological injury, a brain or spinal cord injury.

After four years of graduate school at the University of Maryland, I was now a clinical fellow seeing patients at the hospital while writing my dissertation, just like I'd dreamed. I was making more money than I ever had before: I was awarded a $25,000 annual fellowship stipend, as a 1099 contract employee, which meant my monthly budget was about $1,500 in 2007. My trim income required me to be creative with things like coupons, two-for-one sales, and walking to work three days a week, rather than driving.

Church Hill

I'd move to Church Hill, a neighborhood named for the church where Patrick Henry had given his famous "Give me liberty or give me death" speech at the outset of the revolutionary war. The neighborhood was brimming with history having formerly housed a civil war hospital and claimed Edgar Allen Poe as a resident during his childhood.

Initially, Church Hill was a far cry from being my sanctuary. Some parts of historic Church Hill were beautiful. Other parts had fallen on hard times, and the "hard times" part of Church Hill was the area where I could afford to live on my fellowship salary. The 11 o'clock news did a superb job of covering the shootings that routinely occurred within blocks of my apartment, a newly renovated quadplex, where I occupied one of the two-bedroom units on the 2nd floor. Early on, my new colleagues at the hospital would call me after watching the late-night news to see if I was okay after a shooting was reported particularly close to my apartment.

Within a few days of my arrival, the news began reporting on a (you can't make this stuff up) rabid Pitbull that was roving my neighborhood, having already mauled one person. On my walks to work, I found myself scanning the alleyways and under porches for a dog who might pounce on me at any moment.

After I cleaned up the mess on the floors, I unlocked the kitchen door at the back of the house, and Snowball and I sat outside on the small landing, out of view from the street, overlooking an overgrown lot. I took a deep breath and let it out slowly as I recounted the challenges I'd faced in my new home within days of moving in: the broken air conditioning, the young men on the corner who were making cat calls while dealing drugs, my landlord's unsupportive demeanor, the rabid Pitbull, gun violence, and the mess I had just cleaned up thanks to purchasing a lower quality dog food to fit my slim budget.

Believing In A Better Life

Out on the little unpainted wooden platform, with my back pressed up against the siding of my apartment, I wondered, "Was this the fresh start I'd been planning for all these months?" I was no longer living in a home with a person who was mentally and physically abusive, but my life still felt hard, just a different type of hard. I'd traded feeling unsafe and alone in my own home for feeling alone and unsafe in my neighborhood. "Was this where my hope for a better life brought me? Is this what believing in what was possible, believing in a better life gave me? Were these challenges proof that he was right? Maybe I should just go back to him? Maybe I can't make it out here on my own?", I questioned.

At the thought of all my planning being for not, at not being able to make it on my own, I put my head in my hands and sobbed while Snowball looked on helplessly. These were not delicate graceful sobs with tears gently running down my cheeks. This was a heart-wrenching, chest-heaving, mascara-running, doubled over in pain, anguished sobs racking my whole body, sounding like an animal was dying kinda cry. The magnitude of my feelings, the pain, anger, fear, and frustration felt so vast, that I thought I might never stop crying. Yet, as every disappointment, loss, and betrayal flowed through me, a new perspective emerged within me. This new point of view took up residence in my consciousness, and it felt true enough to simultaneously reframe my fears and allow me to begin to dry my tears.

My new revelation was this: God knew that I was afraid to live on my own because I'd never done it before. So, what if, maybe, just maybe, this adversity I was facing was not a series of signposts meant to reflect my lack of competence? What if, instead, these tests were orchestrated by God himself, divinely conceived to put every conceivable trial before me, so that when all of this was said and done, I would know, deep in my heart, in my soul that I had faced and overcome every difficulty in my path? Then, no matter what happened next, I would know in every fiber of my being that I could make it on my own. That no matter what was happening outside of me, I could handle it, and I would be my own sanctuary.

This new story made sense to me. After this time, stepping into my new story would mean that I would never again have to question my ability to make it on my own. In this new narrative, these challenges were an opportunity to prove my competence, not signals of my incompetence. Wiping the last of my tears, I stood up with a new sense of purpose. I rose up with a fire of belief reignited within me and a determination that I would prevail no matter what happened next.

No Matter What Happened Next

That night, my landlord's handyman did find and fix a glitch in the air conditioning unit despite it being brand new. When I left my apartment to take Snowball for her evening walk, I headed directly for the men on the street corner with an unwavering gaze and unshakeable confidence in my steps. I walked right up to each one of them, the new girl, with her furry Pekinese in tow, and I extended my hand and introduced myself, telling them my name, asking for theirs, and saying that it was nice to meet them. They still didn't know what to make of me. But this time, as I walked away, I could feel them exchange surprised looks, maybe even an initial glimmer of respect, instead of making their cat calls at my back.

All of the challenges I was facing didn't recede, and of course, new concerns continue to emerge to this day, now nearly two decades later. However, the revelation that came to me on my back porch that night, the understanding that I was my own sanctuary, has revolutionized my outlook, choices, and relationships every day since then. Being my own sanctuary, rather than seeking sanctuary outside of myself, meant that I stopped looking to my surroundings, and even other people to provide my security. Becoming our own sanctuary means we all have the ability to find and create our own safety within ourselves, and therefore, as adults, are freed from having to rely on others to provide the security we require.

AFTERWORD BY
TARYN MARIE STEJSKAL, PH.D.

It All Started With A Simple Idea

When I wrote my first book, *The 5 Practices of Highly Resilient People: Why some flourish when others fold*, I began my journey with the simple idea, twenty years before, that I wanted to be in service to my fellow humans by learning the practices that allow each of us to more effectively face the inevitable moments of challenge in our lives. When I began my journey toward understanding resilience, in my early twenties, well before the concept was cool in the pandemic, and long before it became overused, I had already faced a number of significant challenges in my own life ranging from an undiagnosed learning disability to being targeted by a stalker, a person unknown to me, in my early teens that resulted in developing a Post Traumatic Stress response. I found the experience of facing difficulty awful, in part because of the magnitude of the issue at hand, but also in response to the surrounding experiences of fear, uncertainty, and isolation that made things so much worse than they already were. I knew that the human experience of The Big 3 C's: Challenge, Change, and Complexity was part of the fabric of our lives and was not going away, so I wanted to know, "Was there a way to struggle better?"

The 5 Practices is a framework (with two decades of empirical research behind it) that serves as our blueprint to resilience. In the moments of difficulty, just when we're asking ourselves "What am I going to do?", we now have a playbook that gives us a step-by-step guide focused on what to do next. Sharing what I learned about how to be resilient in the face of life's inevitable challenge felt like I was fulfilling my life's calling. I have loved the opportunity to share my work with other people to support them when it matters most.

I Couldn't Have Imagined ...

Stemming from my initial idea to help people navigate challenge better, I never could have imagined the success that would come from publishing that book. It became a #1 Wall Street Journal (WSJ) bestseller, endorsed by people I deeply admire like Arianna Huffington, Daniel Pink, Maria Shriver, Marshall Goldsmith, and more. The 5 Practices was read by tens of thousands of people, won awards, and gave me opportunities to travel the world and speak on big stages to thousands of people that I had previously only dreamed about.

Following the accolades that book received, many people approached me and said they had a resilience story to share with the world. Some of these people had published a book already, others thought they had an entire book to bring into the world, and still others just wanted to share their resilience story with the desire to leverage their experience to uplift and encourage others. *Triumphs of Transformation: Inspiring Stories of Resilience and Life Change* was born from the simple idea that I wanted to support other people in sharing their resilience stories with the world, not only so they could experience measures of success I had enjoyed, but more importantly, so they could harness their own stories to be a beacon of hope for the world. In the most pressing moments when I have faced concerns, I haven't gone on because of my own sheer perseverance or internalized grit. Oftentimes, I've had the strength to pick myself up off of the ground one more time because I heard a story about someone who faced impossible circumstances and somehow managed to triumph. When stories of rising above seemingly impossible odds floated into my consciousness at the exact moment I needed to hear them, I thought to myself, "if they can do it, so can I."

The Awe-Inspiring Power We Rarely Utilize

Each of our resilience stories has an incredible power to inspire, an awesome capacity to uplift, and an uncanny ability to encourage others. Yet, I have found that, too often, our resilience stories go untold, our most meaningful experiences of facing challenges go unspoken. The stories that have the greatest capacity to connect us with our fellow humans, drive cohesion on our teams, and communicate in a way that offers others the wisdom of our experiences are hidden away. Why? Because we fear that despite challenge being our shared universal human experience, that we will be judged, shamed, and not accepted by others if they really knew the truth of our resilience stories.

These fears about others' responses to our resilience stories are unfounded. How do I know? Well, you just finished reading a book where a curated community of authors ranging from everyday people to entrepreneurs, athletic coaches, business executives, a Hollywood actor from an Academy Award-winning film, and members of influential commercial and royal families have all shared their stories of facing difficulties. Harrowing adversity, fantastic loss, and unexpected tragedy doesn't make us unique, they make us a fellow citizen of our interwoven human experience.

Your Story Is Your Superpower

If our resilience stories are our superpower, our fear of being rejected because of our experiences is our kryptonite. Each author in *Triumphs of Transformation: Inspiring Stories of Resilience and Life Change* engaged their courage and dug deep into their vulnerability to share a story that is real and true for the purposes of offering their lessons and to light the paths of so many others who are in their moment of darkness before the dawn. Our authors are just a fraction of the eight billion people on this planet that have a resilience story to share, and you are one of those people. We believe that to be in service to our fellow humans: our friends, family members, colleagues, children, and neighbors, we owe it not only to ourselves, but to others to share our resilience stories. When we share our resilience stories, we get to join the collective army of people who are healing, growing, and evolving, and rather than keeping these stories to ourselves. When we share our resilience stories, we get to share the fruits of our labor, our triumphs and our transformations, with the world so that many more people's paths through their challenges can be illuminated by hearing about our experience. We share our resilience stories so that many other people can be encouraged by knowing that no matter how difficult things get, there is hope. Collectively, we all benefit from the immeasurable impact and influence that each one of us holds within our own resilience stories.

Now, It's Your Turn To Triumph And Transform

If you'd like to learn more about how you can share your resilience story with others in a way that inspires, uplifts, and encourages the people around you, along with spreading positivity beyond yourself, to people you may have never even met, we'd love for you to join us in our Triumphs of Transformation community. Scan the QR code below to learn more. We can't wait to hear your story!